W9-AOS-877

UNGODLY WOMEN

UNGODLY WOMEN

Gender and the First Wave of American Fundamentalism

* * * * * * * *

Betty A. DeBerg

FORTRESS PRESS
MINNEAPOLIS

To my parents,
Dorothy and John DeBerg

UNGODLY WOMEN
Gender and the First Wave of American Fundamentalism

Copyright © 1990 Augsburg Fortress. All rights reserved. Except for brief quotations in critical articles or reviews, no part of this book may be reproduced in any manner without prior written permission from the publisher. Write to: Permissions, Augsburg Fortress, 426 S. Fifth St., Box 1209, Minneapolis, MN 55440.

Cover design: Judy Swanson
Interior design: Ned Skubic

Library of Congress Cataloging-in-Publication Data

DeBerg, Betty A., 1953–
    Ungodly women : gender and the first wave of American
fundamentalism / Betty A. DeBerg.
        p.   cm.
    Includes bibliographical references.
    ISBN 0-8006-2439-4 (alk. paper)
    1. Women in Christianity—United States—History—19th century.
    2. Women in Christianity—United States—History—20th century.
    3. Fundamentalism. 4. United States—Church History—19th century.
    5. United States—Church history—20th century. 6. United States—
    Social life and customs—1865–1918. 7. United States—Social life
    and customs—1918–1945.   I. Title.
    BV639.W7D37   1990
    277.3'0821'082—dc20   90-35589
                                                                           CIP

The paper used in this publication meets the minimum requirements of American National Standard for Information Sciences—Permanence of Paper for Printed Library Materials, ANSI Z329.48-1984. ∞™

Manufactured in the U.S.A.   AF 1-2439

94   93   92   91   90   1   2   3   4   5   6   7   8   9   10

CONTENTS

PREFACE

THE HISTORY OF AMERICAN CHRISTIANITY OFFERS FEW
more interesting chapters than the Fundamentalist-Modernist controversy of the 1920s. The cast was composed of colorful and often bom-
bastic characters, and the issues debated ranged from prohibition to
evolution to the modern theater. The situation becomes especially
interesting if one adds sexual identity and social roles of each gender
into the mix. The fundamentalists began their crusade during a time
in the United States when the gender roles and ideology of the Victorian
middle class were giving way to new configurations, when the norms
for acceptable behavior for, and actual behavior of, women and men
began to change rapidly. Women were getting professional educations,
moving into the white-collar work force, organizing social and political
reform organizations, marching for suffrage, engaging in sex before
marriage, and seeking divorces at a rate that alarmed those who paid
attention to such things. All of these social trends seemed, to conservative evangelical Protestants, to culminate in the flapper of the 1920s,
and the flapper and fear of her permeated fundamentalists' agenda of
theological and social reform.

Locating the origins and urgency of fundamentalism—at least to
a considerable extent—in the drastic changes in gender ideology and
behavior between 1880 and 1930 is a new twist in the historical
interpretation of this widespread religious movement. Many historians,
especially those accustomed to doing their work without consideration
of gender issues, will no doubt find this analysis one sided, strained,
or reductionistic. Yet the evidence from the popular fundamentalist
press is so strong that to hedge the gender issue for the sake of a more
traditional, more "objective" or "balanced" interpretation, in my mind,
does grave injustice to the historical materials themselves. The fundamentalists were not objective or balanced when it came to gender.
In a surprisingly large number of instances, their arguments even about
Christian doctrine or biblical interpretation were simply rhetorical
tactics used to strengthen their case for maintaining Victorian

gender roles well into post-Victorian times. On the gender front, the fundamentalists conducted a complex and multifaceted campaign, the exploration of which is the subject of this book.

I received assistance and support from many quarters as I conducted the research and wrote it up. I am grateful for the help of librarians at Moody Bible Institute, Asbury Theological Seminary, Valparaiso University, Union Theological Seminary in the City of New York, the Jesuit-Krauss-McCormick Library housed at the Lutheran School of Theology at Chicago, the Southern Baptist Historical Society, the New York Public Library, and the Divinity Library at Vanderbilt University. This project began as my doctoral dissertation, and my committee at Vanderbilt University were very helpful, especially Elisabeth I. Perry, who went beyond the call of duty with her careful reading of both drafts, her unflagging support, and her uncompromisingly high expectations of me. My universities have been there with funds when I have needed them. The Graduate School of Vanderbilt University awarded me an Ethel Mae Wilson Dissertation Research Grant in 1986. The Creative Work and Research Committee at Valparaiso University gave me a generous grant in 1988 to support a summer's work making final revisions for publication. My editor at Fortress Press, J. Michael West, has been enthusiastic about the book from our first conversation about it to its appearance on the bookstore shelves, and I am grateful to him for that.

There is no doubt in my mind that I get by with—and only with—help from my friends. Pat Lane and Len Sweet made good comments on draft copies at various stages of the book's composition. Sharon Welch and Wendy Farley shared first-book experiences with me and helped me sort out all the possibilities and pitfalls. I depended and still depend on the care and advice of Mary Ann Tolbert, Sallie McFague, Ed Farley, Dale Johnson, and David Buttrick on the faculty of Vanderbilt Divinity School. I discovered great new cronies at Valparaiso University, especially Rick DeMaris and Jon Pahl, who came new onto the theology faculty with me and who are wonderfully encouraging and fun.

There are three special people who remind me time and time again that scholarly research does not have to be an isolated task performed by lonely or antisocial people. Christine Reilly and I have been studying church history together since 1977, and her friendship, creativity, and good humor, even from Birmingham and St. Louis, are an inspiration. I have learned much about my trade from and with her. Greg Vickers has been my most dependable and knowledgeable conversation partner. He gave the book its most careful reading and its most detailed and honest response, and the book is much better for it. His care for me and appreciation of my work regularly amazed me. Kim Maphis Early is a true and devoted friend and *Ungodly Women* enthusiast. A proofreader from hell, she honed my writing technique as well as my arguments. She was there for me through thick and thin—through writing blocks and crises of confidence, through successes and satisfactions—with her remarkable energy, intelligence, and wit.

Several members of my family deserve special mention. I am grateful to my nephews, Ian and Ned Horsted, for their help on the cover design. (I hope you boys like the color.) My three sisters, Kathy, Sally, and Amy, are—as one would expect three DeBerg women to be—a loud and lively cheering section. And finally, to my parents, Dorothy and John DeBerg, with gratitude and love I dedicate this book.

—*Betty A. DeBerg*

INTRODUCTION

UPON THE PUBLICATION OF ELIZABETH CADY STANTON'S
Woman's Bible in 1898, James H. Brookes, the "founding father and
the controlling spirit"[1] of the premillennialist Niagara Conferences,
called the feminist revision of certain biblical passages "that miserable
abortion . . . that is only the impudent utterance of infidelity."[2] T.
DeWitt Talmage, one of the country's most popular evangelical preachers, in a sermon entitled "The Choice of a Wife," advised his hearers
that a woman who would go to such lectures as Stanton's is *"an awful
creature,* and you had better not come near such a reeking lepress. She
needs to be washed, and for three weeks to be soaked in carbolic acid,
and for a whole year fumigated, before she is fit for decent society."[3]
Arno C. Gaebelein, another prominent premillennialist, warned that
the *Woman's Bible* was "a striking sign" of the approaching tribulation.[4]
This conservative evangelical and premillennialist protest of the *Woman's
Bible* is but a tiny part of a large body of popular fundamentalist and
proto-fundamentalist literature about gender roles and social conventions. That large body of literature has heretofore been largely neglected
by the historians of fundamentalism. This volume attempts to fill the
gap, analyzing the roots and character of fundamentalism in light of
the rapid changes and severe disruptions in gender-role ideology and
in actual social behavior in the United States between 1880 and 1930.

In the last two decades, historians have given an increasing amount
of attention to Protestant fundamentalism in the United States.[5] They

1. Ernest R. Sandeen, *The Roots of Fundamentalism: British and American Millenarianism, 1800–1930* (Chicago: Univ. of Chicago Press, 1970), 134.
2. James H. Brookes, "Good for Miss Willard and the Women," *Truth, or, Testimony
for Christ* 23, no. 1 (January 1897): 6.
3. T. DeWitt Talmage, "The Choice of a Wife," *Christian Herald and Signs of Our
Times* 9, no. 9 (January 1886): 21.
4. "A Striking Sign of the Times: A Chapter from the Woman's Bible," *Our Hope*
2, no. 2 (August 1896): 34.
5. Fundamentalism is a religious movement that seemed all but dead after its heyday
in the 1920s but that has shown rather amazing new strength and appeal for a vast

1

have formulated two basic interpretations of fundamentalism: the religious and theological, and the social and cultural. The first interprets fundamentalism as a religious or intellectual position that took shape in response to and protest of other intellectual and religious currents of its day. Two important historians of fundamentalism, Ernest R. Sandeen and George M. Marsden, have taken this tack. Sandeen argued that fundamentalism was primarily a theological position within mainstream white Protestantism. It emerged out of an exchange between late nineteenth-century dispensationalist premillennialism, which was an apocalyptic strain within some British and American Protestantism, and Princeton orthodoxy.[6] He took issue with previous studies of fundamentalism for giving only a sociological, psychological, or political interpretation of the movement. Marsden began his important book on fundamentalism this way: "From its origins, fundamentalism was primarily a religious movement."[7] He expanded the list of contributing factors beyond Sandeen's and included revivalism and the holiness movement along with premillennialism and Princeton orthodoxy. Although Marsden's goal was to "analyze the impact of the circumstances of America in the early twentieth century on fundamentalism," to discern "how individuals who were committed to typically American versions of evangelical Christianity responded to and were influenced by the social, intellectual, and religious crisis of their time,"[8] he insisted throughout that the social, cultural, and political aspects of fundamentalism that he carefully delineated had nothing to do with its intrinsic nature or character.[9]

But Sandeen and Marsden are certainly not alone. The understanding of fundamentalism as primarily an intellectual or theological response to modernism—whether biblical criticism or evolutionary theory or the new body of social science research—dominates the historiography. Lefferts A. Loetscher defined fundamentalism as a movement that "sought to defend the fundamentals of Christianity against

---

number of contemporary Americans. A Gallup poll in 1982 indicated that there are more Americans—between 27 and 40 million—who are fundamentalists than liberals. See R. Laurence Moore, *Religious Outsiders and the Making of America* (New York: Oxford Univ. Press, 1986), 167–68.

6. See Sandeen, *The Roots of Fundamentalism.*

7. George M. Marsden, *Fundamentalism and American Culture: The Shaping of Twentieth-Century Evangelicalism, 1870–1925* (New York: Oxford Univ. Press, 1980), 4.

8. Marsden, *Fundamentalism and American Culture,* 3.

9. For example, after a discussion of the disruptive impact on dispensationalists of World War I and the scandals in Washington, he concluded, "Yet it would misrepresent the nature of the growing interest in premillennialism in America to characterize it as basically a reaction to social and political conditions." Marsden, *Fundamentalism and American Culture,* 68.

liberalism and ultimately against the outright naturalism which it suspected lurked behind liberalism's compromises."[10] Ferenc Morton Szasz depicted fundamentalism as a movement that emerged to meet three challenges facing the church: evolution, comparative religion, and higher criticism of the Bible. His study of American fundamentalism was a history of thought "because all of these ideas originated in the scholar's study."[11] For Louis Gasper, the movement represented "an interaction against twentieth century liberalism and modernism, particularly against the teachings of science and the higher criticism in Biblical research which tend to undermine certain fundamentalist tenets."[12] Norman F. Furniss labeled the participants in the controversy according to "the individual's attitude toward evolution and modernism."[13] In his study of fundamentalism and the Missouri Synod Lutherans, Milton L. Rudnick followed suit: fundamentalism was essentially a "religious movement concerned with the content of Christian teaching and belief."[14] A recent analysis by Grant Wacker viewed the fundamentalist-modernist controversy as one between conflicting "unit-ideas" (i.e., the ahistorical origin of religious knowledge versus the radically historical origin of religious knowledge).[15] Standard-setting historians of American religion such as Martin Marty and Sydney Ahlstrom labeled it as "chiefly doctrinal"[16] and "a competitive philosophy of history."[17]

Historians of fundamentalism are in general agreement, however, that the movement did not arise independently of its social and cultural context. The second major school of thought on fundamentalism considers the movement primarily as a reaction—only incidentally religious—to significant changes that occurred in American society just

10. Lefferts A. Loetscher, *The Broadening Church* (Philadelphia: Univ. of Pennsylvania Press, 1954), 91.

11. Ferenc Morton Szasz, *The Divided Mind of Protestant America* (University, Ala.: Univ. of Alabama Press, 1982), 1.

12. Louis Gasper, *The Fundamentalist Movement, 1930–1965* (Grand Rapids, Mich.: Baker Book House, 1981), v.

13. Norman F. Furniss, *The Fundamentalist Controversy, 1918–1931* (New Haven: Yale Univ. Press, 1954), vii.

14. Milton L. Rudnick, *Fundamentalism and the Missouri Synod: A Historical Study of Their Interaction and Mutual Influence* (St. Louis: Concordia Publishing House, 1966), 15–19.

15. Grant Wacker, *Augustus H. Strong and the Dilemma of Historical Consciousness* (Macon, Ga.: Mercer Univ. Press, 1985), 17–18.

16. Sydney Ahlstrom, *A Religious History of the American People* (New Haven: Yale Univ. Press, 1972; Garden City, N.J.: Image Books, 1975), 2:275.

17. Martin E. Marty, *Modern American Religion*, vol. 1, *The Irony of It All* (Chicago: Univ. of Chicago Press, 1986), 218.

prior to and during the years in which fundamentalism emerged and gained wide popularity. H. Richard Niebuhr formulated the classic (but now considered obsolete) description of fundamentalism as a reaction to social change. He portrayed fundamentalism as a regional (Southern) and rural protest against urbanization and industrialization.[18] The fundamentalists themselves contradicted Niebuhr's thesis:

> There is no doubt that the God of Fundamentalism is neither upon a mountain in Tennessee nor in a Holy City of the faithful in Minnesota. Fundamentalism is a spirit, unconfined and prevailing more and more. It is everywhere. Into the hinterland of New England, considered by its own folk the impregnable and insulated glory that once was and will be, world without end, the movement made its way.[19]

Most scholars currently agree that fundamentalism was first and foremost a product of the middle-class white[20] urban culture of the Northeast, Middle-Atlantic, east North-Central, and far Western regions of the country.[21] Robert E. Wenger conducted an extensive demographic survey of fundamentalist leaders and lay followers between 1918 and 1933. He concluded that fundamentalism was a nation-wide phenomenon with special strength in northern cities and the far West.[22] Most analysts still rank urbanization and industrialization high on their lists of causative factors.[23] Late nineteenth-century America experienced

18. H. Richard Niebuhr, "Fundamentalism," in *Encyclopedia of the Social Sciences,* 1931–1935 ed.

19. Albert C. Diffenbach, "Christian Fundamentals Association Seeks to Impose Anti-Evolution on the Public Schools by Nationwide Drives, Editor Asserts," *Christian Fundamentalist* 1, no. 5 (November 1927): 5.

20. Along with gender, the sociological variable of race usually has been ignored by historians of fundamentalism as well. Much research remains to be done on the character of fundamentalism in non-white American churches. Such research, while important, is beyond the scope of this study.

21. See R. Laurence Moore, *Religious Outsiders,* 160; Furniss, *The Fundamentalist Controversy,* 28–29; Marsden, *Fundamentalism and American Culture,* 202; Virginia Lieson Brereton, "Protestant Fundamentalist Bible Schools, 1882–1940." (Ph.D. diss., Columbia Univ., 1981), 74; Sandeen, "Toward a Historical Interpretation of the Origins of Fundamentalism," *Church History* 36 (1967): 66–83; Rudnick, *Fundamentalism and the Missouri Synod,* 50; Douglas W. Frank, *Less than Conquerors: How Evangelicals Entered the Twentieth Century* (Grand Rapids, Mich.: Wm. B. Eerdmans, 1986), viii.

22. Robert E. Wenger, "Social Thought in American Fundamentalism, 1918–1933" (Ph.D. diss., Univ. of Nebraska, 1973), 59, 65, 70.

23. See Willard B. Gatewood, *Controversy in the Twenties: Fundamentalism, Modernism, and Evolution* (Nashville: Vanderbilt Univ. Press, 1969), 4–5; Furniss, *The Fundamentalist Controversy,* 20; Marsden, *Fundamentalism and American Culture,* 210; Steward G. Cole, *The History of Fundamentalism* (New York: R. R. Smith, 1931), 17–26; Rudnick, *Fundamentalism and the Missouri Synod,* 10; Frank, *Less than Conquerors,* 38.

vast social and economic disruptions as corporate industrialism gained dominance and as people flocked to the cities. Other sources of social and cultural flux mentioned are professionalization and specialization of knowledge,[24] the militarism and chaos generated by World War I,[25] a new consumer economy,[26] the rise of secular public education,[27] immigration,[28] the labor movement,[29] the decay of traditional moral values,[30] Bolshevism in Russia, and socialism at home.[31]

Neither type of interpretation—the theological or the cultural—has been adequate to explain fully the origins and nature of American fundamentalism. The intellectual and theological interpretation does not account for the popularity of the movement among a general public that knew little about the fine points of Christian doctrine or scientific theory. Even Marsden, a true champion of the model, admitted that "although the [theological] issues were well aired and strenuously debated in the seminaries and among the [Northern Baptist] denomination's leadership, they were not well known on a popular level." Despite there being "deep ideological differences [among Northern Baptists], most American Protestants were not first of all ideological

24. See Szasz, *The Divided Mind of Protestant America*, 132; R. Laurence Moore, *Religious Outsiders*, 163–65.

25. See James R. Moore, *The Post-Darwinian Controversies: A Study of the Protestant Struggle to Come to Terms with Darwin in Great Britain and America, 1870–1900* (New York: Cambridge Univ. Press, 1979), 101–102; Szasz, *The Divided Mind of Protestant America*, 92; Furniss, *The Fundamentalist Controversy*, 23–25; Cole, *The History of Fundamentalism*, 25; Sandeen, *The Roots of Fundamentalism*, xii; Marsden, *Fundamentalism and American Culture*, 141.

26. Frank, *Less than Conquerors*, 167–231; James Davison Hunter, *American Evangelicalism: Conservative Religion and the Quandary of Modernity* (New Brunswick, N.J.: Rutgers Univ. Press, 1983), 37.

27. James R. Moore, *The Post-Darwinian Controversies*, 73; Cole, *The History of Fundamentalism*, 22–24.

28. Rudnick, *Fundamentalism and the Missouri Synod*, 10; Robert D. Linder, "The Resurgence of Evangelical Social Concern (1925–1975)," in *The Evangelicals: What They Believe, Who They Are, Where They Are Changing*, rev. ed., ed. David R. Wells and John D. Woodbridge (Grand Rapids, Mich.: Baker Book House, 1977), 209–30; Brereton, "Protestant Fundamentalist Bible Schools," 80.

29. Brereton, "Protestant Fundamentalist Bible Schools," 80; Rudnick, *Fundamentalism and the Missouri Synod*, 10; Lindner, "The Resurgence of Evangelical Social Concern," 209–230.

30. Furniss, *The Fundamentalist Controversy*, 15–25, 28–29; Brereton, "Protestant Fundamentalist Bible Schools," 80; Timothy P. Weber, "The Two-Edged Sword: The Fundamentalist Use of the Bible," in *The Bible in America: Essays in Cultural History*, ed. Nathan O. Hatch and Mark A. Noll (New York: Oxford Univ. Press, 1982), 101–120; Lindner, "The Resurgence of Evangelical Social Concern," 189–200; Ahlstrom, *A Religious History of the American People*, 2:275.

31. Marsden, *Fundamentalism and American Culture*, 153–56.

in orientation."[32] Issues that seemed compelling in the "scholar's study" did not necessarily move the masses. Furniss concluded that even as late as 1918 "many of the people in the pews had been at best only dimly aware that a dispute over [liberal] theology had ever taken place," and that "static habits of thought, preventing many people from speculating on their faith, provided a vast, sympathetic constituency for the fundamentalist agitator."[33] The danger in portrayals of fundamentalism that are only theological or intellectual become clear in an examination of R. Laurence Moore's explanation of fundamentalism as an "outsider consciousness that developed among average American Protestants [that] was a defensive reaction to intellectual insecurity. In America's best-known centers of learning, they were losing a battle of prestige."[34] Such an argument presupposes that "average American Protestants" knew of the controversies waged in prestigious universities and that, further, they believed that university debates affected them and called them to a particular theological position. That argument does not seem plausible. To understand fundamentalism as a widely popular movement in early twentieth-century America, we must look to causative factors beyond scholarly discourse and denominational meetings.[35] Bill J. Leonard's point is correct: Little has been done that examines any differences between "official" fundamentalism and "popular" fundamentalism and what accounts for such differences.[36] No

32. Marsden, *Fundamentalism and American Culture*, 106.

33. Furniss, *The Fundamentalist Controversy*, 15. William Bryant Lewis, too, argued that the bulk of Americans, "the conservative common people," were "non-theologians who did not particularly fear or favor the liberal [theological] spirit or . . . science and modern thought generally." Lewis, "The Role of Harold Paul Sloan and the Methodist League for Faith and Life in the Fundamentalist-Modernist Controversy in the Methodist Episcopal Church" (Ph.D. diss., Vanderbilt Univ., 1963), 21.

34. R. Laurence Moore, *Religious Outsiders*, 163.

35. LeRoy Moore, Jr., in a response to an early article on the roots of fundamentalism by Sandeen, made some helpful distinctions, too. He called the fundamentalist theological tradition "doctrinaire fundamentalism," and the "intradenominational and interdenominational movements" organized to take control of denominational organizations he called "fundamentalism as a party movement." See "Another Look at Fundamentalism: A Response to Ernest R. Sandeen," *Church History* 37 (June 1968): 202. The purpose of my study is to try to get a closer look at and a better understanding of fundamentalism as a grassroots, or popular, movement.

36. Bill J. Leonard, "The Origin and Character of Fundamentalism," *Review and Expositor* 79, no. 1 (Winter 1982): 14–15. I am also in sympathy with Joel E. Carpenter and Brereton who define fundamentalism as the products of its leaders: Bible schools, magazines, missions, conferences, and revivals. See Carpenter, "The Fundamentalist Leaven and the Rise of an Evangelical United Front," in *The Evangelical Tradition in America*, ed. Leonard I. Sweet (Macon, Ga.: Mercer Univ. Press, 1984), 257–88; and Brereton, "Protestant Fundamentalist Bible Schools," 19–27.

interpretation that fails to examine fundamentalism's broad, popular appeal can adequately explain the movement.

A historian of fundamentalism must reject a purely theological or intellectual approach to interpreting popular fundamentalism, because fundamentalism at that level was primarily a reaction to social change and conditions external to it and to religion in general. Yet there is reason to be dissatisfied as well with the cultural interpretations of fundamentalism that so far have been produced. Current cultural interpretations rest on an incomplete depiction of late nineteenth- and early twentieth-century American society. True, the fifty years between 1880 and 1930 was a time of deep and troubling social change wrought by industrialization, urbanization, immigration, the new consumer economy, and World War I. But probably none of these social factors could affect as many Americans and in such an intimate and intense way as the vast changes in gender roles that also occurred during the period. Yet this flux in cultural symbols and norms relating to gender has not been a factor in most social analyses of fundamentalism.[37] What makes this oversight difficult to understand and harder to excuse is that issues of domestic relations, human sexual identity and behavior, and women's and men's spheres of activity dominated much of the rhetoric in the popular fundamentalist and proto-fundamentalist media. Gender and family issues were not only a major theme independent in themselves, but they also formed part of the rhetorical substructure of fundamentalist writing and preaching on the key theological issues most commonly identified with fundamentalism by the proponents of the religious and theological interpretation—premillennialism, biblical inerrancy, evolution, and modernism.

Any analysis of fundamentalism as a popular movement must look beyond the scholar's study to the popular religious press: periodical literature and addresses and sermons to large lay audiences. The fundamentalism that is the focus of this study is not the carefully constructed and arcane theological positions or body of thought "somewhere in the margins of twentieth century history,"[38] although its more technical theological corpus is also an important part of the phenomenon. Rather this study rests on an analysis of the fundamentalist rhetoric

---

37. The one exception is Janette Hassey, *No Time for Silence: Evangelical Women in Ministry around the Turn of the Century* (Grand Rapids, Mich.: Zondervan, 1986). Her study of the steadily deteriorating support of church women by fundamentalists between 1880 and 1930 is discussed in more detail in chapter 4 of this book.

38. Brereton, "Protestant Fundamentalist Bible Schools," 103–4.

that was most available to and most clearly designed to persuade a larger general public.[39]

The generators of such popular materials were the religious leaders and organizations that have commonly been associated with the origins of fundamentalism in nineteenth-century dispensational premillennialism, the Keswick holiness movement, and the urban revivalism of Dwight Moody and evangelists who came after him. This lead was established by Marsden and followed by most since.[40]

Dispensational Premillennialism

Sandeen traced the theological roots of fundamentalism to two sources—Princeton orthodox theology and dispensational premillennialism.[41] Dispensationalism was a British transplant from John Nelson Darby and the Plymouth Brethren in the 1840s and 1850s. The ideology of the movement rested on several foundations. First, dispensationalism received its name from an understanding of history in which history was divided into seven major periods, i.e., Innocence (Eden), Conscience (Adam to Noah), Human Government (Abraham to Moses), Law (Moses to Christ), Grace (Christ to his second coming), and the Kingdom (or Millennium).[42] The dispensationalist system was based on a "literal interpretation" of biblical "prophecy."[43] Another characteristic was deep pessimism. The premillennial era was to be a time of apostasy and violence. Even the church would fail miserably, and premillennialists believed it was doing so before their very eyes.[44]

Bible conferences promulgated the body of dispensationalist teachings. Most of the conferences between 1868 and 1900 met at Niagara. C. Norman Kraus located the appeal of the conferences primarily in "middle and upper middle-class churches."[45] Leaders of the movement

39. See Martin M. Marty's discussion of rhetorical criticism as historical method in *The Irony of It All,* 12.
40. See Marsden, *Fundamentalism and American Culture,* 3–8; and Frank, *Less than Conquerors,* vii–viii.
41. See Sandeen, *The Roots of Fundamentalism,* 130–31.
42. See several ways in which the ages were charted in Marsden, *Fundamentalism and American Culture,* 53, 58–59, 64–65.
43. Frank, *Less than Conquerors,* 71–72.
44. "Protestantism has unquestionably become a frightful failure, as seen in many of its leading representatives, with regard to the authority, the inspiration and truth of God's holy Word." "Protestantism a Failure," *Truth, or, Testimony for Christ* 11, no. 11 (1895): 528. See also French E. Oliver, "Signs of the Times," *King's Business* 6, no. 9 (September 1915): 769–71.
45. C. Norman Kraus, *Dispensationalism in America: Its Rise and Development* (Richmond, Va.: John Knox Press, 1958), 7.

were James H. Brookes, pastor of the Walnut Street Presbyterian Church in St. Louis; A. J. Gordon, minister of Clarendon Street [Baptist] Church in Boston; William G. Moorehead, President of Xenia Seminary in Ohio; A. T. Pierson, Rueben Torrey, James M. Gray, and William J. Eerdman, associated with revivalist Dwight L. Moody in Chicago; Arno Gaebelein; Charles G. Trumbull; and C. I. Scofield, editor of the *Scofield Reference Bible.* Dispensationalism contributed the largest share of the leadership of fundamentalism proper when it emerged in the 1910s and 1920s.

The Keswick Holiness Movement

This movement, too, was a British import. Although holiness, with its emphasis on sanctification and Christian moral perfection, was not new to the American evangelical scene, the Keswick emphasis on the remainder of a sinful nature even after "the second blessing of the Spirit" made holiness acceptable to Presbyterians and Calvinist Baptists, who could not accept the perfectionistic teachings of most holiness groups.[46] The adoption of Keswick teachings by such evangelists as Dwight L. Moody also made revivalism more acceptable to orthodox Baptists and Presbyterians.[47]

Moody's Northfield conferences became, in the 1890s, a center of Keswick holiness teaching. Charles G. Trumbull founded the Victorious Life Testimony organization in 1910. From 1913 to 1924 this organization held summer holiness conferences on the East Coast, finally settling permanently at Keswick Grove, New Jersey. Other leaders of this movement were F. B. Meyer, Andrew Murray, Reuben Torrey, A. T. Pierson, A. B. Simpson, Harry A. Ironside, W. H. Griffith Thomas, Robert C. McQuilken, Howard Dinwiddie, and Robert F. Horton. Such important fundamentalist institutions as Moody Bible Institute, Wheaton College, and Dallas Theological Seminary had early connections with the Keswick holiness movement.[48]

Revivalism

A new revivalism for the cities emerged in the last quarter of the nineteenth century under the leadership of Dwight L. Moody.[49] His

46. See Marsden, *Fundamentalism and American Culture,* 72–101, and Frank, *Less than Conquerors,* 103–66.
47. Marsden, *Fundamentalism and American Culture,* 77–78.
48. Frank, *Less than Conquerors,* 115.
49. See an account in Marsden, *Fundamentalism and American Culture,* 32–39.

message was a simple one: human sinfulness, redemption by Christ, and regeneration through the Holy Spirit. He concentrated on individual vices and "personal" morality: Sabbath desecration, drinking, amusements, impurity, and unbelief. Moody established an empire consisting of regular revivals, a conference center, training schools for both girls and boys, and the Moody Church and the Moody Bible Institute, both in Chicago. The Moody Bible Institute served as the model for fundamentalist Bible institutes all over the country. As historian Virginia Lieson Brereton has shown in her study of Bible colleges, these schools played an essential role in forming fundamentalist identity and in spreading fundamentalist teachings. Since the schools were essentially middle class, urban, and respectable, they often voiced moderate positions between modernism on one side and the radical conservatives on the other.[50]

Moody's friends and "younger lieutenants" were important fundamentalist leaders in their own right: James M. Gray, A. C. Dixon, C. I. Scofield, William J. Eerdman, George Needham, and A. J. Gordon. Although Moody himself avoided conflict whenever possible and died before the fundamentalist movement became self-conscious as such, Marsden concluded that fundamentalism was "always a subspecies of the larger revivalist movement." About Moody he said:

> Moody was a progenitor of fundamentalism—it could even be argued that he was its principal progenitor. He believed in Biblical infallibility and premillennialism. He did as much as anyone in America to promote the forms of holiness teaching and ethical emphases that were accepted by many fundamentalists.[51]

Other historians—Joel E. Carpenter, Douglas Frank, Virginia Lieson Brereton—also understand Moody and post-Moody revivalism as parents of the later fundamentalist movement.[52]

Billy Sunday best represented fundamentalist revivalism during the first quarter of the twentieth century, with his career peaking for a decade from 1908 to 1918. In 1917, C. D. Moody called Sunday "the most advertised man in the religious world."[53] Like Moody, Sunday's greatest triumphs came in large Northern urban areas. Sunday's

50. Brereton, "Protestant Fundamentalist Bible Schools," 278, 408.
51. Marsden, *Fundamentalism and American Culture,* 39, 33.
52. See Carpenter, "The Fundamentalist Leaven," 281; Brereton, "Protestant Fundamentalist Bible Schools," 9; Frank, *Less than Conquerors,* 167–270.
53. C. D. Moody, "Billy Sunday in Boston," *Western Recorder* 92, no. 28 (April 19,

success in a 1917 revival in New York City was resounding: Attendance was estimated at 1,443,000, and the conversion total at 98,264. William G. McLoughlin, Jr., who has written the best study of Billy Sunday, estimated that Sunday preached over 300 separate revivals, spoke to over 100 million people, brought one million "down the sawdust trail," and collected millions of dollars in contributions from those who heard him.[54]

Countless other Americans heard Billy Sunday imitators who blanketed the country, many of whom were trained in the Bible institutes and colleges. They gave themselves such names as "The Cowboy Evangelist," "The Labor Evangelist," "The Singing Evangelist," "The Businessman's Evangelist," "The Railroad Evangelist," and "The Boy Evangelist." There were, apparently, more evangelists than nicknames: "At one time there were at least three different 'Boy Evangelists,' five 'Singing Evangelists,' three 'Cowboy Evangelists,' and five men, apparently related, each calling himself 'The Gypsy Evangelist.'"[55] McLoughlin cited a report indicating that in 1911 there were about 650 such evangelists active in the United States, and estimating that there were probably at least 35,000 revival campaigns between 1912 and 1918.[56]

Revivalism between 1880 and 1930 appealed to the same people as did premillennialism and the Keswick holiness movement. It was especially popular among the urban middle class.[57]

Periodicals and sermons produced by premillennialist, Keswick, and revivalist strands within late nineteenth-century Protestant evangelicalism and early twentieth-century fundamentalism give insight into fundamentalism's popular appeal.[58] Production and dissemination

---

1917): 2. About Sunday's 1921 Cincinnati Crusade, David L. Calkins wrote: "In scanning the Cincinnati newspapers between March 7 and May 1, 1921, it is impossible to discover a day on which Billy Sunday was not a news item." Sunday was usually covered on the front page, and many of his sermons were printed in the newspapers. "Billy Sunday's Cincinnati Crusade," *Cincinnati Historical Society Bulletin* 27, no. 4 (Winter 1969): 293.

54. William G. McLoughlin, Jr., *Billy Sunday Was His Real Name* (Chicago: Univ. of Chicago Press, 1955), xxviii, 46–47, 293.

55. McLoughlin, *Billy Sunday Was His Real Name*, 262.

56. McLoughlin, *Billy Sunday Was His Real Name*, 260.

57. Brereton documented the middle-class popularity of Moody and his enterprise in "Protestant Fundamentalist Bible Schools," 254. McLoughlin did the same with Sunday in *Billy Sunday Was His Real Name*, 212–13, 220–21.

58. Twenty periodicals published by fundamentalist leaders and organizations between 1880 and 1930 were surveyed for this study, as well as the sermons and published accounts of Billy Sunday's revivals. A detailed description of each can be found in the Appendix.

12 Ungodly Women

of such materials constituted one of the major enterprises of fundamentalist leaders. They edited dozens of newsletters, magazines, and journals. They reached vast audiences from their pulpits. *The Sunday School Times* in the early 1920s surveyed Sunday schools in this country and discovered that all nine with attendance over 2500 were affiliated with fundamentalist churches.[59] Since 1880 about 160 Bible schools have been founded.[60] Conferences were held across the country. For example, Furniss estimated that for the year 1918 to 1919 alone, the leaders of the Philadelphia Prophetic Convention (William Bell Riley, James M. Gray, and A. C. Dixon) held more than one hundred conferences on Christian fundamentals.[61] The fundamentalists were among the first to exploit the potential of radio: In 1925 Charles E. Fuller in Pasadena, California, began the "Old Fashioned Revival Hour." By 1937, it was heard as far east as Indiana.[62] C. Allyn Russell concluded that fundamentalism appealed "to literally millions of people," and that it was and is a major current in American religious life.[63]

Popular fundamentalist rhetoric contained frequent references to gender-related social conventions and beliefs. Close analysis of such rhetoric reveals that conservative evangelical Protestants perceived and reacted to the disruptions in the dominant gender ideology and in social behavior that were occurring all around them. Matters related to human sexual identity and behavior occupied a central place in fundamentalists' moral and religious teaching.

59. The churches, with attendances ranging from 2569 to 6000, were First Baptist Church (Fort Worth), Church of the Open Door (Los Angeles), First Christian (Canton, Oh.), East Calvary Methodist Episcopal (Philadelphia), First Church, United Brethren (Canton, Oh.), First Presbyterian (Seattle), First Christian (Long Beach), Moody Church (Chicago), and Bethany Presbyterian (Philadelphia). "A Contrast and a Comparison," *King's Business* 14, no. 3 (March 1923): 232.
60. Gasper, *The Fundamentalist Movement,* 12.
61. Furniss, *The Fundamentalist Controversy,* 51.
62. Gasper, *The Fundamentalist Movement,* 77.
63. C. Allyn Russell, *Voices of American Fundamentalism* (Philadelphia: Westminster Press, 1976), 215–16.

CHAPTER ONE

Late Victorian Gender Roles

THE SHIFT FROM THE FARM-
land to the cities, from the fields to the factories, resulted in profound
disruptions in gender roles and family life. Historians have called
attention to these disruptions in gender-related traditions—male and
female alike—effected by the industrialization and urbanization of
Western Europe and North America.[1]

This chapter traces, first, the disruptions in traditional gender roles
that occurred with the industrial revolution. The second section de-
scribes the new configuration of gender roles that emerged during the

1. Most of the historical studies of gender roles and ideology have focused on female
roles. This rich and relatively new body of literature is primarily a result of the feminist
movement of the 1960s and 1970s and of the influx into academia of women interested
in uncovering the world and contributions of women, which have been all too long
and often neglected. Because of this new wave of historical research, we know more
than ever before about women's lives and the ideology of female gender identity. See
a description of the rise of this scholarship on female sexuality and gender roles in
John D'Emilio and Estelle Freedman, *Intimate Matters: A History of Sexuality in America*
(New York: Harper & Row, 1988), xii-xiii.

Not as much research has been done on male gender identity and social conventions.
Since most traditional scholarship was done from a male perspective (yet touted as
objective, generic, and genderless or gender inclusive), it was not until women began
producing gender-sensitive critiques and their own body of gender-sensitive research
that historians have turned to male gender roles and identity as primary subject matter.
Few major studies have been produced. Two important among them are Peter G.
Filene, *Him/Her/Self: Sex Roles in Modern America,* 2d ed. (Baltimore: Johns Hopkins
Univ. Press, 1986); Peter N. Stearns, *Be a Man! Males in Modern Society* (New York:
Holmes and Meier Publishing, 1979).

Victorian period in response to the chaos created by industrial capitalism
and the eventual stabilization of a culturally dominant middle class.[2]
The third section examines the late nineteenth- and early twentieth-
century challenges to the reigning middle-class Victorian gender ideology. These cultural disruptions deeply affected the context within
which Protestant fundamentalism emerged.

Industrialization, Urbanization, and Gender Roles

Although changes in gender identity and convention were complex
and uneven, research on the history of gender roles has led scholars to
one general conclusion: "The importance of sex-role definition increased
markedly as an early and durable response to industrial society."[3] With
industrialization and urbanization, gender distinctions assumed unprecedented importance for both men and women. The gender ideology
of the Victorian middle class reflected this new heightened consciousness
of gender distinctions. Fundamentalism was, in part, an expression of
widespread unease during a period in the United States when many
challenged in theory and practice this dominant middle-class gender
ideology and set of social conventions. But it is impossible to understand
the nature of Victorian gender ideology, and the profound discomfort
its destabilization caused, without first examining briefly the origins
of the ideology in early industrial and urban communities.

By 1700, argued social historian Peter N. Stearns, men and women
of Western European descent were heirs to a complex but stable set of
gender roles and conventions. Women's primary roles in the rural and
village structures were as mother, keeper of hearth and home, and
assistant in fields or shops. Men depended for their masculine identity
on several sets of symbols: patriarch within the family, landowner or
skilled laborer, and warrior. Women's functions in childbearing and
housekeeping remained relatively stable despite industrialization and
the move to the cities, and women did not experience as many profoundly disturbing changes as did men. Men had neither childbearing
nor home and hearth to insulate them from the drastic changes in
working conditions and means of production. Men suffered the most

2. With the stabilization of the white middle class, their beliefs about sexuality
"were dominant not only in the sense of being widespread, through an expanding
published discourse, but also because sexual meanings enforced emerging racial and
class hierarchies." D'Emilio and Freedman, *Intimate Matters,* xvi-xvii.

3. Stearns, *Be a Man!* 36.

severe disruptions and, because prevailing cultural norms and symbols, as well as social conventions and institutions, were the products of men, this necessarily brief review of pre-industrial and early industrial gender roles and ideology focuses on male identity and on male-created, dominant cultural symbols and ideology relating to both genders.[4]

Pre-industrial men in Western European societies based their male identity on three major components of their lives.[5] The first was the identification of manliness with work, especially work requiring specialized and carefully honed skill, physical strength, or serious risk to life and limb. In farming, mining, the craftsmen's guilds, and shipping, a man worked with his hands and with his back in an environment in which men shared both a comradeship and a sense of competition.[6] Stearns cited mining as a case in point: The labor was strenuous, the mines hazardous, and women often were banned from the site.[7]

A second support on which traditional manhood rested was an old, even pre-agricultural, set of symbols and cultural expectations that Stearns labeled "warrior" or "hunter."[8] Masculine identity depended not only on physical strength and skill but on ruthless competitiveness and bloody aggression. Such a tradition created and preserved until very recently the "man's army," in which traditional manhood was created, tried, and reinforced through the hazing of basic training; the camaraderie, terror, pain, and joy of battle; and the exclusion of women except as booty and spoils.

The patriarchal family was the third bastion of traditional masculine identity. Although the term *patriarchal* is commonly used to refer to a wide range of family systems in which the father or husband is dominant in some way, in this context *patriarchal* refers to specific ways in which the family was structured to give the father absolute control over his sons and daughters. The primary purpose of the traditional family under analysis here was the production of workers and heirs to whom went the patriarch's land or, if landless, special occupational skill or membership in the guild. The man's main role within the family was as father (rather than husband), with the key emphasis

4. This statement does not deny the existence of culture created and influenced by women. Women have not been the architects of dominant culture and ideology, however.

5. This brief account is dependent primarily on Stearns, *Be a Man!*

6. Women, of course, participated in some of this work, such as farming and spinning, but men derived much of their sense of manhood from their labor. Men's identity as men depended more on the nature of their work than did women's identity as women.

7. Stearns, *Be a Man!* 39.

8. See chapter, "The Tradition of Manhood," Stearns, *Be a Man!* 13–38.

placed on the control of the sons through the promise of economic
security passed on by the father, who was the only source of such
security. Control of the daughters was assured by arranged marriage
and the requirement of a dowry; control of the wife by close proximity
during the work day. Barbara Berg's analysis matches Stearns's:

> In rural or village families, fathers had little difficulty as-
> serting their will. They felt confident that their wisdom
> and experience qualified them to educate their offspring
> . . . and to command their respect. Expecting obedience,
> fathers usually worked near enough to their families . . .
> to see that wives and children followed given directives.[9]

There was a continuity, both economic and domestic, from generation
to generation that was, in fact and in ideology, controlled by the fathers.
The patriarchal family has been called "the ancient citadel of masculine
authority."[10]

The movement to the cities and into a paid labor economy disrupted the day-to-day, generation-to-generation reality on which the
traditional understanding and function of manhood rested and which,
in turn, it molded. As more and more men began to work in the
factories and live in the rapidly expanding cities, fewer and fewer of
them controlled or owned land, which "hit at the essence of masculinity."[11] Sons of these men often had little to inherit and were consequently more difficult for the father to control and intimidate. More
occupational options existed for sons than in traditional society, and
the sons were less likely to follow in their fathers' footsteps, thus
disrupting the economic continuity of the generations. With the male
heads of the family occupied all day in the factories, a division of labor,
found in traditional households but amplified in industrial society,
arose between husband and wife. It gave the wife more responsibility
and power within the household (to compensate for an absentee father)
and further weakened the preserve of patriarchalism.

Men in the business and clerical class had even more difficulty
proving their manhood than did the laboring class. Business required
no physical strength or risk of bodily harm. Also, the new middle
class, faced with a different set of economic demands (saving and
investing capital) and sensibilities (large families were no longer an

9. Barbara J. Berg, *The Remembered Gate: Origins of American Feminism: The Woman
and the City, 1800–1860* (New York: Oxford Univ. Press, 1978), 49.
10. Berg, *The Remembered Gate*, 49.
11. Stearns, *Be a Man!* 44. See also D'Emilio and Freedman, *Intimate Matters*, 66.

economic asset) had, by 1830, begun to reduce the birth rate through birth control.[12] Consequently, the ability to sire heirs declined in importance as a measure of manhood.

Defining and experiencing manhood by relying on the traditional male prerogatives of land, skilled and physically demanding labor, and patriarchy became very difficult over the course of the industrial revolution. By the nineteenth century, men used a new set of cultural signposts to compensate for their losses and insecurities. This set of gender-related symbols, *mores,* and conventions was dominant throughout the Victorian period and is one of the period's most distinguishing marks.

The Victorian Gender Ideology

A new homeostasis in gender roles and an ideology supporting it emerged as the middle class achieved broad economic stability. The process was uneven, but Carroll Smith-Rosenberg estimated that "bourgeois class structure" in the United States had stabilized by the 1860s or 1870s.[13] The primary characteristic of this new set of gender roles and social conventions was a rigid delineation of the genders: each gender was assigned a radically distinct character and a separate sphere of activity and expertise. Given the fragility of the traditional measures of manhood, it became more important to heighten gender differences and to define manliness *via negativa:* men were not women.

> Confused and unsure of themselves, men found a foil for their own ambiguous identities through the specific and stagnant qualities they ascribed to women. Men may not have known who they were or what characteristics they had, but by insisting that women had all the weak and inferior traits, they at least knew what they were not.[14]

By limiting women's participation in the economic and political world, and by permitting a moral and sexual double standard, the symbolic

12. Before the new artificial birth-control technology of the early twentieth century, most couples had to rely on abstinence and *coitus interruptus.* See Daniel Scott Smith, "Family Limitation, Sexual Control, and Domestic Feminism in Victorian America," in *A Heritage of Her Own: Toward a New Social History of American Women,* ed. Nancy F. Cott and Elizabeth H. Pleck (New York: Simon & Schuster, 1979), 222–45.

13. Carroll Smith-Rosenberg, *Disorderly Conduct: Visions of Gender in Victorian America* (New York: Alfred A. Knopf, 1985), 171.

14. Berg, *The Remembered Gate,* 73. See also Filene, *Him/Her/Self,* 93; Barbara Ehrenreich and Deirdre English, *For Her Own Good: 150 Years of the Experts' Advice to Women* (New York: Doubleday Anchor Books, 1979), 109.

roles and the day-to-day lives of the genders became distinct and unrelated.

Men in business, who no longer knew how to demonstrate masculinity when their jobs took them to offices rather than to fields and mines, developed a new measure of manliness. These businessmen, according to Stearns, developed the idea of "business as battle, the business world as the jungle."[15] Businessmen and captains of industry waged campaigns, fought battles, achieved victories, and risked defeat in competition with other businessmen. The world of the breadwinner was depicted as an unsavory and strenuous world in which ruthlessness and aggression were prized. Men sought to eliminate the competition and to exploit workers in order to maximize profits, and hence, to win. Julie A. Matthaei described this new "economic self-seeking" as the "predominant masculine ethic, wiping out the competing ethics of loyalty to firm or family, and religion."[16]

For men in factories and offices, it was even more important to associate the role of breadwinner exclusively with men, since masculinity on the job itself became more tenuous. Men took satisfaction out of simply being able to be the sole support of their families in an economic situation that was so new, unstable, and difficult. Stearns estimated, for example, that the failure rate for new businesses during the first half of the nineteenth century was fifty percent or more.[17] Income replaced property as a sign of successful manhood, and by the late 1800s a wife who did not work outside the home "constituted a visible badge of having achieved middle-class status,"[18] a sign to the outside world that a man was an adequate breadwinner and sufficiently masculine.

The stability of the economic warrior (or breadwinner) symbol depended on keeping women out of the male sphere of business, labor, politics, and government. Women were assigned to the home, where

15. Stearns, *Be a Man!* 83. See also Filene, *Him/Her/Self*, 72.

16. Julie A. Matthaei, *An Economic History of Women in America: Women's Work, the Sexual Division of Labor, and the Development of Capitalism* (New York: Schocken Books, 1982), 103–6. See also Alice Kessler-Harris, "Woman, Work, and the Social Order," in *Liberating Women's History: Theoretical and Critical Essays*, ed. Berenice A. Carroll (Urbana, Ill.: Univ. of Illinois Press, 1976), 332.

17. Stearns, *Be a Man!* 47.

18. William H. Chafe, *Women and Equality: Changing Patterns in American Culture* (New York: Oxford Univ. Press, 1977), 22. See also Lois W. Banner, *Women in Modern America: A Brief History* (New York: Harcourt Brace Jovanovich, 1974), 53; Reay Tannehill, *Sex in History* (New York: Stein and Day, 1980), 351; W. Elliot Brownlee and Mary M. Brownlee, *Women in the American Economy: A Documentary History, 1675–1929* (New Haven: Yale Univ. Press, 1976), 19.

they could not jeopardize, symbolically or practically, the deep and unambiguous sense of manhood fostered in and dependent on an exclusively male workplace and public domain.

Assigning women to the domestic realm helped ease moral conflicts inherent in aggressive capitalism. Uneasy about the profit motive, about exploiting those less fortunate, about using deceptive means to sell their goods, about ruthless and often unfair competition against other businessmen, men created "the home" as a refuge from the dirty work of business. Men also created "the virtuous woman" who would practice the kindness and charity they were unable to in the manly economic world.[19] Sheila M. Rothman called this new ideology of separate spheres "virtuous womanhood."[20] Barbara Welter wrote a landmark study of the same phenomenon, and called it the "Cult of True Womanhood."[21] Filene used the phrase "cult of the lady."[22] Barbara J. Harris gave a succinct description:

> The cult of true womanhood was a compound of four ideas: a sharp dichotomy between the home and the economic world outside that paralleled a sharp contrast between female and male natures, the designation of the home as the female's only proper sphere, the moral superiority of woman, and the idealization of her function as mother.[23]

By the middle of the nineteenth century, Harris argued, the cult of true womanhood represented the dominant values and code of behavior for the middle class and all others who sought upward mobility and middle-class respectability.

Victorian gender ideology represented the home as a private and feminine domain. Men needed a refuge entirely free from the trials and uncertainties of the world of business and politics. The home "was a safe focus for women's energies"[24] because in it women performed tasks that men valued but were no longer allowed to do themselves (i.e.,

19. "The pedestal had, after all, been built by male hands. To be a 'womanly woman' was to play a role before a male audience." Filene, *Him/Her/Self*, 69. See also Stearns, *Be a Man!* 84.

20. Sheila M. Rothman, *Woman's Proper Place: A History of Changing Ideals and Practices, 1870 to the Present* (New York: Basic Books, 1978), 5.

21. Barbara Welter, "The Cult of True Womanhood, 1820–1860," in *Dimity Convictions: The American Woman in the Nineteenth Century*, ed. Barbara Welter (Athens, Oh.: Ohio Univ. Press, 1976), 21–41.

22. Filene, *Him/Her/Self*, 8.

23. Barbara J. Harris, *Beyond Her Sphere: Women and the Professions in American History* (Westport, Conn.: Greenwood Press, 1978), 33.

24. Ehrenreich and English, *For Her Own Good*, 149.

the new middle-class work situation allowed men very little time to rear children and to manage the household). Also, by remaining within the confines of the domestic sphere, women did not challenge masculine identity dependent on rigid and totally discrete gender-role definitions. Men needed to compensate women for being removed from the world of work, so the ideology of the separate spheres named woman "queen of the home," and emphasized the importance of motherhood as a vocation. Consequently, the nineteenth century was the great age of the home, and it was so because much more was at stake than the home itself. At stake was a basic sense of gender identity (especially male identity) and place within the newly established economic and social order.[25]

A second way nineteenth-century men sought to shore up their masculine identity was through a stronger symbolic identification of maleness with sexual activity and aggression. In the last century a startling reversal occurred in the ways in which the culture described human sexuality and attributed it to the genders. Traditional Christian culture portrayed woman as the sexual temptress, the one who had little control over her primal sexual urges and powers. Men were warned constantly to avoid women lest they be seduced and brought down by them. Men were considered creatures of the intellect and spirit, women creatures of the body and earth. A relatively quick turn-around was accomplished in the nineteenth century, when women were transformed from sensual temptresses to "passive partners with little sexual appetite."[26] The man became the location of unbridled and dangerous lust; the woman became the defender of chastity. This new code left the domain of sexual gratification and expertise to men, and sexual conquest became an important symbol of modern manhood.

At the same time, the new theories of female "passionlessness" expressed "tensions over female sexual vulnerability." Because women in the cities lost the traditional protection of family and the arranged marriage, they came to depend on the idea of virtuous womanhood to defend their interests and security.[27]

These Victorian sexual attitudes, with their emphasis on women's sexual restraint and purity, performed another function by reinforcing

25. See William L. O'Neill, *Everyone Was Brave: The Rise and Fall of Feminism in America* (Chicago: Quadrangle Books, 1969), 4–5; Berg, *The Remembered Gate*, 67.

26. Stearns, *Be a Man!* 80.

27. See Nancy F. Cott, "Passionlessness: An Interpretation of Victorian Sexual Ideology, 1790–1850," in *A Heritage of Her Own*, 107–35; D'Emilio and Freedman, *Intimate Matters*, 44–46.

ideologically the attempt to curb legitimate births. A sexual double standard appeared, resulting from the tensions between the ideals of purity and birth control on the one hand, and the new pressures on men to prove themselves through sexual activity on the other. Consequently, the demand for prostitutes increased markedly in the cities, and as could be expected, from 1780 on there was an increase in illegitimate births.[28]

Women's morality was important to men also because it eased the doubts men had about their own sexuality. Norms for manliness dictated a certain sexual prowess and level of activity. Since men could not really be manly *and* preach sexual restraint, it fell to the women to be the guardians of decency. A man worried about controlling his sexual drives could place that burden on women and feel safer from the sin always lurking in him.

The new middle-class masculinity, based on economic warfare and competitiveness, and on the role of sexual aggressor, had no room for Christian morality. Consequently, the church was, along with women, relegated to the private domestic sphere and virtually conceded to women.[29] This change resulted in yet another surprising reversal in Christian history. Victorian society not only portrayed women as the moral superiors of men, but declared religion women's special realm, a lean-to built on to the Victorian home for women to oversee and in which to find work to occupy their leisure time. Barbara Welter called this phenomenon the "feminization of American religion."[30] Ann Douglas gave the topic lengthy treatment in her book, *The Feminization of American Culture*.[31] There she argued that the formal disestablishment of the clergy (with the disestablishment of various colonial churches) and the informal disestablishment of middle-class women (by barring them from business and politics) led to an alliance between Protestant ministers and their female parishioners. Such mutual dependence—

28. D'Emilio and Freedman, *Intimate Matters*. 44.

29. See Barbara Welter, "She Hath Done What She Could: Protestant Women's Missionary Careers in Nineteenth-Century America," in *Women in American Religion*, ed. Janet Wilson James (Philadelphia: Univ. of Pennsylvania Press, 1980), 125. Welter argued that women's advance in such fields as religion and education in the late nineteenth century could represent "less a victory than a strategic retreat by the opposition. Certain areas of societal concern were given over to woman not because of her efforts but because either society or the occupation had changed."

30. See Barbara Welter, "The Feminization of American Religion: 1800–1860," in *Clio's Consciousness Raised: New Perspectives on the History of Women*, ed. Mary S. Hartman and Lois Banner (New York: Harper & Row, 1974), 137–57.

31. Ann Douglas, *The Feminization of American Culture* (New York: Alfred A. Knopf, 1977; Avon Books, 1978).

women dependent on the church and its ministers for a vocation, and ministers dependent on women to fill the pews and do the volunteer work—led to a softening or sentimentalizing of theology and worship. Hence, harsh Calvinism lost some of its influence, and Methodism triumphed not only on the frontier, where camp-meeting Arminianism seemed the most pragmatic way to proceed, but especially among the newly emerging middle class of the urban and industrial Northeast.

As the century progressed, churches baptized infants much earlier, discarded the idea of infant damnation, and interpreted Jesus in a more "feminine" light that stressed his continuity with other human beings, his meekness, and his sacrifice.[32] Nancy F. Cott documented the rapid growth of women's religious clubs and organizations—"prayer groups, charitable institutions, missionary associations"—during the first half of the nineteenth century.[33] The woman of the house became the religious agent of the family—religion was part of the work assigned to the domestic sphere.[34] As religion fell into women's hands, it became less relevant to the male definition of masculinity:

> Increasingly, in a political world, women and the church stood out as anti-political forces, as they did in an increasingly materialistic society, dominated by a new species, Economic Man. . . . Both women and the church were to be above the counting house, she on her pedestal, the church in its sanctuary. Wealth was to be given them as consumers and as reflections of its makers.[35]

This division of labor on the religious front contributed to "a polarization between male and female virtues."[36] Compare the requirements of American manhood described earlier with "the four cardinal virtues of the true woman": piety, purity, submissiveness, and domesticity.[37]

In the history of American Christianity, the segregation of women, religion, home, childrearing, and virtue away from the world of business, politics, commerce, and labor was a historical moment of true significance. This "privatization" of religion limited its relevance to

32. See Welter, "The Feminization of American Religion," 137–57.

33. Nancy F. Cott, "Religion and the Bonds of Womanhood," in *Our American Sisters: Women in American Life and Thought*, 3d ed., ed. Jean E. Friedman and William G. Shade (Lexington, Mass.: D. C. Heath and Company, 1982), 199.

34. See Stearns, *Be a Man!* 50–51.

35. Welter, "The Feminization of American Religion," in *Clio's Consciousness Raised*, 139.

36. Stearns, *Be a Man!* 51.

37. Welter, "Cult of True Womanhood," 21.

"personal or subjective needs" and led "adherents to play down the public import of their world view."[38] It also led to a confusion of church and home that Christopher Lasch referred to as "the cult of the home,"[39] which is explored later in this volume.

Although Victorian gender ideology placed many complex limitations on women and their sphere of activity, it also elevated women to a status they had never enjoyed previously. Because men could not in good conscience entirely brush aside the domestic and religious realms, because they still wanted legitimate heirs who would be raised to value and respect patriarchal authority, and because they sensed that they must make domesticity look sweet in order to keep women within its confines, they produced a sentimental, gushing exaltation of home, woman, and motherhood. Never before had women been praised so highly, nor had their day-to-day lives been described as being so worthy and vital. Women were given an important social role that only they could fill.[40]

The development and dissemination of rigid and precise gender roles did much to stabilize a society that seemed on the verge of total chaos. Historians of gender roles in the United States are in agreement here. Smith-Rosenberg argued that the absolute differences between men and women championed by the dominant culture assured Americans "that they in fact lived in a world of timeless and unambiguous social categories rooted in absolute physiological laws."[41] G. J. Barker-Benfield concluded that in such a fluid and frightening society "men derived their sense of order from the family, and retired home to experience order."[42] Lasch also understood the essential stabilizing function of the separate spheres: "In a society that felt itself on the verge of chaos—a 'frontier' in the broadest sense of the term—they [women] came to represent cohesion, decency, and self-restraint."[43] Although every society needs systems of order and stability, nineteenth-century America chose to place the primary burden of such order and stability

38. James Davison Hunter, *American Evangelism: Conservative Religion and the Quandary of Modernity* (New Brunswick, N.J.: Rutgers Univ. Press, 1983), 14–17.

39. Christopher Lasch, "Woman as Alien," in *The Woman Question in American History*, ed. Barbara Welter (Hinsdale, Ill.: The Dryden Press, 1973), 152.

40. Matthaei, *An Economic History of Women in America*, 106–16.

41. Smith-Rosenberg, *Disorderly Conduct*, 261.

42. G. J. Barker-Benfield, *The Horrors of the Half-Known Life: Male Attitudes toward Women and Sexuality in Nineteenth-Century America* (New York: Harper & Row, 1976), 49.

43. Lasch, "Woman as Alien," 152.

on women, their moral restraint, and their confinement within the domestic realm.

It is important to keep in mind the middle-class urban origin and character of the separate-spheres ideology,[44] for fundamentalism was born of these same urban, middle-class people. And, like fundamentalism, the ideology of separate spheres seemed to thrive on American soil as on no other. Lasch argued that the American situation was both unique and extreme: "In no other country in the world was the distinction between the two [genders], in the popular mind, so uncompromisingly rigid."[45]

Many historians of gender roles and relations in America agree that the Victorian gender ideology contained within it the seeds of its own destruction.[46] Women's command in the home further reduced the chances that men could achieve any sense of manliness from the traditional sources of controlling children and governing a household. More power in the household meant more power for women within the marriage itself. Middle-class women, with the leisure time, money, and experience in organizing they received at home and in their church work,[47] broke out of their domestic sphere into the public and supposedly all-male world of politics, education, professions, and business. And many women did all this as a vocal and self-conscious revolt against the ideology of the separate spheres itself and the limits it placed on women's lives. The next section considers the challenges to the separate spheres that came as a result of the consolidation and expansion of industrialism, the rise of the professions, and the rebellion against the predominant gender ideology present in women's thought and activities.

The Demise of Separate Spheres

Just as middle-class men consolidated their positions as the arbiters of respectable culture, the captains of business and trade, and the keepers of the separate spheres, the United States entered a second stage of its industrial growth and economic development. This stage was marked

44. See Harris, *Beyond Her Sphere*, 33; and Jean E. Friedman, *The Enclosed Garden: Women and Community in the Evangelical South, 1830–1900* (Chapel Hill, N.C.: The Univ. of North Carolina Press, 1985), 6; Chafe, *Women and Equality*, 36.

45. Lasch, "Woman as Alien," 152.

46. See Matthaei, *An Economic History of Women in America*, 185; Friedman, *The Enclosed Garden*, 6; Chafe, *Women and Equality*, 36; O'Neill, *Everyone Was Brave*, 5-6; Harris, *Beyond Her Sphere*, 77.

47. See Gregory K. Vickers, "Woman's Place: Images of Womanhood in the Southern Baptist Convention 1888–1929" (M.A. thesis, Vanderbilt Univ., 1986), 36ff.

primarily by the rise of the professions, professional education, and
large bureaucratic business organizations, and was dated by Stearns
from the 1870s to the 1920s.[48] During this period, the structure of
American industry changed dramatically. Small businesses and man-
ufacturing plants, often family-owned, gave way to giant corporations
with national markets and to finance capitalism and investments. For
example, between the years 1880 and 1900, the following trusts were
organized: Standard Oil Company, United States Steel, American Sugar
Refining Company, American Tobacco Company, Pullman Palace Car
Company, and American Telephone and Telegraph.[49] "Manly" work in
one's own shop, office, vehicle, or factory gave way to employment in
bureaucratized, sterile corporate offices:

> And what could a man measure as his own achievement out
> of the million-dollar annual operations of U.S. Steel or
> Montgomery Ward? As a corporate employee . . . he lost
> touch with the product of his work. He put his hands only
> on the typewriter, the account books, the documents. . . .
> Given this increasing impersonality and efficiency, a middle-
> class man found it harder to acquire the psychological sat-
> isfaction he needed in defining himself as a breadwinner.[50]

When American business became big business, men's ability to play
the "economic warrior" was reduced since many small businesses failed
or were bought out and men became mere bureaucratic cogs in large
business organizations.

Women Move into the Public Sphere. To make matters worse for
men, women began working in far greater numbers both in factories
and in white-collar jobs during the last two decades of the nineteenth
century. Between 1880 and 1910, the proportion of employed women
increased from 14.7 to 24.8 percent.[51] In the ten years between 1900
and 1910, the percentage of married women working outside the home
more than doubled (from 5 to 11 percent).[52] There was also a marked

48. Stearns, *Be a Man!* 39.
49. See Nancy A. Hardesty, *Women Called to Witness: Evangelical Feminism in the 19th
Century* (Nashville: Abingdon Press, 1984), 32; Smith-Rosenberg, *Disorderly Conduct,*
171.
50. Filene, *Him/Her/Self,* 73.
51. Brownlee and Brownlee, *Women in the American Economy,* 23. See also Nancy F.
Cott, *The Grounding of Modern Feminism* (New Haven: Yale Univ. Press, 1987), 129–
31.
52. Banner, *Women in Modern America,* 45.

difference in the kind of employment women sought and held. In 1870, almost 60 percent of all employed women were in domestic service. By 1920, less than 20 percent were. The greatest increases took place in business and the professions, the middle-class male empire. Between 1870 and 1920, the number of women clerks and secretaries increased "a thousand times to one million." The number of women teachers went up eight times to 645,000, and nurses and midwives rose twenty times to 280,000. New technology made physical tasks in factory and shops lighter and thus made possible the employment of more women. The number of women employed as shop assistants during the period increased sixty times to 534,000.[53] This entry of women into the male domain of work outside the home, especially after so many women did so well replacing men at work during World War I,[54] made it less likely that men would be able to see themselves as uniquely capable of earning a living in the modern world. The presence of women in the workplace made it less likely that men could achieve unquestionable masculine identity through their work.

Middle-class men compensated by emphasizing men's special rational nature, "by associating economic manhood with claims to specialized knowledge."[55] During the late nineteenth century, professions such as law, medicine, and ministry adopted new and more rigorous educational prerequisites. Middle-class masculinity came to depend on higher education and professional expertise. By the 1880s, however, women entered institutions of higher learning in ever-growing numbers. Higher incomes and more leisure time for many middle-class women afforded them opportunity for education. By 1890, two-thirds of the country's high school graduates were women.[56] By 1900, only 8 percent of American colleges and universities admitted women, but middle-class women flocked to enroll. By 1908, women outnumbered men in attendance in liberal arts courses of study in Colorado, Kansas, Iowa, Minnesota, Nebraska, and Washington. University presidents began to talk about quotas.[57] Women's colleges fought an uphill battle but became important centers of learning and socialization for women who came of age in the 1880s and 1890s.

53. David Morgan, *Suffragists and Democrats: The Politics of Woman Suffrage in America* (East Lansing, Mich.: Michigan State Univ. Press, 1972), 123. See also Brownlee and Brownlee, *Women in the American Economy*, 19.

54. Morgan, *Suffragists and Democrats*, 58.

55. Stearns, *Be a Man!* 98.

56. Brownlee and Brownlee, *Women in the American Economy*, 19. See also Rothman, *Woman's Proper Place*, 5–6; Matthaei, *An Economic History of Women in America*, 178.

57. Morgan, *Suffragists and Democrats*, 51.

Women, once they were allowed to enter the world of male rationality, succeeded there. Just as education became the mark of the successful middle-class man and the focus of much male energy and activity, so too was education one of the most important contributing factors to the rise in the late nineteenth century of what historians have called the "New Woman." The New Woman was usually college educated, and she married late, if at all. She had fewer children than her counterparts. If employed, she worked in business or the professions, or she volunteered for a myriad of charitable and civic activities. The New Woman chafed under the restrictions imposed upon her by the separate-spheres ideology.[58] Her departure from the private sphere to the public realm constituted yet another significant threat to American masculinity and became the cause of a great deal of alarm. Women's nature and sphere of activity became the battleground on which men fought for their own identity as men. Could men be true men if women were no longer true women?

The woman's rights movement preceded the emergence of the New Woman. The two phenomena are related but not identical. Ellen Carol DuBois traced the origins of the organized movement for equal rights for women to two sources: "women's growing awareness of their common conditions and grievances" and "antebellum reform politics, particularly . . . the antislavery movement."[59] The woman's rights activists were a small but vigorous group led by such women as Elizabeth Cady Stanton and Susan B. Anthony. Before the Civil War, the activists argued for equality on the basis of inherent human rights recognized by the United States Constitution and elucidated in Enlightenment philosophy. They espoused a radical goal: to "break down the wall separating the private sphere, which trapped and isolated women from a rich experience of the world, from the public sphere in which male power reigned."[60] These pioneering feminists were suspicious of all forms of gender ideology: the separate spheres of work and influence, the double standard of morality, the religious foundations of social *mores,* and the traditional Victorian patterns of marriage and motherhood.

58. See Smith-Rosenberg, *Disorderly Conduct,* 176–78; Chafe, *Women and Equality,* 27–29; and Catherine Clinton, *The Other Civil War: American Women in the Nineteenth Century* (New York: Hill & Wang, 1984), 135.
    59. Ellen Carol DuBois, "Women's Rights before the Civil War," in *Our American Sisters,* 292.
    60. William Leach, *True Love and Perfect Union: The Feminist Reform of Sex and Society* (New York: Basic Books, 1980), 133.

The second surge of nineteenth-century feminism occurred after the Civil War and differed from the first in tone and leadership style. William Chafe traced its origins to the "social reform ethos" of the last third of the century.[61] This new generation of women activists, the New Woman, had been born and reared within the limits set by the separate-spheres ideology of the Victorian middle class. They based their work and arguments on the assumptions of gender-specific spheres and character.[62] Women's leadership in the public realm, from temperance to suffrage to church ministry, was desirable and necessary, they argued, because women were uniquely qualified to protect the home and all the virtues associated with it. Late nineteenth-century women's rights activity had wider appeal than its earlier counterpart. And, although it never directly refuted the prevailing notions of male and female gender roles and identity, it was, on the basis of numbers alone, much more startling and obvious evidence that conventional middle-class gender ideology, so fragile and so important to American men, was beginning to crumble.

The only public institution left to women according to the ideology of separate spheres was the church. Contemporary accounts of the abundance of women and the discouraging lack of men in the church and in church activities were numerous, and the situation was a matter of pastoral concern. Herbert J. White, a minister, asked "Why More Women than Men in Our Churches?" He reported that only one-third of the members of Massachusetts Baptist churches were men.[63] Women not only filled the pews each Sunday, but by the end of the century they organized and taught the Sunday schools. They were the most successful supporters of foreign and domestic missions. By 1892, ten of the major denominations organized large national women's missionary societies that raised millions of dollars.[64] Some women had official leadership positions within churches. Julia Ward Howe called a "Woman Preachers' Convention" in 1873 to gather together women who had assumed that role within a church, mission, or revival setting.[65] New and unorthodox religious movements of the late nineteenth century

61. Chafe, *Women and Equality*, 117.
62. See Chafe, *Women and Equality*, 38; Banner, *Women in Modern America*, 92.
63. Herbert J. White, "Why More Women than Men in Our Churches?" *Watchman* 79, no. 26 (June 30, 1898): 13.
64. Virginia Lieson Brereton and Christa Ressmeyer Klein, "American Women in Ministry: A History of Protestant Beginning Points," in *Women in American Religion*, 174–75.
65. See Leach, *True Love and Perfect Union*, 278.

such as spiritualism and Christian Science attracted more women than men. Many of these groups had strong female leadership.[66]

It would be erroneous to conclude that men, by imprisoning the church within the domestic sphere in order to free the political and economic realm from Christianity's moral code and expectations, had given up all claim to power within the church. Although businessmen seemed content with a thoroughly privatized and feminized church, male professionals in the church were not so sanguine. Male ministers were put in special jeopardy because their male identity was dependent in significant ways on a profession that was harbored within an otherwise feminine institution and ethos.

Once woman had been established as the queen of the home, the guardian of virtue, and the mainstay of the church, it was but a short and natural step to the women's temperance movement. Established in 1873, the Women's Christian Temperance Union (WCTU) quickly became the largest organization of women in the nation's history. By 1897, membership stood at over two million, and Frances Willard, the president of the WCTU from 1879 to 1898, has been called "Woman of the Century" by one historian.[67] The WCTU provided for many of its members their first foray into the world of politics and social reform. Although women involved in the temperance movement threatened the male domain of the tavern, the biggest challenge to the separate-spheres ideology contained within the "home protection" agenda of the WCTU was simply the experience in organizing, the social contacts, and the sense of purpose and accomplishment outside the home that these millions of women felt. Many respectable middle-class women were radicalized by their participation in the WCTU. Willard's agenda for the WCTU did not stop at temperance but included social (sexual) purity, child-labor reform, prison reform, homes for unwed mothers, women's suffrage, and socialism. Willard's rhetoric and strategy used an appeal to "home protection," which was an extension and adaptation of the ideology of separate spheres. In 1881, Willard formed the Home Protection Party as a temperance coalition and argued that because women knew best how to guarantee the welfare of the family, home

66. Mary Baker Eddy, founder of Christian Science, is the most notable case in point. Victoria Woodhull, feminist and advocate of "free love," was a national leader of the American Association of Spiritualists. See Leach, *True Love and Perfect Union*, 294.

67. Hardesty, *Women Called to Witness*, 25. See also Ruth Bordin, *Women and Temperance: The Quest for Power and Liberty, 1873–1900*, American Civilization Series (Philadelphia: Temple Univ. Press, 1981), xvi–xvii.

protection was grounds sufficient to give women the vote. A minister reporting on the 1890 Convention of the WCTU in Seattle made the connection between temperance work and women's suffrage clear:

> They declare women should have the ballot because it's right, and also because the dramshop will totter the day she grasps the white missive. Their aim seems to be, not the securing of more politics into religion, but of more religion into politics.[68]

Many of the women active in the suffrage movement came out of the WCTU, although by 1900 the WCTU, without Willard at its helm, narrowed its focus and left the suffrage movement.[69]

The WCTU was perhaps the most popular but certainly not the only large organization of women in the late nineteenth century. Middle-class women left home for clubs of all sorts—civic, religious, intellectual, and artistic. According to Lois Banner, "never before or since have so many women belonged to so many organizations."[70] The General Federation of Women's Clubs was the largest secular alliance. Its membership went from twenty thousand in 1892 to one million by 1915. Women's clubs had significant effect on women, men, and the communities in which they lived, even if the effect is difficult to quantify. O'Neill concluded that the clubs did a great deal of "civic good housekeeping." Many towns owed their pure drinking water or public library to these clubs. In Chicago and Boston clubwomen forced the city to buy and restore tenement houses. They were active in reform movements at the state and federal level as well. Women worked in states like Massachusetts and Rhode Island to pass labor legislation. They exerted pressure on legislatures in Iowa, Ohio, Pennsylvania, and Michigan to create a juvenile justice system. Federal legislation such as the Pure Food and Drug Act, the Child Labor Bill, and "other typical Progressive measures" were passed at the insistence of organized women.[71] In fact, some historians have judged that women's reform organizations were the backbone of the entire Progressive movement.[72]

---

68. Thomas Coyle, "W.C.T.U. Convention in Seattle," *Record of Christian Work* 19, no. 1 (January 1890): 4.

69. See Hardesty, *Women Called to Witness*, 18–23; Clinton, *The Other Civil War*, 177; Filene, *Him/Her/Self*, 81–82.

70. Banner, *Women in Modern America*, 87.

71. O'Neill, *Everyone Was Brave*, 88.

72. See Clinton, *The Other Civil War*, 166–69; Banner, *Women in Modern America*, 96; O'Neill, *Everyone Was Brave*, 84–85.

Perhaps the best way to convey the energy and rapid growth of women's clubs during the period is to look at one example. Twenty-one women formed the Chicago Women's Club in 1876. The club had several departments: reform, philanthropy, home, education, art and literature, philosophy, and science. Club membership increased ten times by 1886 and doubled again by 1892. In 1900, the club set a membership limit of one thousand. By 1890, almost two-thirds of the members worked within the most progressive branches: education, philanthropy, and reform. Other reform groups in Chicago such as the Legal Aid Society, the Public Art Association, and the Protective Agency for Women and Children received assistance from the club.[73] Women's clubs represented a widespread departure from the gender ideology of separate spheres. By joining a club, many women stepped into the male world of politics, government, and social reform.

Although the clubs attracted a wide variety of women—young and old, college-educated and not, Northern and Southern, urban and rural—the settlement house movement of the 1890s represented a noteworthy accomplishment of young female college graduates. Having studied the new social sciences and in search of meaningful and challenging work, settlement house workers lived and worked among the urban poor. Settlement house workers understood their mission to include political reform as well as direct person-to-person aid to the disenfranchised.[74] The social work experience in urban slums was a springboard from which some settlement house leaders went on to highly visible positions in government and social welfare agencies. Katherine Bement Davis was named, in 1914, Commissioner of Corrections in New York City, and three years after that the general secretary of the Rockefeller Foundation's Bureau of Social Hygiene. There she completed studies of prostitution, narcotics addiction, and human sexual behavior. Julia Lathrop became the first director of the federal Children's Bureau in 1912. Mary McDowall was elected first president of the Chicago branch of the Women's Trade Union League, and Florence Kelley was named head of the National Consumers' League. All of these women were trained in settlement house work.[75]

Rural and Southern women organized as well. Mary Ann Mayo toured Michigan, Ohio, and Indiana for the Grange and the populist revolt in the 1880s and 1890s.[76] Significant public involvement of

73. Clinton, *The Other Civil War*, 169.
74. Clinton, *The Other Civil War*, 180–81.
75. Banner, *Women in Modern America*, 98–101.
76. See Clinton, *The Other Civil War*, 196.

women in the Southern Farmer's Alliance has been documented by Julie
Roy Jeffrey.[77] White and black women worked together in the South
on antilynching campaigns, and on day-care and education for black
children.[78]

Through such organizations, women across the country, but particularly urban middle-class women, burst into the public sphere with
a reforming zeal rooted in evangelical religion and the cult of domesticity. These wives and mothers may not have been employed, but leave
the house they did, and men no longer could claim the political world
as their own.

Nowhere was women's intrusion into the political arena more
apparent than in the drive for women's suffrage. It was a radical idea
sometimes using rather conservative strategies, and historians of the
movement tend to emphasize one aspect or the other. For DuBois,
suffrage "was significantly more controversial than other demands for
equality with men" because "the right to vote raised the prospect of
female autonomy in a way that other claims to equal rights could not."
The demand for the vote challenged the prevailing notion of chivalry
because inherent in chivalry was "the idea that women's interests were
identical or even compatible with men's." The women's suffrage movement emphasized a uniquely female political agenda, and that agenda
represented women's autonomous "emergence into public life."[79] In
Friedman's opinion, suffrage evoked fears of the destruction of the proper
relationship between the sexes—male domination and female submis-
sion. Both men and women were afraid of the changes heralded by
women voting—"men feared loss of control and women feared offending
male authority."[80] Barker-Benfield attributed "men's growing sense of
vulnerability after the Civil War" to "the increasingly vociferousness
of women at the same time, most noticeably on the suffrage front."[81]
Certainly, the idea of women at the polls and in political campaigns
must have upset many people.

After 1910, fears of suffrage and its consequences were fueled
when new suffrage leadership brought more aggressive tactics and
nation-wide visibility to the crusade. Around 1910, firebrands, such

77. Julie Roy Jeffrey, "Women in the Southern Farmers' Alliance: A Reconsideration
of the Role and Status of Women in the Late Nineteenth-Century South," in *Our
American Sisters*, 348–71.
78. Friedman, *The Enclosed Garden*, 126. See also Cott, *The Grounding of Modern
Feminism*, 93.
79. DuBois, "Women's Rights before the Civil War," in *Our American Sisters*, 308.
80. Friedman, *The Enclosed Garden*, 121.
81. Barker-Benfield, *The Horrors of the Half-Known Life*, 123.

as Alice Stone Blackwell, Margaret Foley, and Gertrude Cliff initiated bold and highly publicized tactics to push the amendment through Congress. Suffragists began to hold open-air meetings, "a dramatic new tactic" learned from English suffragists. Reporters and photographers covered these meetings closely. Blackwell began in 1909 to sell her *Woman's Journal* on the street, and she and Cliff "invaded the floor of the Boston Stock Exchange and Chamber of Commerce and distributed leaflets." Foley led a group of women to political rallies, where they asked candidates to express publicly their views on suffrage. Again, the press eagerly reported the activities of these "hecklers."[82] The National Women's Party in 1917 began picketing the White House and were imprisoned. Their hunger strikes and forced feedings in prison received national attention. Suffragists began mass demonstrations and street parades in 1910.[83] Such newsworthy and "unwomanly" tactics sparked fears of the suffrage movement that even its most home protectionistic supporters could not quell.

By 1920, however, the movement had mainstream popularity. One reason women's suffrage became palatable to most Americans was that the second generation of feminists, described earlier, used rhetoric that conformed in many ways to the conventions of Victorian gender ideology. Women learned to use the dominant gender ideology for their own purposes. They argued that women should have the vote to protect the home and family (the middle-class, white, "native" family especially), and to eradicate vice and corruption. In addition, by 1920, many more women were educated, had experience in the public sphere, and were less hesitant about their desire for the vote.[84] Yet, even when the women's suffrage activists appealed to the ideology of female domesticity, they dealt yet another blow to it. Women demanded, and received in the ballot, recognition as political equals and, more dangerously, as political agents. They won their prize through toughminded, well-organized, and courageous political activity. The ticket to democracy now carried no gender distinctions.

The identification of men with unbridled sexuality and the resultant sexual double standard, another primary underpinning of nineteenth-century masculinity, also came under sharp attack after 1890.

82. Sharon Hartman Strom, "Leadership and Tactics in the American Woman Suffrage Movement: A New Perspective from Massachusetts," in *Our American Sisters*, 382–85.
83. See Banner, *Women in Modern America*, 122.
84. See Aileen Kraditor, *Ideas of the Woman Suffrage Movement, 1890–1920* (New York: Atheneum, 1965), 19; and Strom, "Leadership and Tactics in the American Woman Suffrage Movement," in *Our American Sisters*, 372–92.

Men and women organized against prostitution and other forms of sexual vice such as pornography, sexual excesses within marriage, and child marriage. David Jay Pivar, in his study of this social purity movement, which he called "the new abolitionism," dated its apex from 1895 to 1900.[85] Although this effort attracted men and women alike, it was the women who were the most radical, attacking not only the crimes of prostitution, rape, sexual molestation, and pornography, but decrying the double standard itself that, they maintained, lent support and a degree of acceptability to such misdeeds. Filene judged that the purity movement, because it dealt a direct blow to the reigning assumptions about sexuality, was more threatening to men than either suffrage or temperance.[86] Indeed, women's purity rhetoric was pointed and radical. Katherine Philips Edson, an active suffragist and purity leader, concluded that some men opposed suffrage because they were afraid that "if women get power they will impose on men the same standards of sexual morality that men have imposed on women."[87] Led primarily by women's rights advocates, the campaign for social purity had a multifaceted agenda: moral (sex) education for young people, especially girls; control of venereal disease; critique of man-woman relationships; adoption of "ideal-roles to usher in the 'new society' ";[88] assistance for rape victims and changes in the way rape trials were conducted (some activists advocated castration as a penalty for rapists); investigation of prostitution and plans for its elimination; increase in the age of consent for marriage; dress reform; and a single standard of morality for both men and women. As Lady Henry Somerset foretold in 1896, "the new woman will demand from man the purity he asks of her."[89] Women were successful in many communities, raising the legal age of consent for marriage in several states. The "women's crusade against social evil" in San Francisco received national attention in 1913 when it launched a campaign to recall a police court judge, Charles

85. David Jay Pivar, "The New Abolitionism: The Quest for Social Purity, 1876–1900" (Ph.D. diss., Univ. of Pennsylvania, 1965), 265. See also Pivar, *Purity Crusade, Sexual Morality and Social Control, 1865–1900*, Contributions in American History, no. 23 (Westport, Conn.: Greenwood Press, 1973).

86. Filene, *Him/Her/Self*, 82.

87. Katherine Philips Edson, "Women's Influence on State Legislation," *California Outlook* 14 (June 14, 1913): 7–8, quoted in Gayle Gullett, "City Mothers, City Daughters, and the Dance Hall Girls: The Limits of Female Political Power in San Francisco, 1913," in *Women and the Structure of Society: Selected Research from the Fifth Annual Berkshire Conference on the History of Women*, ed. Barbara J. Harris and JoAnn McNamara, Duke Press Policy Studies (Durham: Duke Univ. Press, 1984), 149–50.

88. Pivar, "The New Abolitionism," 6.

89. Lady Henry Somerset, "Pure Women," *Watchman* 77 (June 11, 1896): 9.

L. Well, for dealing too leniently with a convicted rapist. The recall was successful.[90]

The germ of the women's crusade for social purity lay embedded in the conventional Victorian gender-role ideology. The ideology of virtuous womanhood gave women who took their moral burdens seriously the incentive and ideological justification to include all of society within their guardianship. As women expressed increasing disapproval of the double standard, men's "sexual quandary," according to Stearns, became intense: the choice was between purity, which was unmanly, and sexual activity, which was impure. Middle-class status brought with it special concern for respectability, so many men within the middle class, or with middle-class aspirations, could depend no longer on the sexual conquest to buttress their gender identity.[91]

Shifting Power Dynamics within the Private Sphere. While the public scrutinized and censured men's extramarital sexual behavior, power relations within the family and sexual practices within marriage continued to change. Two factors widened the generational gap between fathers and their offspring, especially their sons. First, in the closing decades of the last century, fathers spent even less time at home because of long work hours compounded by longer commuting times. Mothers had little choice but to take up the reins of parenting. This concentration of parental responsibility in women's role was recognized and reinforced in a cult of motherhood that gained cultural dominance around the turn of the century. Women, usually with no other choice than to be the primary parent, were complimented anyway as being especially qualified in nature and temperament to rear children. As male participation in childrearing decreased, so did the chances that men could find reinforcement for their masculine identity in family situations, since the patriarchal family depended on the ability of the father to control the actions of his household. As often as not, women had more say in the decisions made about their children than did men.[92] And with the responsibility for the training and guidance of the young came much real and symbolic power.

Second, the new middle-class male focus on education and the professions destabilized the generations within the family even further.

90. See Gullett, "City Mothers, City Daughters," in *Women and the Structure of Society*, 150.

91. See Stearns, *Be a Man!* 92–93.

92. See Rothman, *Woman's Proper Place*, 22; Brownlee and Brownlee, *Women in the American Economy*, 28; Ehrenreich and English, *For Her Own Good*, 183–89; Filene, *Him/Her/Self*, 78.

Education "contributed to widening the gap between fathers and sons," made upward mobility—upward and away from the father's work and expertise—a goal replacing the traditional one of passing on the father's property and special skill. Sons left the world of their fathers behind as they sought education for jobs that were beyond the reach of their fathers, either because their fathers lacked adequate training or because the jobs themselves did not exist when their fathers reached manhood. Sons had more options than their fathers and were not so much dependent on them. Fathers were caught between the old desires of patriarchy to see sons take up the family mantle and a "new ethic of mobility that they should *want* their sons to be different from them, better than they were."[93] After mid-century, daughters became educated and went to work in greater numbers, thus enlarging their worlds beyond the home and their contacts and resources beyond the control of parents. The effect of all this on relations between men and women was that when men had less control over fewer children, patriarchalism came to depend almost entirely on a subordinate *wife* to reinforce masculine identity within the domestic sphere.

Yet there is evidence that subordinate wives became harder and harder to find. Historian Daniel Scott Smith concluded that over the course of the nineteenth century wives gained greater power within middle-class marriage and family life. Smith called this phenomenon "domestic feminism."[94] Linda Gordon studied the voluntary motherhood movement that emerged after 1870 and was closely associated with the social purity movement. Voluntary motherhood was part of the agendas of such diverse groups as the suffragists, moral reformers, church auxiliaries, and the free-lovers or marriage reformers. Gordon argued that the voluntary motherhood movement was a significant feminist cause in that it helped women free themselves of unwanted and dangerous pregnancies and births—to achieve some control over their fertility—by decrying marital rape and sexual abuses and excesses within marriage. These female activists called upon the available cultural symbols of the virtuous woman and the pure mother to inhibit male sexuality.[95] The voluntary motherhood movement advocated the right of women to control frequency of sexual intercourse (they condemned artificial birth control) as the means toward this goal. Aspects

93. Stearns, *Be a Man!* 43.
94. See Smith, "Family Limitation, Sexual Control, and Domestic Feminism in Victorian America," in *A Heritage of Her Own*, 222–45.
95. Linda Gordon, "Voluntary Motherhood: The Beginnings of Feminist Birth Control Ideas in the United States," in *Clio's Consciousness Raised*, 54–71. See also D'Emilio and Freedman, *Intimate Matters*, 154–55.

of Victorian "prudery," consistent on a symbolic level at least with the cult of true womanhood, were women's attempts to take control of the most basic conditions of their lives:

> Until contraception could be taken from the streets and used in the home, and until women won the right to greater mobility outside the home circle, her effort to define—and restrict—her sexual role in marriage was the only sexual freedom available to her and her behavior should be considered an important step in the transition to modern womanhood.[96]

Smith maintained that a major factor in the steady decline of the birth rate throughout the nineteenth century, despite inadequate artificial contraception and a steady high rate of marriage for women (89 to 96 percent of American women surviving past the age of forty-five) was women exerting control over sexual relations and reproductive decisions within middle-class marriages.[97] And while it is certain that many couples shared between them the decision to limit births,[98] there was a "moderation of sexual relations"[99] within marriage, much of which was a result of women regulating the frequency of sexual intercourse, and using the ideology of virtuous womanhood and motherhood as a justification for their new demands. Many middle-class men could no longer assume a sexually submissive wife, nor could they feel entirely comfortable making unilateral sexual demands.

To many observers, the institution of marriage itself seemed to be under attack as well during the late nineteenth century. The educated, career-oriented New Woman often remained unmarried. Carl Degler has labeled this phenomenon a "revolt" against marriage, and estimated that in 1900, 25 percent of female college graduates and 50 percent of women who earned a doctoral degree between 1877 and

---

96. John S. Haller, Jr., and Robin M. Haller, *The Physician and Sexuality in Victorian America* (Urbana, Ill.: Univ. of Illinois Press, 1974), 102. For further analyses of prudery, see David M. Kennedy, *Birth Control in America: The Career of Margaret Sanger* (New Haven: Yale Univ. Press, 1970), 61–62; Linda Gordon, *Woman's Body, Woman's Right: A Social History of Birth Control in America* (New York: Penguin Books, 1977), 16–24; Cott, "Passionlessness," in *A History of Her Own*, 162–81.

97. Smith, "Family Limitation, Sexual Control, and Domestic Feminism in Victorian America," in *A Heritage of Her Own*, 223; Clinton, *The Other Civil War*, 156; Brownlee and Brownlee, *Women in the American Economy*, 24.

98. See D'Emilio and Freedman, *Intimate Matters*, 62.

99. Ann D. Gordon and Mari Jo Buhle, "Sex and Class in Colonial and Nineteenth-Century America," in *Liberating Women's History*, 286.

1924 remained unmarried.[100] Women who married resorted to divorce
at a startling new rate. Between 1870 and 1930 there was a fivefold
increase in the number of divorces obtained in the United States.[101]
Two-thirds of all divorces during the 1920s were initiated by women.[102]
Women, especially educated ones with more opportunities to support
themselves in the workplace, were no longer bound to stay in marriages
and used divorce to escape. The fact that women had more options—
divorce and/or self-support—than they had previously meant that they
gained a better bargaining position within the marriage relationship.
Their stronger position further weakened the supports of male domination and control of family life.

By the close of the century, the middle-class Victorian gender
ideology, still hailed as the right and natural way, was beginning to
unravel. There were simply too many cases, even in respectable middle-
class society, in which the highly differentiated gender definitions and
roles had little congruence with the way in which people actually lived
their lives. Yet it was not until the "revolution in manners and morals"
of the second and third decades of the twentieth century that the
demands of the Victorian gender ideology were flouted so publicly by
so many people that it was left behind, even ideologically, by much
of the middle class. This revolution has been dated by some historians
from 1910, and by others as a phenomenon of the 1920s.[103] However
dated, the center of this "cultural storm," noted Filene, was the sexual
conduct of women. Many women during this period rejected the cultural
stereotype of passivity, passionlessness, and chastity. "The virgin was
on her way to becoming a Victorian period piece." One-half of all
married women who had been born between 1900 and 1910 had sexual
relations with at least one man before marriage; two-thirds of those
born between 1910 and 1920 had done so. Although virginity did not
increase among males after 1890, the statistics for women began to
converge with those for men.[104]

100. Carl N. Degler, "The Changing Place of Women in America," in *The Woman
Question*, 101.
101. Brownlee and Brownlee, *Women in the American Economy*, 24.
102. Degler, "The Changing Place of Women in America," in *The Woman Question*,
138.
103. See James R. McGovern, "The American Woman's Pre-World War I Freedom
in Manners and Morals," in *Our American Sisters*, 479–99; Sondra R. Herman, "Loving
Courtship of Marriage Market? The Ideal and Its Critics," in *Our American Sisters*, 330;
Filene, *Him/Her/Self*, 92–93; Smith-Rosenberg, *Disorderly Conduct*, 177–78; Friedman
and Shade, *Our American Sisters*, 449; D'Emilio and Freedman, *Intimate Matters*, 171–
201.
104. Filene, *Him/Her/Self*, 131–32. See also O'Neill, *Everyone Was Brave*, 298; Cott,
The Grounding of Modern Feminism, 148–51.

Several reasons account for the shift in women's attitudes toward sex and in their sexual behavior. The first was the deterioration of parental controls. Many more young women worked outside the home before marriage than previously. By going to work (or to college) they gained exposure to men and independence of means, which made it easier for them to rebel against parental strictures. Along with the more independent life-style of young people after 1900 came a new world of activity and "amusement" designed to appeal to them. Dance halls, clubs, speakeasies, and movie theaters became popular haunts for this new generation, offering greater opportunity for sexual activity. In the 1920s, young couples began to "date" unchaperoned, sometimes in the privacy of automobiles.[105]

Another factor contributing to the rebellion against Victorian sexual *mores* was the social purity and voluntary motherhood movements. Inherent in women's attack on the nineteenth-century double standard was a leveling of sexual passion between the genders.[106] Also, purity reform helped women and society at large become accustomed to and comfortable with thinking and talking about sex.[107] Nowhere was this process more evident than in the research of the early "sexologists," such as Havelock Ellis. These modernists, as Paul A. Robinson called them, conducted studies of human sexual behavior that left behind the assumptions of the Victorian gender ideology. They "held that sexual experience was neither a threat to moral character nor a drain on vital energies," and "they sought to broaden the range of legitimate sexual activity." In regard to female sexuality, the sex modernists insisted that the female "had sexual parity with the male," and they questioned the wisdom of conventional Victorian marriage and family customs.[108]

Ellis's work, published in the 1910s, was widely read and had significant impact. These new attitudes toward female sexuality helped make artificial means of birth control popular. In the 1920s, nonreproductive sex became acceptable even for respectable women. The public campaign for birth control, led by Margaret Sanger, was in itself testimony to a new day in which middle-class women not only used birth control in their own bedrooms, but also went to the streets to

105. See Banner, *Women in Modern America*, 81; Filene, *Him/Her/Self*, 131–32; Friedman and Shade, *Our American Sisters*, 322, 449.

106. Rosalind Rosenberg, *Beyond Separate Spheres: Intellectual Roots of Modern Feminism* (New Haven: Yale Univ. Press, 1982), 203.

107. See D'Emilio and Freedman, *Intimate Matters*, 155–56.

108. Paul A. Robinson, *The Modernization of Sex: Havelock Ellis, Alfred Kinsey, William Masters and Virginia Johnson* (New York: Harper & Row, 1976), 2–3.

demand changes in public attitudes and in legislation controlling the distribution of birth control information and devices.

This new sexualization of women was very confusing to men who had grown up relying on their mothers and wives "as lighthouses to guide them in the struggle against their stormy sexual drives."[109] The dependable and clear-cut distinctions between the sexes based on the animal lust of the man and the purity of the woman broke down. Also, with greater acceptance in the 1920s of artificial contraception, "pro-creative duty had become recreational performance":

> For women, the change brought new pleasure, for men, it brought a mixed pleasure, the release from inhibition being accompanied by the challenge to be a good lover. The Victorian code of moderation had provided some men a shield for their sense of inadequacy, but that shield was being removed.[110]

For many men, a woman who understood and enjoyed sex was frightening.

The modernization of sex and the revolution in manners was most widely symbolized by the flapper, the "thoroughly modern" woman of the twentieth century who smoked, drank, danced, wore short skirts, petted with young men in automobiles, and bobbed her hair. Filene's point is important here:

> The very fact that the flapper came to be the symbol of the new age underscores the sense in which women were blamed for the rapid change and social upheaval of post World War I America.[111]

Americans were unsettled and threatened by the revolution in manners and morals, particularly because significant changes occurred in understandings of female sexuality and in women's sexual behavior. Because Victorians depended so much on the cult of true womanhood for their sense of identity and social order, civilization itself seemed threatened by the flapper, and she was blamed for all the turmoil.

By 1930, the Victorian gender ideology, with its distinct spheres of activity on which middle-class masculinity depended, was in tatters. Women had invaded the masculine world of higher education, the

109. Filene, *Him/Her/Self*, 144.
110. Filene, *Him/Her/Self*, 145, 92–93. See also Smith-Rosenberg, *Disorderly Conduct*, 115.
111. Filene, *Him/Her/Self*, 129–30.

professions, business, industry, and politics. They had learned to mold the cult of true womanhood to their own purposes within their own sphere as well by assuming ever more power and control over child-rearing, marital relations, household management, and the church. Women claimed their right to sexual pleasure and control over their own reproductive capabilities. The Victorian gender ideology and its rise and fall constituted a major force of change in the lives of the late-Victorian middle class. Amidst this cultural crisis Protestant fundamentalism emerged, and was profoundly shaped and affected by it. An analysis of popular fundamentalist rhetoric reveals just how central gender issues were to this widespread movement.

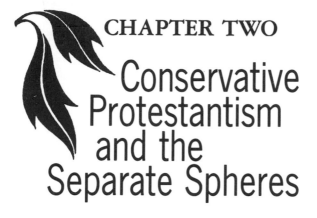

CHAPTER TWO

Conservative Protestantism and the Separate Spheres

"WANTED—MORE MOTHERS," proclaimed the *King's Business.* "We are short on homes; *real* homes. We are short on mothers; *real* mothers. . . . God designed woman as the *homemaker* but somehow she seems to have gotten sidetracked."[1] This is but one of hundreds of expressions in popular fundamentalist literature in support of the Victorian ideology of the separate spheres. Defense of an embattled gender ideology was an important component of the fundamentalist agenda.[2] Fundamentalists used powerful religious symbols and sanctions to legitimize Victorian gender conventions and to attack women's departures from them.

"Enthroned in Glory"

A major component of late nineteenth-century gender ideology was the idea of completely distinct spheres of activity for men and women. Fundamentalist leaders sounded this theme again and again. Woman's place was in the home:

> where she is enthroned in more glory than all beside, where she is to adorn the doctrines of God her savior in the bearing,

1. "Wanted—More Mothers," *King's Business* 12, no. 2 (February 1921): 107–8.
2. The most vocal prior to 1900 were the *Christian Herald and Signs of the Times,* the *Watchman-Examiner and Watchman* (after 1896, the *Watchman;* after 1913, the *Watchman and Examiner*), and the *Western Recorder.* After 1900, the *Western Recorder,* the *King's Business,* the *Record of Christian Work,* and *Our Hope* contained the most rhetoric directly expressive and supportive of the separate-spheres ideology as outlined in the previous chapter.

bringing forth, training, uplifting [of] those who are committed to her keeping.[3]

The compartmentalization of activity and influence was intertwined
with a similar compartmentalization of character traits and virtues.
"The student of nature places men in the public world of work, education and politics, and leaves the domestic realm for the women whose
frailty and spirituality make her unfit for the world of men."[4] Because
the genders differed so much from each other in emotional make-up
and moral character, fundamentalists argued that it was natural and
good to assign each to completely distinct spheres of activity and
expertise. Men represent "the positive or active element," women the
"negative or sympathetic element of life."[5] An editorial in *Bibliotheca
Sacra* made a similar distinction: "Men are primarily interested in affairs,
women in persons. So women are absorbed in the persons they love;
men in the things they love; women in family and friends, men in
affairs."[6] As keepers of the domestic sphere, women were the guardians
of the morality of their families, and, by extension, the rest of society.
T. DeWitt Talmage invested wives with the ability to save unbelieving
husbands: "Paul says the unbelieving husband is sanctified by the
wife . . ."[7]; "A man is no better than his wife will let him be."[8] Billy
Sunday preached that "the devil and women can damn this world, and
Jesus and women can save this old world. It remains with womanhood
today to lift our social life to a higher plane," and that "women have
kept themselves purer than men."[9]

So well defined and discrete were the spheres that Talmage likened
them to the "boundary line between Italy and Switzerland," and one
"can no more compare them than you can oxygen and hydrogen, water

3. M. M'Gee, "Woman's Place in the Kingdom," *Western Recorder* 80, no. 32 (July 6, 1905): 12.
4. Tandy L. Dix, "Sex," *Western Recorder* 52, no. 18 (January 7, 1886): 2.
5. William Parker, "True Womanhood," *Christian Workers Magazine* 16 (November 1915): 184.
6. "Editorial," *Bibliotheca Sacra* 81, no. 323 (July 1924): 256–57.
7. T. DeWitt Talmage, "The Choice of a Husband," *Christian Herald and Signs of Our Times* 9, no. 3 (January 21, 1886): 36.
8. Talmage, "Wifely Ambition, Good and Bad," *Christian Herald and Signs of Our Times* 11, no. 7 (February 16, 1888): 101.
9. Billy Sunday, quoted in William T. Ellis, *"Billy" Sunday: The Man and His Message, with His Own Words Which Have Won Thousands for Christ* (Philadelphia: The John C. Winston Company, 1914), 229, 227. See also Justin D. Fulton, "What a Wife Can Do and Undo," *Watchman* 67 (April 1, 1886): 6.

and grass, trees and stars."[10] Charles Franklin Thwing compared men and women to oak and maple trees: "The oak is superior to the maple, in strength; the maple is superior to the oak in grace."[11] Such overstated descriptions of gender differences were products of a society in which such distinctions were, in practice, giving way. Signs of the strain appeared frequently in popular fundamentalist rhetoric:

> In man, the Scriptures emphasize the active virtues. . . . In woman, they emphasize the passive virtues. . . . When this difference is lost and man becomes womanish, or woman becomes mannish, then the proper balance is lost, and harmony gives way to discord. There is a strong tendency in modern times to regard woman as an exact duplicate of man in her manner of thought, and its balance with feeling, in occupation, and in all sense, save sex.[12]

An important part of the separate-spheres ideology was the glorification of motherhood.[13] Fundamentalists were well aware of the New Woman's relative lack of interest in marriage and motherhood:

> There is a full-fledged rebellion under way not only against the headship of man in government and church but in the home. Statistics of Yale and Harvard show that women of the better homes are not having children, the average showing less than one child to a family. . . . The cultivation of the modern woman's idea of "my individuality" is bound to be a destroyer of the home life. . . .[14]

In response, men, who voluntarily left the domestic sphere themselves, praised it as the place of highest calling and greatest honor. Such an appeal could only have functioned rhetorically to persuade women to remain content within the home. John Milton Williams attributed women's sphere with qualities that made it superior to man's sphere:

> Woman has no call to the ballot-box, but she has a sphere of her own, of amazing responsibility and importance. She

10. Talmage, "Woman's Opportunity," *Christian Herald and Signs of Our Times* 10 (September 1, 1887): 518. See also "The Graces of Womanhood," *Watchman* 75, no. 11 (March 16, 1894): 2; Arthur T. Pierson, "God's Word to Women," *Northfield Echoes* 3, no. 3 (1896): 255; "Church Decorum—Abuses in Connection with Public Worship," *King's Business* 8, no. 12 (December 1917): 1103; J. T. Larsen, "What Is Becoming of the Christian Home?" *King's Business* 19, no. 6 (June 1928): 346.

11. Charles Franklin Thwing, "The Teachings of Christ and the Modern Family," *Bibliotheca Sacra* 61 (January 1904): 14.

12. "Christianity and Woman," *Bible Champion* 32, no. 6 and 7 (June–July 1926): 310.

13. See Gayle Kimball, *The Religious Ideas of Harriet Beecher Stowe: The Gospel of Womanhood* (Lewiston, N.Y.: Edwin Mellen Press, 1982), 73–77.

14. "Woman Suffrage and the Bible," *King's Business* 10, no. 8 (August 1919): 701.

is the divinely appointed guardian of the home. . . . She
should more fully realize that her position . . . is the holiest,
most responsible, and queenlike assigned to mortals; and
dismiss all ambition for anything higher, as there is nothing
else here so high for mortals.[15]

Women's role as mother was the primary reason given for judging
women's sphere more important than men's:

If there be any difference in degree touching the importance
of the spheres assigned the two sexes, surely the palm goes
to woman, since according to God's own decree and word,
she is in a position to mold the character and determine the
destiny of the race.[16]

The exaltation of motherhood is a theme that runs through these
periodicals from the beginning of the period to the end. Fundamentalists
touted motherhood as the "chief function of woman," and the proper
ambition for women is "not to be a great woman, but rather to be the
mother of good men."[17] By bearing and rearing children, women per-
form "the divinest function of life."[18] J. Frank Norris called women
who refused to have children "parasites on society."[19]

Although these religious leaders lauded the domestic realm of
motherhood and virtue as preferable to the male lot, they repeatedly—
and incongruously—urged women to understand female duty and destiny as sacrifice. Ministers told women to give up their own ambitions
and well-being for their families, particularly their husbands and brothers, that women's true mission and fulfillment lay in "self-sacrificing

15. John Milton Williams, "Woman Suffrage," *Bibliotheca Sacra* 50 (April 1893):
343. See also W. Merle Smith, "Mary of Bethany," *Northfield Echoes* 7, no. 4 (1900):
377.
16. "Queen of the Home," *Herald and Presbyter* 82, no. 51 (December 20, 1911):
2.
17. Parker, "True Womanhood," *Christian Workers Magazine,* 185. See also "Woman's
Position," *Western Recorder* 64, no. 15 (December 5, 1889): 6; Frederick Farrer, "The
Mother in the Home," *Western Recorder* 69, no. 10 (January 17, 1895): 11.
18. Spenser B. Meeser, "The Glory and Mission of Motherhood," *Watchman* 86
(December 22, 1904): 9. See also Talmage, "The Christian Mother," *Christian Herald
and Signs of Our Times* 4 (August 1881): 484–85; Lynn F. Ross, "The Honor Due to
Motherhood," *Record of Christian Work* 46, no. 5 (May 1927): 325; Helen Barrett
Montgomery, "The New Opportunity for Baptist Women," *Watchman-Examiner* 11
(July 16, 1923): 950–51; J. Frank Norris, "Son, Behold Thy Mother," *Fundamentalist*
10, no. 27 (May 13, 1927): 2.
19. Norris, "Home Foundation of All Things, Says Rev. J. Frank Norris," *Searchlight*
2, no. 25 (April 22, 1920): 2. See *Searchlight* 1, no. 7 (April 23, 1917): 3, for an
account of the annual Baby Day celebration Norris held in his Fort Worth church. See
also "Mothers Day Next Sunday," *Searchlight* 3, no. 25 (May 6, 1921): 1.

service."[20] Women should emulate the biblical character Ruth, whom William R. Newell, writing for a Moody publication, characterized as "the servant, the unimportant one, the one who feels herself nothing, ever shrinking back from notice."[21] One article written for women advised them to study carefully the nature of love in 1 Cor. 13:

> Paul's chapter on love is the best description of a true woman that the world has ever had. . . . [L]ove . . . never asserts itself; it is always willing to suffer; and in its humility lies its real strength. By enduring all things it overcomes all things.[22]

Stanley White told the women gathered at Moody's Northfield Young Women's Conference in 1906 that suffering is "one of the great privileges of the Christian life."[23] True womanhood resembles Jesus in that "she comes to the world and finds that the crown which awaits her is of thorns, that her throne is a cross":

> Looking upon Him . . . women see the law of their own life, approved of God and glorified as itself the very law of God's life—the law of sacrifice and endurance; for without doubt, to suffer, to serve, to bear . . . is at once the doom and the dignity of woman as God has made her, body, soul, and spirit.[24]

Like the characterization of Jesus in sentimental Victorian Protestantism, the notion of true womanhood found in these religious tracts emphasized death and reward in a future life. Talmage called the death of a good wife in sacrifice and love her final and greatest glory, "a queen's coronation."[25] On the top of his list of women's rights was the

20. "The Mother's Reward," *Watchman* 86 (August 11, 1904): 14. See also Arthur J. Brown, "Paul's Idea of Sacrifice in Serving Christ," *Record of Christian Work* 30, no. 10 (October 1911): 674; "The Three Parts of a Woman's Life," *Herald and Presbyter* 83, no. 32 (August 7, 1912): 30; Mrs. John H. Chapman, "The Young Woman as a Wife," *Watchman and Examiner* 12 (August 28, 1924): 1122–23.

21. William R. Newell, "The Institute Bible Course," *Record of Christian Work* 17, no. 9 (September 1898): 471. See also Mrs. Henry W. Peabody, "The Enlarged Sphere of Woman's Work in Its Relation to the Church," *Record of Christian Work* 37, no. 9 (September 1918): 629.

22. Parker, "True Womanhood," *Christian Workers Magazine,* 184.

23. Stanley White, "A Life Worthy of the Gospel," *Record of Christian Work* 25 (1906): 684.

24. John A. Hutton, "Obscurer Ministries of the New Testament: 'Certain Women'," *Record of Christian Work* 28 (1909): 296.

25. T. DeWitt Talmage, "The Choice of a Wife," *Christian Herald and Signs of Our Times* 9; no. 9 (January 1886): 21.

right to "reach heaven" after a life of suffering and toil:

> Some of you will have no rest in this world. It will be toil
> and struggle and suffering all the way up. . . . But God
> has a crown for you. . . . He is now making it, and whenever
> you weep a tear He sets another gem in that crown; whenever
> you have a pang of body or soul, he puts another gem in
> that crown; until . . . God will say, . . . "The crown is
> done; let her up, that she may wear it." . . . [A]ngel will
> cry to angel, "Who is she?" and Christ will say, ". . . She
> is the one that came up out of great tribulation. . . . She
> suffered with Me on earth, and now we are going to be
> glorified together."[26]

Suffering Jesus and true womanhood were closely identified.

Fundamentalist leaders asked women to forego their own ambitions and opportunities for the sake of the men in their families—their husbands, brothers, and sons. "Daughters and sisters should show loving attention to fathers and brothers in the home. . . ."[27] Dwight L. Moody told his listeners of a special Christian woman who wanted to graduate from Wellesley, "but when her father died, she stepped right out and went to teaching school, and sent her two brothers to the academy and to college."[28] Talmage told women in 1886 "not to begrudge the time and care bestowed on a brother," and that whatever they did for brothers would be repaid in the future:

> Don't snub him. Don't depreciate his ability. Don't talk
> discouragingly about his future. . . . Don't tease him. . . .
> Don't let jealousy ever touch a sister's soul . . . because her
> brother gets more honor or more means. . . . Your brothers'
> success oh sisters is your success.[29]

Held up as a model for all women was a woman who, in 1914, was shot by her husband yet refused to prosecute him.[30] No sacrifice seemed too great.

26. T. DeWitt Talmage, "The Queens of the Home," *Christian Herald and Signs of Our Times* 10 (September 8, 1887): 565.

27. Margaret E. Sangster, "The Christian Woman in the Home," *Northfield Echoes* 5, no. 3 (1898): 331.

28. Dwight L. Moody, "Mary and Martha," *Northfield Echoes* 6, no. 3 (1899): 237.

29. Talmage, "Sisters and Brothers," *Christian Herald and Signs of Our Times* 9, no. 11 (March 18, 1886): 164–65. See also Chapman, "That Girl in the Home," *Watchman-Examiner* 12 (September 25, 1924): 1248.

30. W. H. J., "Saved by a Woman's Love," *Herald and Presbyter* 85, no. 22 (June 3, 1914): 29.

The subjection of wife to husband constituted another important dimension of Victorian gender ideology. All the tension within American families wrought by rapid social change is evident in conservative Protestant literature. Fundamentalists noted that husbands and fathers were away at business all the time, and called men's attention back to home and family.[31] Of more concern, however, was the preservation of patriarchal authority despite absent husbands and fathers. Fundamentalists produced a flood of argumentation, most of its claims based on an appeal to divine revelation, that women were created subordinate to men, no matter what their earthly qualifications and talents. Consequently the wife wielded authority in the household only in the husband's stead:

> And as the state claims authority to dispose of its citizens, within the prescribed limits of the law, because it nourishes and defends them, so the husband and father is naturally the supreme ruler in the family. . . . But we are not left to reason alone on the subject. Revelation has spoken in no uncertain language. . . . I know there are those who will object . . . at the idea of a husband and father being a monarch in his family, whose word is law. But God has made him so. . . .[32]

Against the New Woman of the 1880s, "who desires to be her husband's equal, . . . resents his natural place as the head of the family, and affronts his innate mastery,"[33] conservative religious leaders posited a "federal headship" of Adam over Eve because Adam (and all men) had the priority in creation, or because Adam performed better in Eden than Eve. An important auxiliary argument from creation maintained that men and women were two separate creations, not simply variations of one.[34]

31. See Thurston, "Family Religion," *Western Recorder* 64, no. 30 (March 20, 1890): 1; C. S. Patton, "The Man and the Home," *Western Recorder* 80, no. 35 (July 27, 1905): 12; H. B. Freeman, "Talks to Fathers, " *Western Recorder* 86, no. 40 (August 10, 1911): 2.

32. D. Dowden, "The Family: Supreme Authority—Where Lodged—How Divided—How Used," *Western Recorder* 52, no. 24 (February 18, 1886): 2.

33. "Why Marriages Are Failures," *Western Recorder* 63, no. 45 (July 4, 1889): 2.

34. See "What Is Woman?" *Western Recorder* 94, no. 17 (January 30, 1919): 8; "It Is Wise to Obey God," *Truth, or Testimony for Christ* 21, no. 10 (October 1895): 454; Margaret C. Worthington, "Woman Suffrage—A Reform, But Unto What?" *Christian Workers Magazine* 27 (1916): 112; "The First Three Chapters of the Bible," *Our Hope* 9, no. 1 (July 1902): 19; "Christianity and Woman," *Bible Champion* 32, no. 6–7 (June–July 1926): 310; "Sabbath School," *Herald and Presbyter* 92, no. 19 (May 11, 1921): 17.

Another common model for domestic relations found in this literature equated the husband's relationship with the wife to Jesus' relationship with the church (or with the individual believer). In 1887, James H. Brookes ran an article in the *Truth, or, Testimony for Christ* that called women "the type of the church":

> We are not surprised, therefore, to learn that if order and subordination are to be preserved in the government of God, she is to be officially in subjection.[35]

A premillennialist editor of *Our Hope* reflected the same viewpoint:

> And who is not called upon to be subject? Why our Lord and Savior leads the way and was subject unto the Father. He acknowledged a Head and was subject.
> The Head of Christ is God.
> Man has a Head—Christ.
> Woman has a head—man.
> Wife has a head—husband.
>   In all these natural fixed relationships we are to be "submitting ourselves one to another in the fear of God." The wife is not to be any more subject than every other relationship calls for. But she is especially in subjection to her own husband.[36]

Just as it is "man's duty to glorify Christ, so woman's duty is to glorify the man."[37] In such a way, the patriarchal authority of men within the family was buttressed by the use of central Christian symbolism.

"Do Not Try to Cross Over"

Fundamentalist writers and editors feared the impact on women of club work, suffrage, and other progressive reform organizing; higher

35. "Woman in the Church," *Truth, or, Testimony for Christ* 14 (1887–1888): 255.

36. Mrs. Cyril Bird, *Our Hope* 16, no. 11 (May 1910): 706. See also Worthington, "Woman Suffrage," *Christian Workers Magazine*, 112; G. Campbell Morgan, "Christian Ethics," *Northfield Echoes* 7, no. 4 (1900): 444.

37. "Church Decorum: Abuses in Connection with Public Worship," *King's Business* 8, no. 12 (December 1917): 1104. See also "Woman and the Federal Headship," *Moody Bible Institute Monthly* 22 (January 1922): 765; *Our Hope* 10, no. 3 (September 1903): 212; *King's Business* 9, no. 7 (August 1918): 723; Robert E. Speer, "The Mid-Week Bible Class," *Record of Christian Work* 19, no. 4 (April 1900): 274; "The Masterpiece of God. The Mystery as Seen in the Family," *Our Hope* 20, no. 6 (December 1913): 339–40.

education; and paid employment. Each public activity received significant fundamentalist comment. The growing popularity among middle-class women of club work and other outside activities was noted and generally condemned.[38] Billy Sunday chided women for "neglecting your homes for . . . clubs."[39] Talmage denounced the practice of hiring governesses in order to free women from homebound child-care duties as "heathenish" and irresponsible.[40] The *King's Business* advised women to quit their clubs for the good of their children and for their own "orthodox faith."[41] Women's rights activity and other work received especially harsh criticism. A woman who left home and children for "Woman's Rights Conventions," forcing herself "into public notice," stepped out of the sphere "in which it is evident God himself placed her," and in so doing committed "a sin in his sight."[42] The editor of the *Western Recorder* warned that feminists ("this masculine female tribe") were trying to "unsex and unchristianize," and that "once we have crossed the boundaries established by God's Word, we are already near the city of Sodom."[43]

No part of the women's rights agenda received as much attention from fundamentalists as women's suffrage. Although such popular fundamentalists as Billy Sunday and William Jennings Bryan supported the vote for women,[44] antisuffrage statements in popular fundamentalist periodicals outnumbered prosuffrage statements by a ratio of more than ten to one. Fundamentalists used the ideology of separate spheres and distinct virtues as their main weapon in the suffrage controversy. One well-used argument in the *Western Recorder, Watchman,* and *Watchman-Examiner* was that the majority of women—the true women—did not

38. See "The Home Mother," *Western Recorder 86,* no. 8 (December 29, 1910): 1; "The Change in Home Life," *King's Business* 10 (July 1919): 592.

39. Sunday, quoted in "Sunday Sizzlers," *Trenton (New Jersey) Evening Times* (January 7, 1916): n.p.

40. Talmage, "The Unfaithful Mother," *Christian Herald and Signs of Our Times* 14, no. 32 (August 12, 1891): 502; Talmage, "The Christian Mother," *Christian Herald and Signs of Our Times,* 485; John Roach Straton, "Right Home Life," *King's Business* 12, no. 2 (February 1921): 117.

41. *King's Business* 5, no. 5 (May 1914): 294. See also Talmage, "The Christian Mother," *Christian Herald and Signs of Our Times,* 485; "The Change in Home Life," *King's Business,* 592.

42. Sarah M. Maverick, "Woman's Rights," *Western Recorder* 63, no. 19 (January 3, 1889): 1. See also Talmage, "Duties of Wives to Husbands," *Christian Herald and Signs of Our Times* 9, no. 8 (February 1886): 117.

43. "A Mannish Woman," *Western Recorder* 86, no. 40 (August 10, 1911): 8.

44. See Lee Thomas, *The Billy Sunday Story: The Life and Times of William Ashley Sunday, D.D.* (Grand Rapids, Mich.: Zondervan, 1961), 130; David B. Anderson, *William Jennings Bryan,* Twaynes's United States Author Series, no. 415 (Boston: G. K. Hall, 1981), 177–78.

want to vote. The *Watchman* condemned suffrage for "its injuries to the finer sensibilities of women."[45] Other fundamentalists opposed suffrage because they believed in woman's superiority rather than her equality, a common theme in separate-spheres discourse. This discourse contained a definite note of chivalry: Men should not force on virtuous and delicate women the toil and grime of the political world.[46] "The woman who enters the political arena, must, in the estimation of most men, lose something of her womanly modesty and sanctity."[47] Women were too temperamental, not logical enough, argued revivalist Len G. Broughton.[48] Husbands should represent their wives at the ballot box while wives cast their vote of influence, which "nothing can resist" and which "throbs through the eternities."[49] "Women do not need the suffrage, for they rule the nation without it."[50] "She is most influential when she is most womanly, and farthest removed, in her habits, tastes, and aspirations, from anything coarse, masculine, or unwomanly."[51] A writer for the *Western Recorder* accused suffragists of being untrue women— Christless and childless.[52]

Other fundamentalists argued that Christian homes were more powerful agents of reform than female suffrage. Even reform-minded women should stay in the home, urged John Milton Williams, because the "sweet, well-ordered Christian home is the generic reform, including and superseding all others."[53]

Fundamentalists claimed that suffrage for women would destroy true womanhood and thus jeopardize the home. If wives could vote,

45. "Woman Suffrage," *Watchman* 92, no. 2 (January 13, 1910): 6.
46. See *Watchman* 67 (May 20, 1886): 4; *Western Recorder* 69, no. 36 (July 18, 1895): 8; "Anti-Suffragettes," *Watchman* 90, no. 17 (April 23, 1908): 6; "Anti-Female Suffragist," *Western Recorder* 86, no. 34 (June 29, 1911): 8; "As You Like It," *Western Recorder* 87, no. 5 (December 7, 1911): 8; G. K. Chesterton, "On Female Suffrage," *Western Recorder* 88, no. 40 (August 7, 1913): 5; "Votes for Women," *Watchman-Examiner* 2 (March 12, 1914): 327.
47. "Woman Suffrage," *Watchman* 85, no. 42 (August 25, 1910): 8.
48. "Len G. Broughton on Suffrage," *Western Recorder* 92, no. 26 (April 5, 1917): 3.
49. Talmage, "Woman's Opportunity," *Christian Herald and Signs of Our Times,* 518.
50. "American Women," *Watchman* 81, no. 9 (March 1, 1900): 17. See also Francis J. Dyer, *Western Recorder* 64, no. 45 (July 3, 1890): 6; Senex, "Questions Answered," *Western Recorder* 88, no. 26 (May 1, 1913): 2; Williams, "Woman Suffrage," *Bibliotheca Sacra,* 332.
51. Williams, "Woman Suffrage," *Bibliotheca Sacra,* 338. See also Talmage, "The Queens of the Home," *Christian Herald and Signs of Our Times,* 564.
52. "Needs Fixing," *Western Recorder* 88, no. 11 (January 16, 1913): 8. See also "Decay of the Home," *Western Recorder* 69, no. 34 (July 4, 1895): 2.
53. Williams, "Woman Suffrage," *Bibliotheca Sacra,* 337.

there would be political strife within the household; the home would
no longer be "neutral ground, the quiet retreat from battles without,"
on which middle-class men had come to depend. It was unthinkable
to some of them that the "strife of politics" be carried "into the sacred
enclosure," "the charmed spot of the world."[54] Warnings sounded that
suffrage would discourage women from marriage and childbearing.[55]

After 1910, Americans got word of the more aggressive and
sometimes violent battle for women's suffrage in England. When American suffrage activists used some of these new tactics, fundamentalists
launched sharp attacks on the English suffragettes and their American
counterparts. They called suffrage activists "unsexed solecisms of the
twentieth century."[56] The editor of *Our Hope* was particularly harsh. In
four issues between October 1913 and August 1914, he called British
suffragettes "demon-possessed" and "criminal":

> The situation in England is serious. These satanic instru-
> ments seem to stop short of nothing. Like their master, who
> is a murderer from the beginning, they may resort to poison
> and destroy human life. It is significant how Satan uses
> woman in these closing days of our age. . . . He goads them
> on to perpetrate these wicked actions. Woe unto this world
> when they get the leadership they desire.[57]

Women's "great political agitation" was a chief factor in the downfall
of Pompeii, the editor surmised, and would be so for modern nations.
"Woman leaving her sphere, becomes by it an instrument of Satan. . . .
Corruption of the vilest kind must follow."[58] In 1913, J. H. Grimes
wrote about an increase in the number of female criminals, most commonly charged for murdering their husbands. He linked the crime

54. Williams, "Woman Suffrage," *Bibliotheca Sacra,* 336. See also H., "Woman
Suffrage," *Western Recorder* 86, no. 52 (November 2, 1911): 7; "Women in Politics,"
Truth, or, Testimony for Christ 21, no. I (January 1895): 6; Talmage, "Home," *Christian
Herald and Signs of Our Times* 6 (January 11, 1883): 20–21.

55. "Woman Suffrage," *Watchman,* 6. See also "Len G. Broughton on Suffrage,"
Western Recorder, 3.

56. "Suffragettes," *Western Recorder* 88, no. 16 (February 20, 1913): 8. See also
"Editorial Comments on Current Events," *Watchman-Examiner* 1, no. 4 (September 25,
1913): 105.

57. "Demon Possessed Women Continue Their Crimes," *Our Hope* 21, no. 2 (August
1914): 109. See also "Current Events and Signs of the Times—in the Light of the
Word of God," *Our Hope* 20, no. 4 (October 1913): 239–40; "They Are Still at It,"
Our Hope 20, no. 11 (May 1914): 693–94; "The Outrageous Mrs. Pankhurst," *Our
Hope* 20, no. 7 (January 1914): 435–36.

58. "The Women Suffragist Movement," *Our Hope.* 19, no. 3 (September 1912):
169.

wave to the New Woman, who shunned marriage and large families
and was infected with "the craze for notoriety and newspaper publicity,"
which "is to be greatly deplored, whether it be in the name of politics
or religion." Women's "seeking political suffrage and performing all
kinds of unseemly doings in pursuit of it" were represented as the fruits
of women leaving their proper sphere.[59]

The education of women, especially higher education, was of
greatest concern from 1880 to 1900, although the issue nearly dropped
from view by the turn of the century. Although there were a few
scattered comments in favor of identical education for males and fe-
males,[60] most commentary took one of two approaches. The first supported education for women *within their sphere.* Women should be taught
to be "teachers to their children"[61] and better housekeepers, and they
should receive "some careful instruction regarding the beauty of girlhood as shown by modesty, by unselfishness, by unostentatious care
for others."[62]

The other line of argument was even more negative: Higher education for women was inappropriate and dangerous. One set of articles
warned that a college education for women would alienate them from
the attitudes and work that were properly feminine. In 1915, the *King's
Business* reported that many fewer college-educated women marry than
their relatively uneducated sisters and that married, college-educated
women had fewer children. Editorial comment always accompanied
such statistics:

> There has been a growing feeling . . . that there was some
> radical defect in the education of women as now carried on,
> that the average college education . . . alienated them from,
> rather than prepared them for, the work God has set before
> most women. . . . [W]omen as a rule should be trained for

59. J. H. Grimes, "Female Criminals," *Western Recorder* 88, no. 13 (January 30,
1913): 2. See also "Women and Crime," *Western Recorder* 86, no. 44 (September 7,
1911): 8.
60. I found two. See A. B. Cabaniss, "Our Field Votes: Religious Herald and Higher
Education of Women," *Western Recorder* 51, no. 47 (July 30, 1885): 4; *Western Recorder*
92, no. 17 (February 1, 1917): 1.
61. "Women and High Culture: The Injury Done When Weak Girls Study beyond
Their Strength," *Watchman* 71 (September 18, 1890): 6.
62. "Our Girls," *Western Recorder* 51, no. 45 (July 16, 1885): 6. See also "Co-
Education of the Sexes," *Western Recorder* 47, no. 5 (October 7, 1880): 4; "The Training
of Daughters," *Western Recorder* 47, no. 16 (December 23, 1880): 6; "Training for
Marriage," *Western Recorder* 64, no. 5 (October 3, 1889): 6; "Plain Words about Women,"
Western Recorder 64, no. 25 (February 13, 1890): 6; Thurston, "Self-Culture for Mothers,"
Western Recorder 63, no. 47 (July 18, 1889): 1.

motherhood. . . . Sad to say . . . in colleges . . . the office
of motherhood has been spoken of very lightly and con-
temptuously in comparison with . . . "the higher calling
of women," or "a career."[63]

In 1886, Talmage, probably in jest, noted in a sermon that women
"are better educated than the majority of men; and if they continue
. . . before long the majority of men will have difficulty in finding in
the opposite sex enough ignorance to make appropriate consort."[64]
College athletics for women seemed particularly threatening:

. . . it is high time to . . . revolutionize or abolish college
athletics for girls. That some of our women aspire to . . .
mannishness is painfully evident, but we can hardly afford
to facilitate this tragic transition. . . . An unsexed man, or
woman, is a solecism worthy of withering contempt. Ev-
ermore may we pray to be delivered from the masculine
woman and the feminine man.[65]

For the most radical premillennialists of the late nineteenth century, education for women threatened Christian faith itself. The editors
of the *Truth, or, Testimony for Christ* made much of a link they perceived
between educated women and heathenism. They suspected that education rendered women "a ready prey to the wiles of the devil," and
that "the eagerness with which they [educated women] rush off into
heathenism" such as Buddhism, theosophy, ethical culture, and Christian Science, "raises grave doubt whether they have sense enough to
stand the higher education, unless they are first converted to Christ,
and become subject to His word."[66] The *Truth, or, Testimony for Christ*
sounded an alarm about a wave of "infidelity" among middle- and upper
middle-class women, and blamed the "godless" public schools that
educated these women.[67] Equating Victorian notions of gender-based

63. "The Education of Women," *King's Business* 7, no. 4 (April 1916): 293–94. See
also "Sex in Education," *Watchman* 73, no. 21 (May 26, 1892): 1; "The Popular Woman,"
Watchman 75, no. 38 (September 20, 1892): 21; James C. Fernald, "A Womanly
Woman," *Christian Cynosure* 24, no. 19 (January 21, 1892): 10; Billy Sunday, "Samson
and Delilah," *Trenton (New Jersey) Evening Times* (February 15, 1916): 10.
    64. Talmage, "The Choice of a Wife," *Christian Herald and Signs of Our Times,* 20.
    65. "Athletics for Girls," *Western Recorder* 86, no. 5 (December 8, 1910): 8.
    66. "Heathenism in America," *Truth, or, Testimony for Christ* 13 (1886–1887): 297–
98.
    67. "Infidelity among Women," *Truth, or, Testimony for Christ* 25 (1888–1889): 245.
See also "The Vile Corruption of the Young," *Our Hope* 34, no. 8 (February 1928):
466–67.

separate spheres and sacred law, fundamentalists claimed that the education of women was an offense before God, one of the ways "man
invades these sacred fields" of metaphysical and spiritual law.[68]

Fundamentalists expressed equal discomfort with women invading
the male world of paid employment. An article published in the *Western
Recorder* in 1913 reinforced the cultural myth of the male economic
warrior:

> The burdens are his—and the world is merciless: the trials
> are his—and the world is a hard judge. Of course she has
> her troubles and annoyances, but . . . they seem trifling
> and petty compared to his. What is she doing to repay
> him? . . . The debt is there. . . . When the sacrifice is in
> his side of the balance, does she place love in the other?
> When he meets sharp criticism does her tenderness coun-
> teract its effects?[69]

Talmage, in a sermon "Duties of Wives to Husbands," told his female
hearers to "remember in what a severe and terrific battle for life her
husband is engaged." Women do "more for God" by staying out of the
workplace and off the public platform.[70] American women did not
know how lucky they were not working when so many of the women
in the world suffered daily from back-breaking toil:

> America is the paradise of women, and it becomes them to
> preserve that paradise . . . lest rash and restless spirits,
> under the name of reform, should make it a pandemonium
> of contending passions, and a trampled arena of political
> strife.[71]

Women working in factories and business lived in "an unfortunate and
unnatural state of affairs" for "the normal place for men, with exceptions,
was at the head of a home, making enough by his personal labor to
support that home."[72] When women showed skill in industry during

68. Dix, "Sex," *Western Recorder*, 2.
69. "Is Woman Paying Her Debt?" *Western Recorder* 88, no. 15 (February 13, 1913):
10.
70. Talmage, "Duties of Wives to Husbands," *Christian Herald and Signs of Our
Times,* 116.
71. "Women in the East," *Western Recorder* 64, no. 14 (November 28, 1889): 4.
72. "The Normal Home," *Herald and Presbyter* 84, no. 42 (October 15, 1913): 1.
See also "The Home and Virtue and Vice," *Herald and Presbyter* 84, no. 18 (April 30,
1913): 4; "Why Many Young Men Do Not Marry," *Watchman* 2 (March 12, 1914):
336–37; Norris, "Husbands, Love Your Wives," *Fundamentalist of Texas* 7, no. 40
(August 16, 1929): 6.

World War I, a plea was made to save the home at the expense of industry. The Great War, according to the *Watchman-Examiner:*

> got women involved in . . . industry, and industrialists
> found them good workers. . . . At the same time it is true
> that the distinctive function and the supreme mission of
> woman is home-making. . . . And homes are fundamental,
> where the home breaks down the Nation breaks down. . . .
> We shall purchase our shops and our factories at too high
> a cost if we give our homes for them.[73]

Given the extent to which middle-class men had come to depend on the separate-spheres ideology for their sense of manliness and gender identity, fundamentalists' reaction of alarm at the deterioration of gender distinctions and discrete fields of activity should not be surprising. Any hint of androgyny—a world without gender limits—seemed very frightening. Talmage, for example, censured the masculine women and the womanish men he observed around him. About the women he said that "they copy a man's stalking gait and go down the street with the stride of walking beam." "O woman, stay a woman!" he pleaded. "Do not try to cross over."[74] The *Bibliotheca Sacra* told its readers that:

> The world needs a fresh conviction of the nature, the
> stability, and the obligations of the family. The general
> unsettlement of belief and institutions which have charac-
> terized the past decade or two has had its effect upon the
> theories of the family. At a rapid rate we have been removing
> all the hedges and boundary lines, and filling up
> the ditches that marked the limits of our life in days
> gone by.[75]

Several years later the *Western Recorder* echoed the theme: "More and more we are removing the old landmarks, and differences and distinctions are being rapidly obliterated."[76]

In 1880, Henry W. Battle, an evangelical minister, gave the commencement address for the Starkville Female Institute. In the address he sounded another important fundamentalist theme. Women

73. "Women and the Industrial Situation," *Watchman-Examiner* 8, no. 9 (February 26, 1920): 271–72.
74. Talmage, "Dominion of Fashion," *Christian Herald and Signs of Our Times* 12, no. 5 (February 2, 1888): 68.
75. Jesse Hill, "A Plea for the Family," *Bibliotheca Sacra* 62 (1905): 629.
76. "Female Football," *Western Recorder* 86, no. 6 (December 15, 1910): 8. See also Parker, "True Womanhood," *Christian Workers Magazine*, 185; A. R. Funderburk, "Serving the God of Fashion," *Moody Bible Institute Monthly* 25 (July 1925): 500.

outside their proper sphere were, in his view, threatened with sin and ruin. He told those young women to exert their power "within its appropriate sphere." If their influence "be womanly," it was "God's greatest blessing to man. Beyond that sphere, all history proves it to be an unmitigated evil—a blighting withering curse." Speaking of the suffrage movement, he warned them of its pernicious results:

> Though you be endowed with vigorous minds, nature never intended that you should become *masculine*. . . . "It is from the soil of meekness that true strength of womanhood grows." It is not woman's mission to revolutionize by radical means, but to ameliorate and beautify . . .[77]

Battle was not a voice crying alone in the wilderness. The *Christian Workers Magazine* told its readers that when woman assumes:

> the prerogative of power which belongs to the man and seeks to dominate the world or all of its activities, as she is doing today, she then possesses the spirit of the beast and is like an angel of light fallen from heaven.[78]

Even several decades later, an article in the *King's Business* said that even though women were superior to men intellectually, morally, and spiritually, "her divinely appointed position is that of subordination, and it is her ruin to fight against that which God . . . had ordained for her." Women were warned that "man does not suffer as much as woman does when she gets out of her place."[79]

Fundamentalist popular literature is full of the separate-spheres ideology supported by religious commandment and taboo. Given the strength of Protestant evangelicalism in nineteenth-century American culture,[80] particularly among women who were religion's special guardians, this "religious" rhetoric must have been among the strongest defenses of the Victorian gender ideology.

77. Henry W. Battle, "Address: To Graduates of Starkville Female Institute, Class of 1880," *Western Recorder* 46, no. 49 (August 19, 1880): 1.
78. Parker, "True Womanhood," *Christian Workers Magazine*, 185.
79. *King's Business* 8, no. 11 (November 1917): 1046.
80. Filene concluded that religion was the "framework of Victorian women's lives." Peter G. Filene, *Him/Her/Self: Sex Roles in Modern America*, 2d ed. (Baltimore: Johns Hopkins Univ. Press, 1986), 14.

CHAPTER THREE

The Divinized Home

I N 1886, T. DEWITT TALMAGE
used an extended metaphor to express serious concern:

> Yonder comes . . . a ship having all the evidence of tem-
> pestuous passage: salt water-mark reaching to the top of the
> smoke-stack; . . . bulwarks knocked in; . . . main shaft
> broken; all the pumps working to keep from sinking. That
> ship is the institution of Christian marriage.[1]

Like conservative Protestant evangelicals everywhere, Talmage believed
in the sacred quality of the Victorian home, and he was alarmed by
what he perceived as its decay. The idea of a sacred, or divinized, home
was not an original creation of Talmage and his generation. Rather,
this theme emerged decades earlier as a natural extension of the ideology
of virtuous woman and worldly man and as a major defense of separate
spheres of activity.[2]

    1. T. Dewitt Talmage, "Clandestine Marriage," *Christian Herald and Signs of Our
Times* 9, no. 4 (January 28, 1886): 52–53.
    2. Lawrence Foster concluded, "Perhaps the most common response . . . was the
attempt to control potentially anarchic social and sexual tendencies by attributing
enormous, even cosmic, importance to 'the home.' The sense of boundless potentiality
and undefined limits that had characterized the 1830s and 1840s gradually gave way
after about 1850 to a period of consolidation and to the introduction of new intellectual
and institutional forms of control." *Religion and Sexuality: Three American Communal
Experiments of the Nineteenth Century* (New York: Oxford Univ. Press, 1981), 13–14.
    Colleen McDannell wrote, "That the proper Christian home worked toward the
salvation of the family was . . . crucial to Victorian society. . . . Under the impact

Colleen McDannell documented this elevation of the home in nineteenth-century American culture in her book *The Christian Home in Victorian America*. McDannell's portrait of Victorian Protestant family life included family worship (Bible reading, hymn singing, prayers) once or twice a day; parlor altars and brackets for displaying the family Bible; handmade religious samplers, table crosses, and bookmarks. According to McDannell, family religious leadership often alternated between the "paternal model" and the "maternal model," with the father's leadership often more formal and limited to the context of family worship, the mother's usually oriented more toward the religious education of the children and the use of religious symbols throughout the home.

McDannell rejected a purely denominational or official interpretation of American religion. American religion consisted, she argued, of three strands running parallel to each other—official denominational religion, civil religion, and domestic religion. Domestic religion—the divinized home—became so popular over the course of the nineteenth century, in McDannell's view, because of the heightened individualism of industrial capitalism and the inability of institutionalized denominations to command allegiance and to provide meaning. Her argument is valuable so far as it goes. McDannell paid little attention, however, to the ways in which divinized home symbolism and rhetoric functioned to sustain Victorian gender ideology.

"The Blessed Family"

The symbolic divinized home as presented in the popular fundamentalist press justified, through the use of religious appeal and sanction, the traditional patriarchal family and the gender-based division of labor on which men's gender identity rested. This chapter contains a description of the divinized home that appeared regularly and forcefully in fundamentalist discourse.

Conservative evangelicals of the 1880s, fundamentalists in the 1920s, and those of similar ilk in between claimed that the middle-class Victorian family structure was sacred because God ordained it:

The family that is united in the bonds of true religion . . . [is] of immeasurable importance and influence for good. It is one of the divine institutions devised by God . . . ,

---

of industrialization, consumerism, and the growth of urban centers, the quality of domestic Protestantism took on a particularly Victorian form." *The Christian Home in Victorian America, 1840–1900* (Bloomington, Ind.: Indiana Univ. Press, 1986), 19.

instituted in the Garden of Eden . . . preserved through
all the centuries . . . and carefully maintained according
to God's own plan.[3]

Billy Sunday called the home "the most sacred spot on the globe."[4]

When these conservative Protestants used the term *family*, they
referred to a monogamous marriage between a man and woman with
intent to have children reared in an evangelical Protestant environment:

> The family founded on the ordinance of marriage between
> one man and one woman, is designed not only for the
> perpetuation of the race, but for its social and religious
> welfare. . . . There is no satisfaction or purity where the
> family does not exist. All other relationships of men and
> women and children, except as God directs, fail to secure
> the proper welfare of the race.[5]

Conservative evangelical clergy presented Christian marriage as the
specific divine institution undergirding Christian domesticity. In 1880,
the *Watchman* proclaimed marriage "a relation of sacredness,"[6] and "the
sanctity of the nuptial bond . . . one of the principal, if not the chief
cause of the superior refinement, freedom and prosperity enjoyed at
the present time by Christian nations."[7] A. C. Dixon reminded his
audience that "marriage came from Paradise and let us remember that
Paradise still lingers in the home where the marriage relation is hon-
ored."[8] In 1900, G. Campbell Morgan set marriage above all other
human relationships and institutions: "The most sacred thing after the
soul's relationship to God is the marriage relation."[9]

Despite the fact that a growing segment of the American middle
class sought divorces,[10] the divinized home rhetoric changed little by

3. "Prayer Meeting: The Blessed Family," *Herald and Presbyter* 91, no. 24 (June 16,
1920): 19. See also "The Festival of the Home," *Watchman* 75 (October 22, 1894): 7;
Thurston, "Order in the Family," *Western Recorder* 64, no. 3 (September 12, 1889): 1;
John S. Sewall, "The Social Ethics of Jesus," *Bibliotheca Sacra* 52 (April 1895): 283.

4. Billy Sunday, "Home," *Trenton (New Jersey) Evening Times* (January 7, 1916): n.p.

5. "Prayer Meeting," *Herald and Presbyter*, 19.

6. "Charles Dickens Marriage Scandal," *Watchman* 61 (January 15, 1880): 19. See
also John F. Kendall, "The Family," *Truth, or, Testimony for Christ* 11 (1884–1885):
187.

7. "Morality of Divorce," *Western Recorder* 67, no. 8 (October 28, 1880): 4.

8. A. C. Dixon, "The Message of Jesus Concerning Marriage and Divorce," *Watchman*
86 (December 29, 1904): 9–10.

9. G. Campbell Morgan, "Christian Ethics," *Northfield Echoes* 7, no. 4 (1900): 445.
See also Jesse Hill, "A Plea for the Family," *Bibliotheca Sacra* 62 (1905): 631; James I.
Vance, "The Supreme Social Need of Modern Life—The Christian Home," *Record of
Christian Work* 35, no. 10 (October 1916): 654.

10. Between 1870 and 1930 there was a fivefold increase in divorce in the U. S.

1930.[11] A lead editorial that year in the *Bible Champion* declared that "it is obvious that, according to the Holy Scriptures, marriage is a divine institution. That marriage is to be monogamous."[12] J. Frank Norris, a very popular voice in the 1920s, had a similar message: "Marriage is God's first institution," the sacredness of which is revealed in the Bible.[13] The *King's Business* editorialized that "marriage is a sacred institution, ordained of God, sanctioned and commended by our Lord Jesus Christ, and is fraught with tremendous obligations and consequences."[14]

So complete was the translation of the domestic into the sacred that the home replaced the church in fundamentalist literature as the primary location of religious meaning and as the cornerstone of Christian civilization.[15] Given traditional Christian ecclesiology, this was a remarkable move, especially for ministers who were theologically trained. Popular fundamentalism related the home to the church in different ways, but always the home was superior in holiness and importance to the church.

One strand in the literature depicted the home as the foundation of the church. John Roach Straton preached that "out of the home, at last, flow all the forces that make our educational system, our religion, and our society what they ought to be."[16] In a sermon, Norris said that "the home is the first institution that God instituted—and as goes the home so goes the church."[17] F. C. Woods called the family "the

---

W. Elliot Brownlee and Mary M. Brownlee, *Women in the American Economy, 1675–1929* (New Haven: Yale Univ. Press, 1976), 24.

11. By the 1920s mainline Protestants, as represented by the Federal Council of the Churches of Christ, had given up part of the Victorian gender ideology. The Council declared that the mother "needs to be out of the home as well as in it, for her children's sake as well as her own." Quoted in David M. Kennedy, *Birth Control in America: The Career of Margaret Sanger* (New Haven: Yale Univ. Press, 1974), 138.

12. "The Church, Marriage and Divorce," *Bible Champion* 36, no. 7 (July 1930): 337.

13. J. Frank Norris, "5,000 Hear Norris Speak at Tabernacle," *Searchlight* 7, no. 25 (May 9, 1924): 1; Norris, "Marriage and Desertion," *Searchlight* 6, no. 12 (February 2, 1923): 1–2.

14. "Homeless Houses," *King's Business* 17 (May 1926): 253. See also Dixon, "Marriage and Divorce as Taught by Christ," *King's Business* 11 (July 1920): 644.

15. Gayle Kimball noted that in nineteenth-century America "the family replaced the older institutions of court and church as symbols for stability, order, and moral purpose." *The Religious Ideas of Harriet Beecher Stowe* (Lewiston, N.Y.: Edwin Mellen Press, 1982), 84.

16. John Roach Straton, "Right Home Life," *King's Business* 12, no. 2 (February 1921): 116.

17. Norris, "Husbands, Love Your Wives," *Fundamentalist of Texas* 7, no. 40 (August 16, 1929): 1. See also Norris, "Home Foundation of All Things," *Searchlight* 2, no. 25 (April 22, 1920): 2; John Balcom Shaw, "Domestic Evils," *Western Recorder* 69, no. 19 (March 21, 1895): 6.

foundation of all other institutions, both civil and religious,"[18] and he warned his audience that "no godly church life can exist without their roots beneath Christian hearth stones and family altars."[19] In some instances, the home was described as the kernel or germ from which the church grew: "The family is the first institution of God on earth. It has in it the germ and something of the development of the church."[20] Fundamentalists described the home as the original and permanent social reality from which all others emerged. Contrary to the findings of the "sex modernists" like Havelock Ellis in the 1910s that the Victorian family was both culturally relative and seriously flawed, fundamentalists reasserted its permanence and inevitability. On the solid bedrock of the eternal, Victorian family fundamentalists placed the foundation of the church:

> The family is the earliest organization into which human beings have been gathered. . . . It was the original state, of which the father was the lawgiver, judge and executive. As the human race increased, and the separate church was organized it retained many of the characteristics of the family. . . . But the family still exists, as fundamental, as necessary, and as abiding as ever. Upon its rightful development and maintenance depend the success of the Church. . . .[21]

In this rhetoric, the home or family altar "finds its larger expression in the church"[22] and was actually more important than the church. Charles Franklin Thwing concluded that "of all social institutions, Christ apparently judged the family to be the most important."[23] The *Watchman* told its readers in 1894 that the home

> is the finest flower of Christian civilization. Our success in home-making better than anything else measures our attainment of Christian culture. . . . Before Church and before State is the Divine institution of the family, and the family has rights and wields influences to which every thoughtful Christian and patriot concedes precedence.[24]

18. F. C. Woods, "The Divorce Question," *Watchman* 71 (April 3, 1890): 2.
19. T. L. Cuyler, "The Home," *Western Recorder* 63, no. 33 (April 11, 1889): 2.
20. Edward Trumbell Hooker, "The Family and the Church," *Bibliotheca Sacra* 63 (1886): 487.
21. "Sabbath School," *Herald and Presbyter* 92, no. 19 (May 11, 1921): 17.
22. Charles R. Compton, "The Home, the School," *Herald and Presbyter* 83, no. 2 (January 10, 1912): 6–7.
23. Charles Franklin Thwing, "The Teachings of Christ, and the Modern Family," *Bibliotheca Sacra* 61 (January 1904): 1.
24. "The Festival of the Home," *Watchman,* 7.

In a speech at the Northfield General Conference for Christian Workers in 1916, the home was described as "something more sacred than a Church," and that even more important than a revival of the church was a revival of the Christian home.[25] Fundamentalist popular literature from 1880 to 1930 described the middle-class Victorian home as God's first institution, as the base on which the church rested and on which the church's continued well-being depended.

Another way in which fundamentalists divinized the home was to describe it as the primary agent on earth for the fulfillment of the kingdom of God. Earlier Christian tradition had often designated the church as such. Nineteenth-century American evangelical revisions insisted that "the Christian home is the unit in the earthly development of the kingdom of God among us."[26] The home was held up as the earthly type of the kingdom:

> If God has told us earthly things so nearly and incessantly touching our earthly happiness and perennial life in the home and we are unbelieving and dull in understanding them, how shall we believe and understand if He tells us the heavenly things themselves which are purified so far above these?[27]

Talmage referred to the home as "a type of heaven."[28]

Throughout this literature the Christian home, rather than the invisible church of Protestant tradition, constituted "a church within a church."[29] And like the church invisible, "a house is not a home. Home is a spiritual fact; home is an atmosphere."[30] Gender roles within the traditional household were described in the theological language of priesthood and the ministry. Talmage told his listeners and readers that "the greatest sermons are not preached on celebrated platforms" but "with an audience of two or three, and in private home life."[31] In 1907, Moody's Young Women's Conference heard a speaker proclaim

25. Vance, "The Supreme Social Need," *Record of Christian Work*, 653.

26. "Fathers and Sons," *Herald and Presbyter* 90, no. 10 (March 5, 1919): 1. See also Charles H. Richards, "Some Needed Factors in the 'New Evangelism'," *Bibliotheca Sacra* 62 (April 1905): 362.

27. Hooker, "The Family and the Church," *Bibliotheca Sacra,* 491.

28. Talmage, "Home," *Christian Herald and Signs of Our Times* 6 (January 11, 1883): 21.

29. Talmage, "Matrimonial Harmony and Discord," *Christian Herald and Signs of Our Times* 9, no. 5 (February 4, 1886): 68.

30. Straton, "Right Home Life," *King's Business,* 119.

31. Talmage, "The Queens of the Home," *Christian Herald and Signs of Our Times* 10 (September 8, 1887): 564.

that "God has given to motherhood the gift of interpretation, beyond
the genius and power of the priesthood, of translating to childhood
the life of the Nazarene."[32] Another minister described the husband as
"the priest of the household," but that "at times the mother may
substitute for her husband."[33] Robert E. Speer told women at another
Moody conference that they must resolve to make each home "a little
church. I do not know a more sacred institution than the home, nor
any priesthood higher than that of the Christian father as he sits at the
head of the table."[34]

Fundamentalists believed that the home was the primary location
of moral authority and character formation. In language nearly identical
to that used to describe the special virtue of pure womanhood, William
E. Biederwolf argued that "the life of the nation will never rise higher
than the life of the home." Religion in the home—that is, the conservative Protestant evangelicalism of traditional white middle-class
families—"will settle every problem—the problem of anarchy, of gambling, and the saloon problem, and every other curse which blights
our land today."[35] Billy Sunday preached that "home is on a level with
the women; the town is on a level with the homes."[36] Those who
attended the Northfield General Conference of Christian Workers in
1913 were told that "if the home life is pure, all is pure. The home
is the center of everything."[37] Talmage preached that "if things go right
there [in the home], they go right everywhere; if things go wrong
there, they go wrong everywhere."[38] All kinds of evils, personal and
social, ran rampant whenever the Christian home broke down:

So there is no sin against God or man . . . which does not
follow in so-called society (but soon to be anarchy) where

32. James E. Freeman, "Serving and Following," *Record of Christian Work* 26 (1907):
772.
33. J. T. Larsen, "What Is Becoming of the Christian Home?" *King's Business* 19,
no. 6 (June 1928): 346.
34. Speer, "The Church in the House," *Record of Christian Work* 31, no. 9 (September
1912): 572–75.
35. William E. Biederwolf, "The Family Altar League," *Institute Tie*, new series, 9,
no. 8 (April 1909): 666.
36. Sunday, quoted in William T. Ellis, *"Billy" Sunday: The Man and His Message,
with His Own Words Which Have Won Thousands for Christ* (Philadelphia: The John C.
Winston Company, 1914), 770.
37. George R. Stuart, "The Christian Home," *Record of Christian Work* 32, no. 10
(October 1913): 706. See also Thwing, "The Teachings of Christ and the Modern
Family," *Bibliotheca Sacra*, 8.
38. Talmage, "Matrimonial Harmony and Discord," *Christian Herald and Signs of
Our Times*, 68.

the home becomes hollow or discordant with heartless selfishness, deceit, false and capricious choosings or alien af-
fections. . . .[39]

In an article entitled "Family Religion," the subscribers to the *Western
Recorder* read, "without the home, promiscuous living, lawlessness,
rapine, murder, would prevail."[40]

According to fundamentalists, the middle-class Victorian home
should be defended not only because it was holy but because society
and nations depended on the home for strength and stability. This was
not a theological but rather a sociological argument. The rhetoric used
remained virtually unchanged from 1880 to 1930. Charles Franklin
Thwing contended that "the family represents an institution fundamental, essential, structural to human society. It is impossible to con-
template the higher society without the family."[41] Straton surmised
that "out of the home, at last, flow all the forces that make our
educational system, our religion, and our society what it ought to be."[42]
Norris called traditional marriage the "cornerstone of society. On it
everything depends and everything falls if it goes down."[43] J. W. Loving
warned that

> no nation or people can long survive in power, influence or
> greatness if the home be destroyed. . . . Every blow at the
> home is at the same time a blow to the whole social, eco-
> nomic, political, and religious fabric.[44]

The health of the nation was linked to the welfare of the evangelical
home. In the destruction of the home lay the republic's peril:

> No more important problem confronts the workers for righ-
> teousness than how to preserve our homes. . . . It is the

39. Hooker, "The Family and the Church," *Bibliotheca Sacra,* 501.

40. "Family Religion," *Western Recorder* 52, no. 28 (March 18, 1886): 4. See also
"Editorial Comments on Current Events," *Watchman-Examiner* 1, no. 10 (November
16, 1913): 10.

41. Thwing, "The Teachings of Christ, and the Modern Family," *Bibliotheca Sacra,*
41. See also Stuart, "The Christian Home," *Record of Christian Work,* 706–7; "Fathers
and Sons," *Herald and Presbyter,* 1; Woods, "The Divorce Question," *Watchman,* 2; P. S.
Henson, "The Illuminated Home," *Watchman* 86, no. 23 (June 9, 1904): 10–11;
"Prayer Meeting," *Herald and Presbyter,* 19; Shaw, "Domestic Evils," *Western Recorder,*
6; "The Sanctity of Marriage," *Watchman-Examiner* 4 (March 9, 1916): 296.

42. Straton, "Right Home Life," *King's Business,* 116.

43. Norris, "Marriage and Desertion," *Searchlight,* 2. See also Norris, "Home Foundation of All Things," *Searchlight,* 2; Norris, "Check Divorce, Save Homes, Norris'
Plea," *Searchlight* 1, no. 18 (March 16, 1923): 3.

44. J. W. Loving, "Jesus and the Home," *Western Recorder* 75, no. 5 (January 4,
1900): 3.

one remaining institution of Paradise, the secret of all sociology, the beginning and the end of all reformations, and
the unity of society, whose redemption means the redemption of the world. The home is the corner-stone of the
Republic![45]

"Domestic Evils"

The supposed corruption and decline of the family disturbed fundamentalists. They assumed that the family and Christianity were
inexorably linked. Just as the home was the germ or foundation of the
church, so "religion is the bond of home life."[46] One could not flourish
without the other; to weaken or transform one was to weaken or
transform the other. The consumers of popular fundamentalist literature
were frequently warned of a decline of this "home religion," and were
chastised for the disappearance from many of their homes of the "family
altar":

> Every Christian family should have daily the reading of
> God's Holy Word and prayer. Yet this blessed privilege is
> sadly neglected by hundreds of fathers and mothers. . . .
> The first thing every child of a Christian family should
> remember is the sight of father and mother on their knees
> and the reading of the Holy Scriptures. . . . The hurried
> life we all live . . . is in good part responsible for the
> neglect of family worship. If . . . our readers have failed
> in this . . . begin at once and *make time* . . . , and blessing
> upon the home will surely come.[47]

45. Hill, "A Plea for the Family," *Bibliotheca Sacra,* 639. See also Compton, "The
Home, the School," *Herald and Presbyter,* 6–7; "Morality of Divorce," *Western Recorder.*
4; "Family and Home Life," *Herald and Presbyter* 94, no. 5 (January 31, 1923): 4;
"Rome and Marriage," *Western Recorder* 86, no. 35 (July 6, 1911): 8; "Editorial,"
Bibliotheca Sacra 83, no. 329 (January 1926): 9; "Divorce," *Western Recorder* 86, no. 29
(May 25, 1911): 8; Cortland Myers, "What Will Save Religion in These United
States?" *King's Business* 12, no. 10 (October 1921): 970–71; George Loring Thurlow,
"Thou Shalt Not Commit Adultery," *Watchman* 94, no. 15 (April 11, 1912): 9–11;
Alexander R. Merriam, "Some Relations of Divorce to Social Morality," *Bibliotheca
Sacra* 65, no. 177 (January 1888): 33; "Sabbath School," *Herald and Presbyter,* 17;
Montgomery, "Women and the New World Movement," *Watchman-Examiner* 8 (April
15, 1920): 503.
46. F. B. Meyer, "Laxity in Religion," *Watchman-Examiner and Watchman* 77 (August
27, 1896): 14. See also Norris, "Cleaning Out the Wells," *Baptist Fundamentalist* 11,
no. 10 (January 13, 1928): 6.
47. "Family Worship," *Our Hope* 18, no. 1 (July 1911): 5. See also "The Family
Altar," *Western Recorder* 85, no. 38 (July 28, 1910): 1; Robert C. Patrick, "Family

"Domestic religion" had been corrupted and was on the decline.[48]

Fundamentalists were even more alarmed by the increasing divorce rate. The attack on divorce constituted a major fundamentalist defense of Victorian domestic ideology. The frequency with which the issue was treated in the literature reached a high point after 1900 and began to decline after 1920; it was treated with more frequency before 1900 than after 1920. Every periodical carried editorials, articles, or sermons on the topic, with the *Watchman/Watchman-Examiner*, *Western Recorder*, and *Bibliotheca Sacra* having the most. Divorce was decried as the "deadliest foe to the home,"[49] and a "monster of iniquity" that "threatens to destroy the American home."[50] More frequently and histrionically these magazine editors and writers called divorce the "single greatest menace to our national welfare."[51] In 1904, the *Western Recorder* editorialized that

> the chief social question of the day, more than in labor and capital, more than in municipal government, more even than in temperance . . . is . . . the permanence and sanctity of the marriage relation.[52]

Talmage warned his audience that "the frequency of divorce always goes along with the dissolution of society," and that divorce was the cause of the fall of Rome.[53]

Fundamentalists cited divorce statistics over and over again as evidence of an extreme and dangerous trend.[54] They noticed that more

Worship," *Western Recorder* 69, no. 26 (May 9, 1895): 1; "No Family Altar," *Western Recorder* 62, no. 24 (February 18, 1886): 4; "The Family Altar," *Western Recorder* 85, no. 36 (July 14, 1910): 7; Richards, "Some Needed Factors in the 'New Evangelism'," *Bibliotheca Sacra*, 362; "The Christian Home," *Our Hope* 30, no. 4 (October 1923): 202–3; H. K. Sherrill, "The Christian Home," *Record of Christian Work* 43, no. 9 (September 1924): 626–29.

48. See "Family Religion," *Western Recorder*, 4; Sherrill, "The Living Christ and Daily Living," *Record of Christian Work* 44, no. 9 (September 1925): 602; Straton, "The Only Way Out of Our Troubles," *American Fundamentalist* 2, no. 9 (1925): 3.

49. "Divorce," *Western Recorder*, 8. See also "Editorial Notes," *Moody Bible Institute Monthly* 23, no. 11 (July 1923): 507–8.

50. "Divorce," *Western Recorder* 85, no. 49 (October 13, 1910): 8.

51. "Grounds for Divorce," *Watchman* 84, no. 34 (August 21, 1902): 7.

52. *Watchman* 86, no. 41 (October 13, 1904): 5. See also Thurlow, "Thou Shalt Not Commit Adultery," *Watchman*, 9–11; "Divorces in the U.S.," *Herald and Presbyter* 85, no. 42 (October 21, 1914): 2; "Rome and Marriage," *Western Recorder*, 8; "The Divorce Evil," *Watchman-Examiner* 4 (October 4, 1916): 1287; "France Is Disgusted with American Divorces," *Our Hope* 30, no. 10 (April 1924): 611–12.

53. Talmage, "Easy Divorce," *Christian Herald and Signs of Our Times* 7 (April 24, 1884): 260–61.

54. See "The Divorce Peril," *King's Business* 7, no. 8 (August 1916): 679; "Is the

women were beginning to seek divorces than previously and that more women than men were petitioning for divorce:

the sex which is most deeply interested in the security of the home and maintenance of social purity has taken the lead in the war upon both through our perverted legal machinery.[55]

To curb divorce, fundamentalist leaders argued that divorce laws should be tightened, divorced individuals be treated as criminals and brought to trial, and the public censure and ostracize those who had divorced outside of the law of Jesus.[56]

The primary strategy these conservative Protestants employed against divorce was the use of religious sanctions. The first line of the argument was to claim that divorce was a religious question rather than a purely civil matter. The editors of the *King's Business* advocated a "Divorce Sunday" on which ministers throughout the nation would preach on divorce, "the great American sin. It is America's crying and burning shame."[57] In a more scholarly article published in 1888, Alexander R. Merriam concluded that the state would be of little help

---

World Growing Better?" *King's Business* 8, no. 11 (November 1917): 966; "France Is Disgusted with American Divorces," *Our Hope*, 612; "Work at Home and Abroad," *Record of Christian Work* 26, no. 4 (April 1907): 327; "A Remedy for the Divorce Evil," *Watchman* 90, no. 51 (December 24, 1908): 6; Woods, "The Divorce Question," *Watchman*, 2; "Some Startling Facts," *Truth, or, Testimony for Christ* 13 (1886–1887): 14; Norris, "Check Divorce, Save Homes," *Searchlight*, 3; Sunday, quoted in Ellis, *"Billy" Sunday*, 228; Larsen, "What Is Becoming of the Christian Home?" *King's Business*, 346; "Marriage and Related Problems," *Record of Christian Work* 47, no. 4 (April 1928): 209; "Ghastly Divorce Record," *Christian Cynosure* 56, no. 9 (January 1924): 272.

55. "Our Divorce Laws," *Watchman* 61 (February 12, 1880): 52. See also Robert Morris Rabb, "The Awful Question of Divorce," *Western Recorder* 92, no. 46 (August 23, 1917): 1.

56. See Charles L. Morgan, "Is Desertion a Scriptural Ground for Divorce?" *Bibliotheca Sacra* 43 (1886): 334; Rabb, "The Awful Question of Divorce," *Western Recorder*, 1; "Ministers and Marriage Reform," *Watchman* 73, no. 44 (November 10, 1892): 4; "Divorce," *Western Recorder* 90, no. 10 (December 16, 1915): 8; Joe C. Johnson, "Divorces," *Western Recorder* 88, no. 13 (January 13, 1913): 12; "Divorce and Imprisonment," *Watchman* 90, no. 25 (June 18, 1908): 5–6; "A Remedy for the Divorce Evil," *Watchman*, 6; Noah Lathrop, "The Holy Scriptures and Divorce," *Bibliotheca Sacra* 56 (April 1899): 266–77; Ralph E. Prime, "Critical Notes: Do We Want a Uniform Divorce Law: Or What Is the Remedy?" *Bibliotheca Sacra* 69 (January 1912): 136–41; John G. Reid, "Shall I Marry Them?" *Moody Bible Institute Monthly* 24, no. 1 (September 1923): 12; Sunday, quoted in Ellis, *"Billy" Sunday*, 228.

57. "A Divorce Sunday," *King's Business* 7, no. 12 (December 1916): 1059. See also T. E. Richey, "Should Ministers Marry Divorced Persons?" *Western Recorder* 64, no. 27 (February 27, 1890): 5; "Current Events," *Christian Herald and Signs of Our Times* 4 (September 1881): 552.

in fighting the divorce evil, but that because divorce is "a religious and moral issue, more than a political one," the "Christian church, at least, must try to show to the public law a bold and loyal response to Christ's aims for the home, by knowing his law so clear and strict."[58] The religious and moral grounds of their opposition to divorce lay, they argued, in the teachings of Jesus recorded in the New Testament. Divorce was permissible only on the grounds of adultery, and remarriage of the adulterer was prohibited.[59] Ministers who had a tolerant attitude toward divorce and the remarriage of divorced persons were taken to task:

> The re-marriage of those who have transgressed every word of Christ's utterance has sometimes been accomplished by prominent ministers. . . . A minister who winks at the outraging of divine law . . . cannot be faithful to his or-dination vows. The church and the minister who sanction and bless an unscriptural marriage are guilty of matrimonial blasphemy.[60]

Interestingly, late nineteenth-century evangelicals sided with their sworn enemy, Roman Catholicism, against divorce.[61] This alliance on gender issues between Rome and the "first wave" of fundamentalism has gone unnoticed in previous histories of the movement. Such prominent historians as George Marsden have characterized early fundamentalists as lacking "fully developed or carefully articulated political

58. Merriam, "Some Relations of Divorce to Social Morality," *Bibliotheca Sacra*, 51. See also Hill, "A Plea for the Family," *Bibliotheca Sacra*, 631; Kendall, "The Family," *Truth, or, Testimony for Christ*, 190.

59. See Merriam, "Some Relations of Divorce to Social Morality," *Bibliotheca Sacra*, 32–50; Dixon, "Marriage and Divorce as Taught by Christ," *King's Business*, 644–45; "The Scripture and Divorce," *Christian Cynosure* 23, no. 38 (June 4, 1891): 8; Rueben A. Torrey, "Jesus' Teaching Concerning Marriage, Divorce and Children," *Institute Tie*, new series, 9 (May 1909): 758–59; Rabb, "The Awful Question," *Western Recorder*, 1; Lathrop, "The Holy Scriptures and Divorce," *Bibliotheca Sacra*, 266–77; Morgan, "Is Desertion a Scriptural Ground for Divorce?" *Bibliotheca Sacra*, 318–34; J. C. Burkholder, "That Divorce Question," *Western Recorder* 51, no. 49 (August 13, 1885): 5; Richey, "Should Ministers Marry," *Western Recorder*, 5; Thwing, "The Teachings of Christ, and the Modern Family," *Bibliotheca Sacra*, 30–41; Randolph H. M'Kim, "Our Lord's Teaching on Marriage and Divorce," *Bibliotheca Sacra* 67 (January 1910): 143–56; Charles Caverno, "The Divorce Problem: A Rational Religious View," *Bibliotheca Sacra* 69 (April 1912): 242–53.

60. Hill, "A Plea for the Family," *Bibliotheca Sacra*, 632. See also "Marriage and Divorce," *Watchman* 86, no. 22 (June 2, 1904): 6.

61. See Merriam, "Some Relations of Divorce to Social Morality," *Bibliotheca Sacra*, 38.

views," and, instead, reflected typical anti-Catholicism: "the conventional slogans of the day," which "could have been summarized under such headings as 'Rum, Romanism, and Rebellion.' "[62] Wenger claimed that even fundamentalists' strong distaste for Roman Catholic theology was eclipsed in the 1920s by their fear of "Rome's political influence in America."[63] Yet on divorce and several other issues that are discussed in later chapters, the support of Victorian gender conventions and domestic patterns was more important to fundamentalists than their theological differences with, and nativist prejudices against, Roman Catholics.[64]

In the 1920s, the defenders of the traditional Christian family and the permanent, monogamous marriage diverted some of their wrath from divorce to the "companionate marriage," a term used to describe a relationship between a man and a woman who lived together, childless and economically independent, for renewable periods of five years. Judge Ben B. Lindsey proposed it as a means of bringing the divorce rate down. His suggestion drew heavy fire from fundamentalists, and they denounced it in at least five of their periodicals between 1928 and 1930:

> It is highly significant that in all the discussion of companionate marriage, the name of Jesus never occurs. His legislation is never consulted. His teachings are ignored, or sneered at as medieval superstitions. . . . [A]ll are swept away, that men and women may be as free as the beasts of the field in the indulgence of their lower natures. The slaughter of the innocents at Bethlehem is renewed on a universal scale. . . .[65]

62. George M. Marsden, *Fundamentalism and American Culture: The Shaping of Twentieth-Century Evangelicalism, 1870–1925* (New York: Oxford Univ. Press, 1980), 66.
63. Robert E. Wenger, "Social Thought in American Fundamentalism, 1918–1933" (Ph.D. diss., Univ. of Nebraska, 1973), 167–76.
64. Hence, Marsden incorrectly concluded that the Evangelical-Roman Catholic alliance in support of conservative gender issues emerged only in the 1970s resurgence of fundamentalism. See *Fundamentalism and American Culture*, 228.
65. "Companionate Marriage," *Christian Fundamentalist* 3, no. 10 (April 1930): 616. See also "What about 'Companionate' Marriages?" *Bible Champion* 34, no. 4 (April 1928): 194; Leander S. Keyser, "True Marriage," *Christian Faith and Life* 37, no. 4 (April 1931): 180; "College Students of Both Sexes Favor Companionate Tie," *Christian Fundamentalist* 1, no. 10 (April 1928): 25; "So 'Tis—With Companionate Marriages," *King's Business* 19, no. 3 (March 1928): 142; "The Vile Corruption of the Young," *Our Hope* 34, no. 8 (February 1928): 466–67; Sunday, "Christian Scientists Scored by Sunday," *Trenton (New Jersey) Evening Times* (January 7, 1916): n.p.

Just how common men and women responded to these fundamentalist appeals to save the Victorian family we do not know.
McDannell uncovered the widespread appeal of the divinized home in
both Protestant and Catholic circles until the 1910s or so.[66] Also,
evidence in popular fundamentalist literature indicates that lay people
were very perplexed about the status of marriage and the propriety of
divorce, and that they turned to their ministers for answers. For example, between 1910 and 1919 divorce and remarriage were the most
frequently discussed issues in the write-in question and answer column
of the *Western Recorder*.[67] Fundamentalist advertising indicated that the
divinized home rhetoric was an effective sales technique. Publishers of
these periodicals knew that an appeal to the idealized Victorian home
of yesteryear would sell their magazines. The *King's Business*, for example, used on the front cover drawings of "Christian families" sitting
around tables together reading the Bible.[68] Also, about this time the
King's Business was subtitled, "The Bible Family Magazine," and it used
the idealized Christian home as a primary marketing strategy on sub-
scription solicitation pages:

> A Wholesome Home Atmosphere is made possible in part
> by providing the family with the really helpful things to
> be found in good periodical religious literature. . . . With
> the Bible as the necessary foundation of the Christian home,
> and with such a publication as *The King's Business* making
> regularly monthly visits, a mantle of protection is thrown
> around the household, which tends to unify the family
> interests, and imposes a real safe-guard against the many
> insidious influences which are having such a baneful effect
> upon family life today. Make sure that YOUR subscription
> is renewed promptly![69]

If the *King's Business* was in tune with its constituency, and there is
every indication that it was, then we must conclude that part of the

66. McDannell, *The Christian Home in Victorian America*, xv–xvi.
67. See Senex, "Questions Answered," *Western Recorder* 85, no. 16 (February 24,
1910): 2; 85, no. 34 (June 30, 1910): 2; 85, no. 52 (November 2, 1910): 2; 86, no.
12 (January 26, 1911): 2; 86, no. 18 (March 9, 1911): 2; 86, no. 52 (November 7,
1911): 2; 88, no. 16 (February 20, 1913): 2; 90, no. 20 (February 25, 1915): 2; 91,
no. 1 (October 14, 1915): 2; 92, no. 13 (January 4, 1917): 2; 92, no. 29 (April 26,
1917): 2; 92, no. 48 (September 6, 1917): 2; 94, no. 31 (May 8, 1919): 2.
68. See *King's Business* 16, no. 8 (August 1925): n.p.; 16, no. 10 (October 1925):
n.p.
69. *King's Business* 18, no. 1 (January 1927): n.p. See also *King's Business* 18, no. 3
(March 1927): n.p.

appeal fundamentalism had for millions of Americans lay in its defense
of middle-class Victorian domestic conventions against the tempests of
modernity. A major part of that defense was the idea of the divinized
home.

From the beginning of the period to its end, the defenders of
traditional households had little peace. The rapid changes in family
patterns—absent fathers, educated sons and daughters, working wom-
en, divorces, the refusal of college-educated women to marry, domestic
feminism, the revolution in morals—affected many Americans and
touched them, literally, where they lived. One of the casualties was
patriarchal marriage, in which the wife had little power and no economic
independence. Wives more and more frequently sought freedom from
marriages through divorce.[70] For Christians who linked religion and
gender roles—a natural phenomenon given the isolation and mutual
dependence of women and religion within the domestic sphere—issues
such as divorce had religious as well as social import.[71] For middle-
class men, whose gender identity and social domination were at stake
in the battle to preserve the prevailing Victorian gender ideology, the
use of religious discourse was an available and effective defensive strategy. Given the ideology of virtuous womanhood, the impact on good
evangelicals, both male and female but especially female, was powerful.
Fundamentalist ministers told women that they tossed aside Victorian
social conventions at the risk of sin, damnation, and the corruption of
the republic and Christian civilization. A departure in practice from
the ideal Christian home meant a desecration of the land's first, last,
and most sacred institution.

It must be noted that women themselves supported and found
comfort and self-esteem in the domestic religion of the sacred home
and the priesthood of parents. The cult of domesticity and virtuous
womanhood offered women more power within the home and in religious circles than they had ever previously enjoyed.[72] Women's new

70. Also, Leach discovered that a common topic for discussion by feminists in their
"clubs, congresses, and social science associations" in the 1870s was a repudiation of
"the idea that married women should rely at all on their husbands for an independent
source of income." *True Love and Perfect Union*, 195, 198–99.

71. Barbara Welter, *Dimity Convictions: The American Woman in the Nineteenth Century*
(Athens, Oh.: Ohio Univ. Press, 1976), 126.

72. "The assertion of Woman's moral superiority had important implications. For
the first time, women as a group had been attributed an independent power of moral
guardianship which, however intellectually degrading, contained the potential of a
hidden challenge to woman's traditional political and social passivity." Ann D. Gordon
and Mari Jo Buhle, "Sex and Class in Colonial and Nineteenth-Century America," in
Liberating Women's History: Theoretical and Critical Essays, ed. Bernice A. Carroll (Urbana,
Ill.: Univ. of Illinois Press, 1976), 287.

power and independence led, by the close of the nineteenth century, to the spoiling of the separate spheres. Yet fundamentalists used divinized-home language for decades after the idealized Victorian home was tarnished by the new economic realities of middle-class life and by new marriage patterns and family habits.[73] Theirs was a late attempt to glamorize the home (and hence, to keep women more satisfied in it) with the trappings of the sacred. Only by keeping women at home could men reclaim the public realm. In the next chapter, we examine their effort to reclaim the church as well.

73. McDannell argued that "domestic piety" increased between 1820 and 1870, became firmly entrenched by 1880, and fell off rather sharply after World War I. McDannell, *Christian Home in Victorian America,* xv–xvi.

CHAPTER FOUR

Reclaiming the Church for Men

I N 1892, ALBERT G. LAWSON asked, "Why are there not more men in our churches?" He claimed to have done a survey of eight churches in three denominations (which he did not specify in the article) and discovered that only 28 percent of total congregational membership and only 38 percent of the crowd "on a given Sunday morning" were male.[1] Conservative Protestant clergy and editors were well aware of the preponderance of women in most congregations. A speaker at the 1906 Northfield Young Women's Conference expressed dismay that "the best men . . . never go to church."[2] Another minister noted that "in every church the women are more numerous than the men." He worried that there would not be enough Christian men to make husbands "for the growing number of our fine Christian women."[3]

Protestant leaders of the 1880s inherited a feminized church. The church's relegation to the domestic sphere, the province of women, led to the dominance of women in the church's activities, and to a softening of some traditional Christian doctrines. Few writing for fundamentalist periodicals seemed comfortable with the concession of the church to women:

> The Church of Christ . . . may have to look to women
> and to depend on their labors and on their testimony as has

1. Albert G. Lawson, "Why Are There Not More Men in Our Churches?" *Watchman* 73, no. 38 (September 22, 1892): 1. See also "The Church and Men," *Watchman-Examiner* 1, no. 8 (October 23, 1913): 235.
2. White, "A Life Worthy of the Gospel," *Record of Christian Work* 25 (1906): 682.
3. W. T. Elsing, "A Pastor at Camp Northfield," *Northfield Echoes* 8, no. 1 (1901): 68.

not been the case since apostolic times. It would seem . . .
western civilization were to bring about a division of work
. . . which will put the practical work entirely in the hands
of men and leave the spiritual side [to women]. . . .[4]

A careful reading of the popular fundamentalist press indicates that at
least one part of the fundamentalist agenda was to regain the church
for men. To achieve that end, fundamentalist ministers, uncomfortable
within a feminized institution, worked on two fronts. They attempted,
first, to diminish women's influence and power by calling into question
the legitimacy of women speaking and holding positions of authority
within the church. Second, they replaced feminized Christianity with
a language of virility, militarism, and Christian heroism.

"Woman's Work in the Church"

Conservative Protestants debated among themselves about whether
the Bible forbade women to speak in the church or any other mixed
assembly. The controversy raged throughout the period under study.
James H. Brookes and his journal *Truth, or, Testimony for Christ* were
among the most prominent and the most vocal against women speaking
in the church. In regard to 1 Cor. 14:34–35, he argued against those
who contended that the injunction was limited to Corinthian women
only, and that it referred to chattering and whispering during the
service rather than to teaching, praying, and preaching. Woman was
to be silent because:

> she is a type of the Church, that has no right to teach
> anything, but only to be taught, and to be found sitting
> at the feet of Jesus, hearing His word. . . . There is no
> proof from the New Testament that the Lord Jesus . . .
> selected women for any public office and ministry, although
> much used in service, and then, as now, more devoted and
> even courageous than proud and insolent man.[5]

Brookes reiterated his position in 1887 and held up an inerrant Bible
against the more expedient position that women had talents that the
church needed and, consequently, should be allowed fuller participation
in ministry:

> Unless it can be proved that the [Biblical] order was sub-
> sequently repealed, all the arguments that may be urged

---

4. John A. Hutton, "Obscurer Ministries of the New Testament: 'Certain Women',"
Record of Christian Work 28 (1909): 297.
5. "Question Drawer," *Truth, or, Testimony for Christ* 6 (1879–1880): 29.

from the piety and eloquence of women, and from the blessed results of their public preaching, and from the affecting recollection of a sainted mother's teaching, go for nothing. That is to say, such arguments do not have a feather's weight against the authority of God's word in any mind subject to that word.[6]

In 1897, he protested the celebration of the WCTU convention held in St. Louis by churches in that city that invited eighty WCTU members to preach from their pulpits one Sunday. He praised both the Episcopal and the Roman Catholic churches in town for refusing to let temperance women speak from their pulpits.[7] In 1895, he took to task A. T. Pierson and A. J. Gordon, editors of the *Missionary Review* and premillennialists like himself, for publishing an article supporting women's work in "a missionary apostolate" and their right to preach. In his article, Brookes expanded his case against women speaking to include several additional points: no woman was chosen to author a biblical book; no woman was chosen to be an apostle; Old Testament passages about daughters prophesying are not relevant to the current dispensation; woman is subordinate to man just as man is subordinate to Christ; no "true woman will complain that her sphere is narrowed, because she is told to keep silence in the churches."[8]

The *Western Recorder* also voiced strong opposition to women speaking in church. Such practice by women and the churches who allowed them to speak constituted "signs admonishing as in thunder tones, of the coming tide of innovations, which is pressing down hard upon us."[9] In 1890, the magazine's editors wrote against the Young People's Christian Endeavor Society because the group allowed women to conduct meetings. The same article condemned the practice of allowing women to recite Bible verses or pray aloud in worship services.[10]

After 1910, an explosion of articles against women speaking in church or in any other mixed assembly was printed in the *Western Recorder*. This excitement was prompted by the placement of two women speakers on the program of the meeting of the Baptist World Alliance

6. "Woman in the Church," *Truth, or, Testimony for Christ* 14 (1887–1888): 252–53.
7. "W.C.T.U. Convention," *Truth, or, Testimony for Christ* 23, no. 1 (January 1897): 6.
8. "Ministry of Woman," *Truth, or, Testimony for Christ* 21, no. 2 (February 1895): 87–92.
9. S, "Let Your Women Keep Silence in the Churches," *Western Recorder* 65, no. 11 (November 6, 1890): 1.
10. Senex, "Questions Answered," *Western Recorder* 64, no. 29 (March 13, 1890): 1. See also Senex, "Questions Answered," 69, no. 19 (March 21, 1895): 3.

in the early part of 1911,[11] and the admission of women as messengers to the Southern Baptist Convention in 1918.[12]

Some conservative evangelical leaders spoke in favor of women's right to speak. In 1885, the *Western Recorder* ran several articles on the subject of women teaching or speaking in public. Four of the articles constituted a series written by A. B. Cabiniss supporting a more public role for church women.[13] Publications by Moody in 1890 and 1891 urged women to consider careers as missionaries, and in so doing judged that women had a "commission to tell the story of a risen Savior."[14] From 1910 to 1921, the *Christian Workers Magazine,* the *Record of Christian Work,* and the *Moody Bible Institute Monthly,* all published by the Moody Bible Institute, argued that the New Testament did not command contemporary women to keep their heads covered nor to keep silence in Sunday school classes or prayer meetings.[15] The *King's*

11. H. B. Taylor, "New Testament Restrictions of Women," *Western Recorder* 85, no. 27 (May 12, 1910): 2; Senex, "Questions Answered," *Western Recorder* 86, no. 6 (December 15, 1910): 2; John A. Broadus, "Should Women Speak in Mixed Public Assemblies?" *Western Recorder* 86, no. 14 (February 9, 1911): 6; E. H. Garner, "The Women Preaching and Praying in Public Gatherings," *Western Recorder* 86, no. 32 (June 15, 1911): 4; A. C. Dorris, "Women's Sphere in the Church," *Western Recorder* 86, no. 35 (July 6, 1911): 3; "The Women Also," *Western Recorder* 86, no. 37 (July 20, 1911): 8; Sonor Bellicoa, "Need Scripture Proof for Women Speaking," *Western Recorder* 88, no. 35 (July 13, 1913): 3; "The B.Y.P.U." *Western Recorder* 90, no. 25 (April 1, 1915): 8; Senex, "Questions Answered," *Western Recorder* 92, no. 25 (March 29, 1917): 2; Senex, "Questions Answered," *Western Recorder* 92, no. 18 (February 8, 1917): 2; "Paul and the Women," *Western Recorder* 94, no. 17 (January 30, 1919): 8; Senex, "Questions Answered," *Western Recorder* 94, no. 31 (May 8, 1919): 2.

12. See Gregory K. Vickers, "Woman's Place, Images of Womanhood in the Southern Baptist Convention 1888–1929" (M.A. thesis, Vanderbilt Univ., 1986): 20.

13. See A. B. Cabiniss, "Ought Women to Speak, Teach or Pray in Our Churches, or in Public?" *Western Recorder* 51, no. 22 (February 5, 1885): 4–5; 51, no. 23 (February 12, 1885): 5; 51, no. 25 (February 26, 1885): 4. Another article in support of women speaking included the following poem:
Not she with a trait'rous kiss her Savior stung,
Nor she denied him with unholy tongue;
She, while apostles shrank, could danger brave,
Last at his cross and earliest at his grave.
See George Dana Boardman, *Western Recorder* 52, no. 3 (September 17, 1885): 6.

14. "An Appeal from More than Two Hundred Ladies," *Record of Christian Work* 11, no. 9 (September 1890): 4. See also Arthur T. Pierson, "God's Word to Woman," *Northfield Echoes* 3, no. 3 (1896): 256–57.

15. See *Christian Workers Magazine* 11, new series, no. 2 (October 1910): 107; "Practical and Perplexing Questions," *Christian Workers Magazine* 15, new series, no. 10 (June 1915): 626; "Women Preaching," *Christian Workers Magazine* 16 (March 1916): 532; Mrs. Henry W. Peabody, "The Enlarged Sphere of Woman's Work in Its Relation to the Church," *Record of Christian Work* 37, no. 9 (September 1918): 627–33; *Record of Christian Work* 40, no. 9 (September 1921): 643–44; Grant Stroh, "Practical and Perplexing Questions," *Moody Bible Institute Monthly* 21, no. 8 (April 1921): 365.

Business, the publication of the Bible Institute of Los Angeles that, like the Moody Institute, trained women for lay ministry, supported publicly women's right to teach and speak.[16] In 1918, the *Watchman-Examiner* published an article entitled "Using the Woman-Power in Our Churches," which expressed a belief in the equal rights of women within the church.[17] William Bell Riley editorialized in 1928 that women were sometimes called by God to become evangelists.[18]

No matter what the position expressed concerning women speaking in church or in any other mixed assembly, all writers and editors of these magazines opposed ordaining women to traditional parish ministry. They argued primarily that God's and nature's order would be disrupted by placing women in positions of authority over men, thereby destroying the integrity of the gender-based hierarchy and the separate spheres of activity.[19] "God has ordered it. Hers is the narrower and more quiet service. Her throne of power is the home."[20] A. C. Dorris declared that "women are barred from preaching," and that "women are not called to ministry."[21] Mark A. Matthews, a fundamentalist leader in Seattle, called the "female pulpiteeress" an "unscriptural monstrosity" that "belongs to the zone of ecclesiastical freaks." He insisted that "God has never called a woman."[22] Brookes interpreted 1 Tim. 2:11–12 as a prohibition against women that "extends to public ministration, or preaching or praying in the church, and she cannot thus teach, nor exercise dominion over the man, because it would be at variance with the order of God's house."[23]

16. See Torrey, "Light on Puzzling Passages and Problems," *King's Business* 6, no. 1 (January 1915): 71; *King's Business* 7, no. 4 (April 1916): 304.

17. "Using the Woman-Power in Our Churches," *Watchman-Examiner* 6 (February 21, 1918): 230.

18. William Bell Riley, "Women in the Ministry," *Christian Fundamentalist* 1, no. 11 (May 1928): 21.

19. See W. C. Taylor, "A Woman Preacher," *Western Recorder* 69, no. 10 (January 17, 1895): 4; "Women Preaching," *Christian Workers Magazine* 16 (March 1916): 532; A. B. Cabiniss, "Ought Women to Speak, Teach or Pray in Our Churches, or in Public?" *Western Recorder* 51, no. 22 (February 15, 1885): 4–5.

20. "Ordination of Women," *Western Recorder* 61, no. 35 (May 7, 1885): 4.

21. A. C. Dorris, "Women's Sphere in the Church," *Western Recorder* 86, no. 35 (July 1911): 3.

22. Matthews, quoted in "Why Women in the Pulpit?" *Our Hope* (May 1930): 651.

23. "Ministry of Woman," *Truth, or, Testimony for Christ* 21, no. 2 (February 1895): 91. See also Margaret C. Worthington, "Woman Suffrage—A Reform, But Unto What?" *Christian Workers Magazine* 27 (1916): 112; Stroh, "Practical and Perplexing Questions: Concerning Women," *Moody Bible Institute Monthly* 23 (March 1923): 302; *King's Business* 8, no. 11 (November 1917): 1045; Stella Davis, "A Woman's Appeal to Women," *Western Recorder* 93, no. 5 (November 8, 1917): 10; J. M. Pendleton,

In the context of this debate, fundamentalists stressed a "priestly" understanding of the ordained ministry, the authority of the clergy over the laity. An article in the *Western Recorder* rejected a feminized understanding of ministry:

> The theory that the pastor is the servant of the church is anti-scriptural. His office is one of direction, authority, earthly headship and the scriptures expressly declare that these are positions which women are not suffered to occupy. . . . They can gain nothing by ordination which they ought to have, but rather put themselves where the Lord has said they ought not be.[24]

For ministers eager to reassert the manliness of their work, the authority and dominance of the profession itself had to be salvaged. They rejected any understanding of the ordained minister as subservient to the laity, most of whom were women.

Although all expressed opposition to women usurping male authority by being ordained to ministry, none of these religious leaders declared a desire to remove women from church work altogether. These ministers and their churches across the country were far too dependent on the skill, dedication, time, and money women gave readily to the church. For example, word came back from foreign missions that women were needed as missionaries to native women.[25] By 1906, 90 percent of the Sunday school teachers were women.[26] In 1926, A. W. Beaven admitted to the young women gathered at Northfield in conference that the church had to compete with social agencies for women's energies. He urged them to consider careers in missions and Christian education.[27] Throughout this period, a shortage of male ministers persisted, especially for rural congregations.[28]

"The Woman Question," *Western Recorder* 61, no. 28 (March 19, 1885): 1; Rueben A. Torrey, "Light on Puzzling Passages and Problems," *King's Business* 6, no. 1 (January 1915): 71; *Christian Workers Magazine,* new series, 11, no. 2 (October 1910): 107; *King's Business* 7, no. 4 (April 1916): 304.

24. "The Ordination of Women," *Western Recorder* 61, no. 40 (June 11, 1885): 3.

25. "An Appeal from More than Two Hundred Ladies," *Record of Christian Work,* 4.

26. Leonard I. Sweet, *The Minister's Wife: Her Role in Nineteenth-Century American Evangelicalism* (Philadelphia: Temple University Press, 1983), 227.

27. A. W. Beaven, "The Church and the New Day," *Record of Christian Work* 46, no. 2 (February 1927): 117–23.

28. See G. Frederick Wright, "The Country Church," *Bibliotheca Sacra* 47 (April 1890): 267–84; "Dearth of Ministers," *King's Business* 10, no. 9 (September 1919): 879; "More Ministers Needed," *Herald and Presbyter* 92, no. 25 (June 22, 1921): 2; T. LeRoy Muir, "An Appeal for *Rural* Evangelism," *Moody Bible Institute Monthly* 22, no. 11 (July 1922): 1104.

Because of the shortage of available manpower, it was necessary to rely on women. Yet male ministers had a stake in preserving their work as a source of masculine identity, so they encouraged women only as lay workers performing tasks that seemed consistent with women's role in the domestic sphere, with an emphasis on sacrificial service. In 1887, women were told that the ordination of women was wrong because Christ recognized the "original law" of subordination, but that "in her appropriate sphere of Christian work and Christian usefulness, how lovely a woman, how worthy of honor, and how beneficent their services!"[29] Talmage described the ministry of women as comforting the sick, taking care of the poor, visiting the "haunts of iniquity," soliciting charity, and rearing children.[30] Brookes concluded that home, Sunday school, prayer meeting, house-to-house visitation, and "numerous organizations among Christian women" were "wide enough field" for women.[31] Robert E. Speer made the distinction between public preaching, which was "inimical" to women's sphere, and women's legitimate sphere within the church, which he called "ministration."[32] In 1918, Mrs. Henry W. Peabody told the Northfield General Conference for Christian Workers that women had two great missions: to help and support male ministers and to rear children as good Christians.[33] Another list of women's appropriate activities within the church published in the *Herald and Presbyter* in 1921 included Sunday school teachers; leaders of prayer meetings, missionary societies, and temperance organizations; missionaries; and "teachers and physicians and leaders in Christian activities of many lines and departments."[34] Another author surmised that "women are not to be in authority in the church over their husbands," but that "it is wholly scriptural for women to be Sunday school teachers, Bible readers, missionaries, and evangelists."[35]

29. Pendleton, "The Woman Question," *Western Recorder*, 1.

30. T. DeWitt Talmage, "The Queens of Home," *Christian Herald and Signs of Our Times* 10 (September 8, 1887): 564.

31. "Woman in the Church," *Truth, or, Testimony for Christ*, 266.

32. Robert E. Speer, "The Mid-Week Bible Class," *Record of Christian Work* 19, no. 4 (April 1900): 275.

33. Peabody, "The Enlarged Sphere of Woman's Work and Its Relation to the Church," *Record of Christian Work*, 61.

34. "Prayer Meeting: Woman's Work in the Church," *Herald and Presbyter* 92, no. 5 (February 2, 1921): 10.

35. Stroh, "Practical and Perplexing Questions," *Moody Bible Institute Monthly*, 302. See also "Why Women in the Pulpit," *Our Hope* 36, no. 11 (May 1930): 651–52; Norris, "The Purple, Scarlet-Robed Woman of Prophecy and History," *Searchlight* 7, no. 36 (July 18, 1924): 1; Dixon, "Sermon," *Western Recorder* 92, no. 20 (February 22, 1917): 6–7; Charles H. Brent, "The Challenge of Capacity," *Record of Christian Work*

The Bible institutes and colleges, such as Moody Bible Institute and the Bible Institute of Los Angeles, had something else at stake in women's lay ministry: They needed students for their classrooms. Virginia Lieson Brereton, who conducted an extensive study of Bible schools, discovered that women outnumbered men in the schools that stressed "abbreviated" forms of training for religious work, but that women were virtually excluded from ministerial and graduate study at Bible institutes that had such pastoral training programs and at conservative seminaries.[36] The Bible Institute of Los Angeles advertised itself to men "called of God into Christian work"—the pastorate, graduate study, evangelism, teachers, and professors, and special ministries such as pastors' assistants, missionaries, Sunday school superintendents, evangelists, and YMCA secretaries. In the same statement of purpose, the school described itself as intended for women who feel "called of God to enter some form of Christian work" such as pastors' assistant, home and foreign missionaries, YWCA secretary, deaconesses, rescue workers, Bible class leaders, and wives of ministers. There was no mention to women of pastorates, graduate study, or places on college faculties.[37]

Some scholars have assigned feminist motives to fundamentalist leaders, particularly the founders and officers of the Bible institutes and colleges, because they recruited women for their student bodies and church programs. Janette Hassey recently argued that heavy participation of women in turn-of-the-century evangelical church work and missions indicates a prowoman impulse within late nineteenth-century proto-fundamentalism that dried up during the first decades of the twentieth century.[38] True, twentieth-century fundamentalists were considerably less tolerant of female leadership of any kind in the church than their nineteenth-century counterparts.[39] Yet evidence in

35, no. 8 (August 1916): 472–77; A. J. D., "Woman's Work in the Macedonia Churches," *Western Recorder* 80, no. 32 (July 6, 1905): 12; Floyd W. Tompkins, Jr., "Religion in Daily Life," *Northfield Echoes* 2, no. 3 (1895): 331; "Ordination of Women," *Western Recorder*, 4.

36. Virginia Lieson Brereton, "Protestant Fundamentalist Bible Schools, 1882–1940" (Ph.D. diss., Columbia Univ., 1981), 309–10.

37. "The Purpose and Methods of the Bible Institute," *King's Business* 3, no. 5 (May 1912): 101–2.

38. See Janette Hassey, *No Time for Silence: Evangelical Women in Ministry around the Turn of the Century* (Grand Rapids, Mich.: Zondervan, 1986), 125–37.

39. Sweet documented the decreasing power given to evangelical ministers' wives from 1880 to 1900. See *The Minister's Wife*. Vickers documented the declining feminist edge within the Southern Baptist Women's Missionary Union after 1900. See Vickers, "Woman's Place."

popular literature from both the nineteenth and twentieth centuries indicates that ministers tolerated the leadership and participation of women within conservative Protestantism only because it was needed and could be justified within the boundaries previously established by the ideology of separate spheres and virtues. The claim that the support by men of the separate-spheres ideology constitutes feminism—even evangelical feminism—is highly suspect. Fundamentalists readily admitted that women possessed special virtues and talents for all kinds of church work and service—all kinds of church work, that is, except for ordained ministry. Women were not to have authority over men. Just as administrative appointments in the public education system became a symbol of male authority and prerogative when the teaching profession became feminized,[40] so did ordination remain, except in rare circumstances, an unbreachable barrier against women's equal participation with men in positions of authority within the church.[41] Hassey's careful research of even the most moderate within the conservative evangelical camp, Moody Bible Institute, revealed few instances of women ordained for the ministry they performed. Generally the women she discovered in nineteenth-century evangelical periodicals were lay workers performing "auxiliary" work, such as domestic and foreign missions, revivals, and Christian education and seldom the "core" Protestant ministerial duties of shepherding a congregation. The women Hassey cited who did have charge of a congregation usually worked in rural churches far from the mainstream and the power of the large churches in the cities.[42] Essentially, women were not permitted equal authority, except perhaps in a handful of situations when a shortage of men willing to take rural churches left a woman minister the only alternative to the closure of these churches.

By the end of the period little doubt remained of the fundamentalists' opinions concerning women participating in the church. When the Independent Fundamental Churches of America (formerly the American Conference of Undenominational Churches) drew up its bylaws in

40. See Sheila M. Rothman, *Woman's Proper Place: A History of Changing Ideals and Practices, 1870 to the Present* (New York: Basic Books, 1978), 58–59, 156.

41. In 1910, three-tenths of 1 percent of all ordained clergy were women; in 1920 1.4 percent were women. Hassey, *No Time for Silence*, 9.

42. For example, William Bell Riley's Northwestern Bible and Missionary Training School was established to meet the need for pastors in small-town and rural churches. It has been reported that 90 percent of the 300 Baptist churches in Minnesota at that time had no minister. Also, the Bible Institute of Los Angeles was founded because of an urgent perceived need: "hundreds of small churches closed without pastors." Hassey, *No Time for Silence*, 23–25.

1930, it officially excluded women from membership in the association.[43] In the same year, A. J. Gordon's Gordon College voted to restrict
the number of women students to one-third of the total.[44] The last
woman graduated from the Pastor's Class at Moody Bible Institute in
1929.[45]

Another rhetorical strategy employed in the popular literature to
limit women's growing power and authority within the church was to
link churchwomen's demands for equality and positions of leadership
to two other contemporary social currents: the women's rights movement and sectarian religious movements. Both were unpopular and
generally suspect. In the 1880s, Brookes warned his female followers
of the "worldly, fashionable, skeptical woman." Unlike such a woman,
"every believing woman" should find "wide enough field opened before
her for effective work, without insisting upon her right to speak":

> A Christian woman will do well to keep herself aloof from
> . . . these ungodly women, either in temperance work or
> in other needed reforms, remembering the divine command,
> "Be ye not unequally yoked together with unbelievers." . . .
> Thank God, there are thousands and tens of thousands of
> humble and faithful Christian women in the land, who are
> content with their lot, and have no desire to be dragged
> into the glare of notoriety.[46]

The *Western Recorder* in 1895 urged women to protest "whenever an
'advanced' woman attempts a harmful innovation in one of our
churches."[47] In 1917, the same magazine published "A Woman's Appeal
to Women," warning readers that feminism, which had already
"wrought such evil in social and domestic life," was "invading the
sacred realm of the church." Women, so went the appeal, should not
seek prominence within the church.[48] During the controversy over
women's status in the Southern Baptist Convention in 1919, the *Western
Recorder* linked the prowomen faction within the Convention to Susan
B. Anthony and, especially, to the kind of biblical interpretation found

43. James O. Henry, *For Such a Time as This: A History of the Independent Fundamental Churches of America.* (Westchester, Ill.: The Independent Fundamental Churches of America, 1983), 49.
44. See Brereton, "Protestant Fundamentalist Bible Schools," 309–10.
45. Hassey, *No Time for Silence,* 44.
46. "Woman in the Church," *Truth, or, Testimony for Christ,* 266.
47. *Western Recorder* 69, no. 39 (August 8, 1895): 8.
48. Davis, "A Woman's Appeal to Women," *Western Recorder,* 10.

in Elizabeth Cady Stanton's *Woman's Bible*.[49] An editorial in a 1919
issue of the *King's Business* likened women's efforts to win ordination
within the Presbyterian Church to woman suffrage and "rejection of
the Word" and "rebellion against Bible teaching."[50]

After the turn of the century, fundamentalists also associated
female religious leadership with sectarian religious groups such as theosophy, spiritualism, Christian Science, and Pentecostalism. Women,
in fact, did play important roles within these religious movements,
and that dynamic was not ignored by conservative evangelicals. The
editors of *Our Hope* in 1908 wrote against Pentecostalism, arguing that
the movement, by allowing women to speak, disobeyed the Bible:

> Indeed it is a fact, significant and striking, that nearly all
> the leaders of these "isms" are women. These with their
> public teaching and leadership are disobeying the Word of
> God. If they were to take the place which Nature and the
> Word of God assigns to them, some of these movements
> would come to an end.[51]

H. B. Taylor advanced arguments against women assuming leadership
roles in the church based on his analysis of certain New Testament
texts and the association of women leaders with sectarian groups:

> The Holy Spirit here seemed to say that woman is too easily
> beguiled to be a leader. . . . A casual observer may see the
> wisdom of this prohibition if he will but observe Christian
> Science, Theosophy, Spiritualism, and practically all union,
> high pressure, claptrap evangelism.[52]

J. Frank Norris criticized Christian Science for its female leadership.[53]
In 1920, A. C. Gaebelein referred to these sectarian movements as
"witcheries" carried on by "demon-possessed women."[54] Another writer

49. See "Paul and the Women," *Western Recorder*, 8; "Hard to Say," *Western Recorder*
94, no. 25 (March 27, 1919): 8; "Notes," *Watchman* 77, no. 2 (January 9, 1896): 8;
"New Woman's New Bible," *Truth, or, Testimony for Christ* 21, no. 6 (June 1895): 249;
"Miss Willard and the Woman's Bible," *Truth, or, Testimony for Christ* 22, no. 1 (January
1896): 25.

50. "Woman Suffrage and the Bible," *King's Business* 10, no. 8 (August 1919): 700.

51. "1 Corinthians xiv:34," *Our Hope* 9, no. 12 (June 1908): 770.

52. Taylor, "New Testament Restrictions of Women," *Western Recorder*, 2. See also
Peabody, "The Enlarged Sphere of Woman's Work," *Record of Christian Work*, 628–29.

53. "J. Frank Norris Visits the Largest 'Christian Science Church' in Los Angeles,"
Searchlight 3, no. 39 (August 12, 1921): 1. See also Norris, "Spiritualism," *Searchlight*
2, no. 37 (May 15, 1919): 1–4.

54. A. C. Gaebelein, "The Apostasy Sweeping over the Churches," *King's Business*
11, no. 1 (January 1920): 18. See also Gaebelein, "Christianity vs. Modern Cults,"
Moody Bible Institute Monthly 22 (March 1922): 861.

for the *King's Business* saw evidence of the apostasy of the woman suffrage movement in the fact that "so many of the prominent characters in the movement are identified with Christian Science, Theosophy, New Thoughtism, Socialism, Unitarianism and rationalism."[55] The editors of the *Herald and Presbyter* were concerned about "heathenism at home," and noted that the "followers of these cults are largely women."[56]

Fundamentalists and their predecessors within conservative evangelicalism produced popular literature that undermined women's efforts to achieve some equality of position and authority within the church. In the late nineteenth century, some argued that women should be permitted to speak in church or in other mixed assemblies; others argued that women should keep silent at all times. Some sought to render women's ambitions suspect by associating them with feminism and the women's rights movements and with sectarian groups. All recognized the predominance of women on membership rolls and in lay ministry, but none supported full ordination of women for that ministry. Even in the church, the one institution men conceded to women, some remnant of the separate-spheres ideology was consistently preserved in order to grant men both actual and symbolic authority within religious activities and organizations.

"Manly Christianity"

The second major campaign to regain the church for men consisted of a dismissal of feminized Christian symbols and doctrine. Feminized religion was replaced with what historians have called "muscular Christianity."[57] Historian Leonard I. Sweet wrote a brief description of the phenomenon. He noted "an overwhelming fear of effeminacy and an exaggerated attention to masculinity," a "re-entry of men into American religious life," and a reassertion of male authority in the church in the decades between 1880 and 1920.[58] A strong current of the rhetoric of masculine Christianity runs through popular fundamentalist literature of the period.

One key aspect of this masculine rhetoric was a depiction of the current age, especially the current church and its ministers, as effeminate. In 1912, the *Herald and Presbyter* told its readers that:

> America needs iron in her blood. Her age is effeminate. . . .
> Men don't have the nerve to execute the laws, and the women

55. "Woman Suffrage and the Bible," *King's Business,* 701.
56. "Heathenism at Home," *Herald and Presbyter* 90, no. 13 (March 26, 1919): 5.
57. See Colleen McDannell, *The Christian Home in Victorian America, 1840–1900* (Bloomington, Ind.: Indiana Univ. Press, 1986), 116.
58. Sweet, *The Minister's Wife,* 232–35.

and the clergy, by overworking the cult of mercy, are making it impossible for men to do so, if they should feel themselves strong enough.[59]

Francis L. Patton, too, expressed special discomfort with feminized Christianity:

> It may well be a question whether we have not gone too far in the practice of the passive virtues, whether it has not made us a little too soft, whether Christianity carried to an extreme would not make a very chicken-hearted set of people, and result in the production of the wrong kind of patriotism.[60]

Warren A. Candler, one of the strongest fundamentalist voices within Southern Methodism, wrote about "the need for manly vigor" in the church "not diminished by the fact that the sphere of conflict is spiritual, not material."[61]

The masculinity of the clergy was of special concern, and a call went out through this periodical literature to "real men" to take up the mantle of the ministry and to reestablish that profession as irrefutably male. In 1895, the *Western Recorder* published an article that concluded that the church needed ministers like our pioneer heroes to withstand the slings and arrows of modern American society.

> For it is in the pioneer days of every civilized country that its people are bravest. . . . We want men who can calmly endure slow martyrdom for propagating and defending acknowledged truth. . . . To resist the popular pressure and endure the darts of guerilla warfare, he needs to have the dauntless courage and persistless [sic] endurance of a martyr.[62]

In an article entitled "Virility in the Ministry," Matthews argued in 1919 for a male ministry and related fundamentalist theological positions to masculine identity:

> Only a man can preach the Gospel. . . . It takes courage . . . to preach the infallible Bible and the vicarious atone-

59. "Iron in Her Blood," *Herald and Presbyter* 83, no. 27 (July 3, 1912): 2.

60. Francis L. Patton, "The Present Assault on the Bible: The Issue between Supernaturalism and Atheism," *Bible Student and Teacher*, new series, 1, no. 5 (May 1904): 271.

61. Warren A. Candler, "What Is AT STAKE?" *Call to the Colors* 1, no. 4 (July–August 1925): 49.

62. Paulus, "Moral Heroism," *Western Recorder* 69, no. 20 (March 28, 1895): 2.

ment. . . . It takes no courage to go to pink teas and present
to the world social service platitudes. There isn't anything
effeminate about the Gospel nor . . . about a real . . .
preacher of the Gospel. . . . The pulpit offers a greater
opportunity for real men, who possess real manhood, than
any other position in the world.[63]

J. Frank Norris, who was called a "real man" by the editors of the
King's Business,[64] published an article by William Bell Riley in 1927
in which Riley identified the apostles with nineteenth-century American notions of masculinity:

> They [the apostles] were no weaklings. The Gospel ministry
> was never meant for weaklings. . . . Do I speak to any
> young man who is about to enter the ministry? Any gentle,
> delicate, pale, frail creature who is going to take up the
> Apostolic banner . . . ? Wherever this Gospel is preached
> it must create antagonism. . . . Christianity began as a
> fighting religion. When did it lay aside its first charter?
> When did it pass through a transformation which robbed
> it of its combativeness and made it as other faiths? When
> was this Samson shorn?[65]

An article about fundamentalist leader L. W. Munhall, published on
his death, was entitled "A Manly Methodist." He was manly because:

> In his youth he was a blacksmith, and learned how to handle
> the sledge hammer and has never forgotten the art of hitting
> good and hard. . . . He was in thirty-two battles in the
> Civil War and left a remunerative practice to take up Chris-
> tian work.[66]

This description of Munhall combined many themes important to
American masculinity: strenuous labor, the successful breadwinner, and
the warrior.

Billy Sunday was the prime example of an exaggerated masculine
demeanor. A contemporary critic of Sunday wrote this about him:

63. Matthews, "Virility in the Ministry," Western Recorder 94, no. 38 (June 26,
1919): 2. See also "Regarding Effeminate Fools," King's Business 12, no. 11 (November
1921): 1070–71; "The LACK of Leaders," King's Business 10, no. 10 (October 1919):
893.
64. "The Tiger from Texas, King's Business 13, no. 11 (November 1922): 1100.
65. Riley, "The Persecution of the Premillennialists," Fundamentalist 10, no. 23
(April 15, 1927): 5.
66. "A Manly Methodist," King's Business 12, no. 4 (April 1921): 313.

"Billy" lionizes himself by threatening physical violence to many offenders, favorite expressions being, "They will get a fight out of me; I will put my fist under their nose."[67]

Sunday threatened violence, even the murder of his theological opponents:

They tell me I am a marked man by these God-forsaken anarchists and cutthroats. . . . I'll shoot the first one of them that starts anything so full of holes that he'd pass for a sieve anywhere.[68]

In a sermon entitled "The Fighting Saint," which Sunday regularly preached at his revivals, his language was militant and abusive.

Jesus Christ intended his church to be militant as well as persuasive. It must fight as well as pray. . . . The prophets all carried the Big Stick. . . . Strong men resist, weaklings compromise. . . . Lord save us from off-handed, flabby-cheeked, brittle-boned, weak-kneed, thin-skinned, pliable, plastic, spineless, effeminate, sissified, three-caret Christianity.[69]

Sunday's excessive language and posturing was a key to his spectacular popularity. Historian William G. McLoughlin, Jr., noted that Sunday's revivals were unusually attractive to men, especially young men. One male college student wrote this after he heard Sunday speak at the University of Pennsylvania: "He appeared to me to be a man in every way, and by his sheer personality he made me strive to be all that is best in manhood."[70] McLoughlin also concluded that Sunday appealed to women as "a preacher, a father, a husband, and a knight-errant who would defend American womanhood against all enemies":

No one, "not even Mr. Roosevelt himself," said one observer, "has insisted so much on his personal militant masculinity." His well-cut clothes accentuated his slim, athletic figure,

67. Scott Anderson, "Billy Sunday, Prophet or Charlatan," *Overland Monthly*, 2d series, 71 (January–June 1918): 77.
68. Sunday, *(Cincinnati) Commercial Tribune* (May 1, 1921): 5, quoted in Calkins, "Billy Sunday's Cincinnati Crusade," *Cincinnati Historical Society Bulletin* 297–98. See Douglas W. Frank for more documentation of Sunday's violence. *Less than Conquerors: How Evangelicals Entered the Twentieth Century* (Grand Rapids, Mich.: W. B. Eerdmans, 1986), 256–66.
69. Sunday, "The Fighting Saint," *Trenton (New Jersey) Evening Times* (January 6, 1916): n.p.
70. Sunday, quoted in McLoughlin, *Billy Sunday Was His Real Name*, 173.

and he posed as the example, par excellence, of good health through clean living.[71]

Sunday represented a new kind of revivalism. In manner and metaphor, Sunday was a far cry from gentle Dwight L. Moody. McLoughlin stressed the difference between the two by comparing the music each used during revival meetings. Moody liked the humility of the hymn "Oh, To Be Nothing." Sunday preferred "Onward, Christian Soldiers," "The Battle Hymn of the Republic," and "The Fight Is On."[72]

Historian Douglas W. Frank offered the most provocative analysis so far of Sunday's obsession with "manhood." He correctly concluded that Billy Sunday "spoke intuitively to the deepest confusion of his age and to the realities most troubling his evangelical audiences,"[73] but Frank's own perceptual horizons did not include the grave uncertainty about gender identity that plagued Sunday's audiences, especially the men. For Frank, Sunday's manhood rhetoric had only generic import and meaning: "to speak of humanity and its possibilities for strength and heroism and goodness."[74] But Sunday's espousal of the Victorian cult of true womanhood makes it inconceivable that Sunday intended to persuade women to take on such clearly defined masculine identity and behavior. Sunday usually preached Christian manhood on "men only" nights, and he most certainly spoke to and of men and their supposedly unique potential for strength and heroism.[75]

Similarly, Frank painted a genderless picture of Sunday's use of violent language about beating and killing by linking it to the supposedly universal mythological and literary tradition of the hero. "This," argued Frank, "is the tragic meaning of The Hero in human history: The Hero is a killer. The Hero's task is to affirm his invulnerability and thus ours in the face of death."[76] Yet, since Victorian culture did not affirm women's invulnerability, emotional or physical, this interpretation needs gender distinctions. Sunday's violence is more easily interpreted in light of omnipresent uneasiness over male gender identity, and as an attempt to reestablish it. Sunday's violent warrior language and personal demeanor reassociated the middle-class male evangelicals in his audience with the warrior aspect of traditional masculine identity.

71. Sunday, quoted in McLoughlin, *Billy Sunday Was His Real Name,* 173.
72. Sunday, quoted in McLoughlin, *Billy Sunday Was His Real Name,* 84, 141, 179.
73. Frank, *Less than Conquerors,* 215.
74. Frank, *Less than Conquerors,* 193.
75. See McLoughlin, *Billy Sunday Was His Real Name,* xxvi, 93, 98–99, 187.
76. Frank, *Less than Conquerors,* 257–58.

Frank described a Billy Sunday revival in such terms: "the carnival atmosphere, the building excitement, the seizure and execution (symbolically) of the hated enemy, the sense of power and triumph, the joy of victory over evil." This may be, as Frank suggested, a good description of a lynch mob (another nineteenth-century male activity), but it is an apt description as well for traditional warfare.[77]

Just as virility was associated with fundamentalists and their cause, so effeminacy was associated with the godless. Adam Beaseley attributed his failure to let God into his life as a child to his "sissiness."[78] In the struggle they waged within the denominations against the more moderate and modernist men, and in the debates with the higher critics and evolutionary theorists, the fundamentalists sometimes expressed the differences between the two parties in the terms of gender identity. The fundamentalists were masculine; the modernists were effeminate. B. F. McLendon called college professors "effeminate, sissified,"[79] and "effeminate ginks."[80] J. Frank Norris called professors "sissy."[81] The editors of *King's Business* called modern theology "emasculated Christianity."[82]

Lodged as they were in a feminized institution, and dependent as they were on female support, male fundamentalist ministers often vented their anger, frustration, and fear in theological debates with other male ministers. Because gender identity was at stake, the differences were expressed in degrading gender terminology. Liberals and modernists were identified with the women whom male ministers had come to resent.

In contrast to womanish liberalism, fundamentalists described the ideal Christian life and the ideal Christian in terms of Christian manhood. They associated the ability to live untroubled by doubt with true manliness and true faith:

> To be manly is to be strong, and if we would be really strong, we must be steadfast in the faith. . . . Some people nowadays, seem to imagine that it is very manly to parade

77. Frank, *Less than Conquerors*, 261.
78. Adam Beasely, "Girl-Boy Religion," *Watchman* 84, no. 12 (March 20, 1902): 13.
79. B. F. McLendon, "Where Art Thou?" *Searchlight* 6, no. 18 (March 16, 1923): 3.
80. McLendon, "The Efficiency and Sufficiency of the Blood," *Searchlight* 6, no. 20 (March 30, 1923): 2.
81. Norris, "Latest and Best Book on Evolution," *Searchlight* 6, no. 24 (April 27, 1923): 6.
82. "Emasculated Christianity," *King's Business* 13, no. 4 (April 1922): 330.

their doubts about the truth of the Bible. . . . But to be
content to live in an atmosphere of uncertainty . . . is a
proof of weakness of character, whilst it imperils our eternal
safety.[83]

The *Watchman* warned Christians not to assume that "the so-called
feminine virtues are the sole characteristics of a Christian spirit," and
assured them that "the valiant, militant, masculine spirit has its place
in the souls of the true servants of God."[84] Charles H. Richards in
1905 had great hopes for what he called the "new evangelism" because
it would be masculine and appeal to men in ways that the old evangelism
had not:

There will be a virility in song and sermon which will appeal
to all that is manliest in men. A masculine vigor will throb
through its presentation of truth which will lay hold on
manhood and greatly increase the proportion of men in our
churches and congregations.[85]

True Christianity, these religious leaders argued, was an ingredient of
true manliness:

Christianity emasculates no man, makes no man effeminate,
depreciates no manly virtue. There is nothing that puts so
much iron into the blood; nothing that tones and builds
up the manly nature; . . . nothing that emphasizes and
exalts manliness, as does Christianity. The purpose, the
incarnate idea of Christianity is to make magnificent manhood; to make men like Christ, the manliest of all men.[86]

Fundamentalists rejected the feminized Jesus of Victorian evangelical piety and identified Jesus with traditional notions of masculinity.
Norman Maclean admitted that everyone had become used to thinking
of Jesus "as if he were effeminate." He assured his readers that things
were changing in that regard. "Today we think of him as strong. It is
not the ascetic but the athletic in Jesus that grips the heart today."[87]
Charles G. Wright protested the effeminate Jesus of religious art:

The world has had a perfect example of a manly man and
yet medieval art . . . pictured him with long hair parted

83. William Burnet, "Manly Christianity," *Watchman* 71 (May 1, 1890): 2.
84. "Christian Militancy," *Watchman* 79 (August 6, 1896): 7.
85. Richards, "Some Needed Factors in the 'New Evangelism'," 360.
86. Isaac W. Grimes, "Manliness," *Watchman* 88, no. 2 (January 11, 1906): 15.
87. Norman Maclean, "The Founder of Democracy," *Record of Christian Work* 42,
no. 5 (May 1923): 351.

down the middle, large dreamy eyes, and an expression that
can only be described by the word effeminate. But that is
not the Christ of the Gospels . . . strong, virile, resourceful,
commanding. Because Christianity's Christ was a man, and
a manly man, Christianity has a masculine side. It is religion
not only for the hour of weakness, dependence and sorrow,
but a religion for strength and athletic faculties as well.[88]

Fundamentalist ministers asserted their masculinity by presenting
Christianity as a faith for real men and the prime Christian example,
Jesus, as a manly man.

Another way in which fundamentalists asserted their masculinity
and related Christianity to manliness was their use of aggressive language and military metaphors. Conservative evangelical clergy chose
to understand and to depict themselves as warriors in God's army,
taking on any assault—biblical criticism, immorality, evolutionary
theory, communism and infidelity. Historians of fundamentalism have
called attention to its militancy. Wenger contended that "militant
method" was "inherent in fundamentalism."[89] Marsden attributed the
rise of more aggressive and shrill fundamentalism in the 1920s to the
sense of crisis precipitated by World War I.[90] James R. Moore made
his analysis of the fundamentalists' use of "the military metaphor"
central to his interpretation of the movement. He concluded that the
use of military metaphors by evangelical Christians in the last decades
of the nineteenth century and the first three decades of the twentieth
century revealed, "most obviously, . . . the absence of any deep moral
aversion from war." He also theorized that Christians employed military
metaphors after World War I to depict "their intellectual and moral
stance towards the world."[91] Yet his description of the violence and

88. Wright, "The Masculine in Religion," *Watchman-Examiner* 5, no. 12 (March
22, 1917): 363–64. See also Hutton, "The Resources in Christ for Those Who Have
Failed," *Record of Christian Work* 42, no. 2 (February 1923): 105; James E. Freeman,
"Serving and Following," *Record of Christian Work* 26 (1907): 769.

89. Robert E. Wenger, "Social Thought in American Fundamentalism, 1918–1933"
(Ph.D. diss., Univ. of Nebraska, 1973), 46.

90. George M. Marsden, *Fundamentalism and American Culture: The Shaping of Twentieth-Century Evangelicalism, 1870–1925* (New York: Oxford Univ. Press, 1980), 141,
170.

91. J. R. Moore, *The Post-Darwinian Controversies: A Study of the Protestant Struggle
to Come to Terms with Darwin in Great Britain and America, 1870–1900* (New York:
Cambridge Univ. Press, 1979), 101–102. See also Furniss, *The Fundamentalist Controversy*, 36, 41; Marsden, "From Fundamentalism to Evangelicalism: A Historical
Analysis," in *The Evangelicals: What They Believe, Who They Are, Where They Are Changing*,
rev. ed., ed. David F. Wells and John D. Woodbridge (Grand Rapids, Mich.: Baker
Book House, 1975, 1977; paperback, 1977), 158.

extravagance of the militaristic language used by fundamentalists does not adequately account for it. The battle mentality and violent language are best understood not so much in relation to Christian ethical thinking about war but from the perspective of gender-role disruptions and a threatened sense of male identity within a feminized church. Also, these military metaphors were a part of fundamentalist popular literature decades before the militarization of American society and the sense of crisis prompted by World War I and, therefore, cannot be adequately explained by it. Already in 1895 the inroads made by modernism were called "the darts of guerilla warfare."[92] The *Watchman* published a piece in 1896 in which "the valiant, militant, masculine spirit" and "masculine self assertion" were praised.[93] In 1904, the *Bible Student and Teacher* told its readers to "glorify the Soldier and let the Saint take the back seat."[94] W. W. Moore, in 1907, described Paul as "essentially a soldier, strenuous and devoted and courageous," who became in his old age "weatherbeaten, warworn, his body covered with honorable scars."[95] In a speech designed to recruit college men for the ministry, Harold Arnold Walter described ministry as "a great battleground where tremendous forces are at war, and leaders of imperial mould are demanded."[96] Christians were told to be good soldiers,[97] that the "church is a regiment,"[98] and that "Christian life is a warfare."[99]

The military metaphor became more frequent by 1920, and the Great War became a topic of discussion. At the Presbyterian General Assembly of 1924, William Jennings Bryan, in his nominating speech for Clarence E. McCartney, told his audience that "our church is one of the great fighting units of the Army of our Lord, and we are here to plan its campaign for the coming year."[100] The Bible Crusaders of

92. Paulus, "Moral Heroism," *Western Recorder*, 2.

93. "Christian Militancy," *Watchman*, 7.

94. Patton, "The Recent Assault," *Bible Student and Teacher*, 271.

95. W. W. Moore, "A Good Soldier of Jesus Christ," *Record of Christian Work* 26 (August 1907): 733.

96. Harold Arnold Walter, "A College Men's Conference on the Christian Ministry," *Record of Christian Work* 28, no. 3 (March 1909): 172.

97. John Y. Ewart, "Drilling the Church Army," *Herald and Presbyter* 85, no. 19 (May 13, 1914): 6–7.

98. T. T. Eaton, " 'All These Men of War That Could Keep Rank'," *Western Recorder* 86, no. 12 (January 26, 1911): 1.

99. E. P. Marvin, "Moral Courage," *Western Recorder* 86, no. 11 (January 19, 1911): 1.

100. William Jennings Bryan, "When Bryan Nominated McCartney," *Christian Fundamentals in School and Church* 6, no. 4 (July–September 1924): 28. See also "The Conflict and How to War," *Our Hope* 30, no. 8 (February 1924): 459–62; Candler, "What Is AT STAKE?" *Call to the Colors*, 49; "The Making of Real Men," *King's Business* 16, no. 6 (June 1925): 246.

America publicized their mission as a military one. Their enemy was modern biblical criticism:

> This is the greatest uprising of this century and will over-
> throw the blighting influence of German philosophy, just
> as German militarism and imperialism were overthrown in
> the World War. [101]

Rank-and-file supporters of fundamentalism were reminded regularly that "a true soldier of Christ does not run away from difficulty," and that "opposition only determined the apostles to stay longer." [102] Using holy war imagery, J. Frank Norris likened the struggle for the true faith of the fundamentalists to the "age-long war with Amalek." [103]

A concern to remasculinize the church is also apparent in the practical suggestions made to increase male attendance at and interest in church functions. Fundamentalists were aware of the role the separate-spheres ideology played in creating the gender imbalance in the churches. In 1890, an article in the *Watchman* described the new "economic warrior" that historians Stearns and Filene discovered in their research of turn-of-the-century male gender roles.

> Financial, commercial, political business is the prerogative
> of the stronger sex. Immersed in worldly care and ambition,
> they are inaccessible to spiritual motives. [104]

Charles E. Jefferson suggested that the church could attract men by the potential for heroism contained within its mission and activities. W. T. Elsing advised church leaders to take young men on hunting, fishing, and swimming excursions, hoping that Christian outdoor camping would compete with such secular spectacles as baseball and shooting matches. [105] Charles H. Richards believed that the vigorous new evangelism of conservative evangelicalism would be attractive to men because it would "bring to proper prominence this neglected half":

> It will arouse conscience, exalt duty, and summon men to
> live nobly the life that now is. It will not be weakly sen-
> timental, nor unduly emotional, seeking conversions chiefly

101. "The Bible Crusader's Challenge," *Christian Fundamentals in School and Church* 8, no. 2 (June 1926): 55.

102. "Sunday School Lesson Course," *Fundamentalist* 10, no. 23 (April 15, 1927): 7.

103. Norris, "The Age-Long War with Amalek," *Baptist Fundamentalist* 10, no. 49 (October 14, 1927): 6.

104. "Women in the Church," *Watchman* 71 (May 15, 1890): 4.

105. Elsing, "A Pastor at Camp Northfield," *Northfield Echoes,* 68.

by appeals to the feelings. It will appeal to the intellect to
receive the truth, to the heart to desire a noble life, to the
will to choose the right because it is right.[106]

Harold Arnold Walter was convinced that strong men could be recruited
for the ministry by "strong speakers with strong appeal" who issued a
call to ministry "as to a great battle ground where tremendous forces
are at war."[107] A widely publicized effort of evangelicals around the
country, the Men and Religion Forward Movement, was organized to
bring men back into the church. The program of the 1912 Boston
meetings of this movement contained an official statement of its ob-
jectives: "to emphasize masculine Christianity," "to energize the Christian manhood of Greater Boston," "to stimulate specialized work for
men and boys," "to win many men and boys to Christ," and "to double
enrollment in Bible School."[108]

Evidence exists that conservative evangelicals during our period
attracted men in unusually large numbers. Elijah P. Brown, an un-
critical biographer of Billy Sunday, noted that, although revivals were
usually most successful winning women and children as converts,[109]
Sunday drew more conversions from men than from women, especially
from young men.[110] An editor of the *Moody Bible Institute Monthly*
claimed in 1923 that his Sunday morning and Bible class crowds were
five-eighths men, and that he had heard A. C. Dixon "say the same."[111]
Perhaps the Moody editor was referring to a sermon by Dixon published
in 1917 in which Dixon reported:

> Gipsy Smith [a revivalist in the Billy Sunday mold] said,
> that among his converts there are seven men to one woman.
> And so far as I could learn, the universal testimony of
> evangelists in America is that [*sic*] at least five men to one
> woman. And I am sure in the Moody Church during the
> five years and a half of my ministry there were at least five

106. Charles H. Richards, "Some Needed Factors in the 'New Evangelicalism',"
Bibliotheca Sacra 62 (April 1905): 360.
107. Walter, "A College Men's Conference on the Christian Ministry," *Record of
Christian Work,* 172–73.
108. "The Boston Men and Religion Campaign," *Watchman* 94, no. 4 (January 25,
1912): 9.
109. Hardesty documented the appeal to women of the earlier evangelical revivalism
of Charles G. Finney. See *Women Called to Witness,* 10.
110. Elijah P. Brown, *The Real Billy Sunday: The Life and Work of Rev. William
Ashley Sunday, D.D., the Baseball Evangelist* (New York: Fleming H. Revell Company,
1914), 104.
111. "Mothers to Blame?" *Moody Bible Institute Monthly* 23 (1923): 556.

men to one woman who accepted and confessed Jesus Christ.[112]

Sweet, in his discussion of muscular Christianity, cited religious census figures from the period that showed an "advance in the proportion of males in the total membership of all the churches."[113]

Conservative evangelicals during the period employed a rhetorical strategy that consisted of contradictory claims and a double-sided message. At the same time that their leaders championed the home as the bastion of true religion and expressed reservations regarding the efficacy of the church, they also waged a passionate battle for control of the church against both modernists and women and promoted a manly Christianity to replace the perspective and practices of feminized evangelical Protestantism. Such a rhetorical strategy accomplished several things. The divinization of the home urged women to view the home as the most appropriate location for their religious activities and influence and, hence, encouraged them to remain at home and away from the male sphere. The battle for the church against women reestablished male dominance in an important social institution earlier conceded to women. The remasculinization of the church was accomplished without, at the same time, taking the burden of private morality away from women, since women were supposed to be religious leaders in the divinized home.

The fierce and rhetorically violent battle against modernists gave the cause of fundamentalism a masculine character and appeal because such language harkened back to traditional male identification with the warrior and with competition against other men. At that level, the controversies created or joined by the fundamentalists accomplished their purpose no matter what the outcome of these controversies were in denominational deliberations, state legislatures, public debates, or the courtroom.[114] Although earlier nineteenth-century Protestant clergy could be defined as feminized, there was no doubt in the public mind that fundamentalists such as Billy Sunday, J. Frank Norris, and John Roach Straton were manly. These fundamentalist leaders paraded their

112. Dixon, "Sermon," *Western Recorder*, 6.
113. Sweet, *The Minister's Wife*, 234–35.
114. As Gatewood noted, when the fundamentalists "were not waging war on modernists and other 'infidels,' they were usually squabbling among themselves." *Controversy in the Twenties: Fundamentalism, Modernism, and Evolution* (Nashville: Vanderbilt Univ. Press, 1969), 17.

pugnaciousness for all the world to see.[115] The controversy with the modernists gave them cause, arena, and arsenal for a war, the stakes of which were the male identity of the fundamentalist ministers and their male followers, an identification of the church with the ethos of male professionalism, and the exclusive right of church men to the office of ordained ministry.

115. James Davison Hunter noted the "uninhibited brashness of their social demeanor and the aggressive bellicosity with which they proffered or defended their beliefs." *American Evangelicalism: Conservative Religion and the Quandary of Modernity* (New Brunswick, N.J.: Rutgers Univ. Press, 1983), 37–38.

CHAPTER FIVE

Fundamentalists and the Flapper

I N 1928, WILLIAM BELL RILEY preached a sermon entitled "Is Society Rotting?"[1] Riley, like many Americans in the 1920s, was concerned about the revolution in manners and morals, especially among the young and more particularly among young women. The corruption of conventional morality was a prominent theme in fundamentalist literature of the period.

Although prominent social historians have disagreed about the exact dating of this revolution, all saw it as an early twentieth-century phenomenon. Specific disruptions in social norms and behavior such as unchaperoned dating, dancing, movie-going, short skirts and bobbed hair, and an increase in premarital sex did, indeed, capture early twentieth-century headlines in the conservative Protestant press. Yet conservative Protestant evangelicals sounded an alarm throughout the last twenty years of the nineteenth century—an alarm calling attention to "undisciplined homes" that were "the cauldrons of great iniquity."[2] Talmage coached parents on the "perils of childhood," and warned them of the "many traps . . . set for our young people" and the "temptations for every form of dissipation and every stage of it."[3] The Reverend

1. William Bell Riley, "Is Society Rotting?" *Christian Fundamentalist* 1, no. 9 (March 1928): 4–12. See also A. Z. C., "Living in Revolt," *Bible Champion* 35, no. 6 (June 1929): 282–83.
2. T. DeWitt Talmage, "Poison," *Christian Herald and Signs of Our Times* 5 (September 21, 1882): 596.
3. Talmage, "The Perils of the Children," *Christian Herald and Signs of Our Times* 9, no. 47 (November 25, 1886): 741.

John F. Kendall stressed parental authority in his article in James Brookes's *Truth, or, Testimony for Christ,* the leading premillennialist journal in the nineteenth century. For Kendall, parental authority over children in the home had biblical sanction, and the subjection of child to parent, like subjection of wife to husband, ensured the "good order of the family" and the "welfare of the child."[4] Already in 1880, the writer of an article entitled "The Girl of the Period" described a new generation of "fast girls" who are forgetful of "maidenly modesty and reserve."[5] Evident in late nineteenth-century religious literature is worry about the younger generation who had strayed from social conventions and *mores.* Of special concern were young women.

"Worldly Amusement"

The rhetoric of parental authority and youthful rebellion intensified after the turn of the century. Billy Sunday, whose evangelistic career peaked in the 1910s, generalized that "in the home authority is needed today more than at any time in the history of this nation. . . . Neither law nor gospel can make a nation without home authority and home example."[6] Departures from the true faith, from conventional morality, and from parental authority went hand in hand, and were seldom distinguished. In 1905, conservative theologian Henry A. Stimson declared that the "best equipment for the young men starting out" was "a good stock of conventional virtues."[7] The World's Christian Fundamentals Association resolved in 1924 that "a revival is the only hope of saving the youth of the land" from the "maelstrom of modern infidelity."[8] George R. Stuart believed that American youth could be saved only by "the proper combination of wholesome authority and a Godly example" set by their parents.[9]

Parental authority and example in the home was especially important to fundamentalists because they believed that the schools—

4. John F. Kendall, "The Family," *Truth, or, Testimony for Christ* 11 (1884–1885): 236.
5. "The Girl of the Period," *Western Recorder* 66, no. 37 (May 27, 1880): 4.
6. Billy Sunday, quoted in William T. Ellis, *"Billy" Sunday: The Man and His Message, with His Own Words Which Have Won Thousands for Christ* (Philadelphia: The John C. Winston Company, 1914), 246.
7. Henry A. Stimson, "The Place of the Conventional in Morals," *Bibliotheca Sacra* 72 (October 1905): 746.
8. "Resolutions and Reports: The Coming Revival," *Christian Fundamentals in School and Church* 6, no. 4 (July–September 1924): 9–10.
9. George R. Stuart, "The Christian Home," *Record of Christian Work* 32, no. 10 (October 1913): 708.

from elementary schools to colleges and universities—were controlled by modernists and infidels. Readers of the *Herald and Presbyter* were told in 1918 that "a highly moralized state cannot be maintained on a secular basis," and that such morality was entirely dependent on an educational system that was "steeped with spirituality."[10] In 1911, the *Record of Christian Work* attributed the "growth of juvenile criminality" to "the absence of all religious ideas" in schools.[11] Christian parents were warned that youth suicides were the tragic but logical outcome of the breakdown of authority at home and the incursions into the schools of modernistic and atheistic teachings.[12]

Fundamentalists also believed that new kinds of "worldly amusement" threatened young people because such activities would "destroy love for God and His worship."[13] This reaction to new leisure-time opportunities for the middle class is evident in nineteenth-century fundamentalist criticism of the theater. The treatment on the contemporary stage of such topics as marital infidelity, courtship, sexual relations, and divorce alienated the conservative Protestant clergy. Talmage described the theaters in 1884 as "fetid and malodorous chapters in which dishonest womanhood is chased from iniquity to iniquity."[14] W. A. Betts, a minister, decried theater in 1890 for its "blighting affect on the sensibilities produced by artificial excitement."[15] Another condemned theater as "a sensuous spectacle,"[16] and another because theater showed women in improper dress: in men's clothes or in skimpy women's attire.[17]

10. *Herald and Presbyter* 89, no. 17 (April 24, 1918): 5. See also "Where Education Should Focus," *Herald and Presbyter* 88, no. 29 (July 18, 1917): 2; "Religion in the Schools," *Herald and Presbyter* 84, no. 34 (August 20, 1913): 3.

11. "The Fruit of Atheist Teaching in French Schools," *Record of Christian Work* 30, no. 10 (October 1911): 647.

12. See Riley, "Is Society Rotting?" *Christian Fundamentalist,* 5; Hervin U. Roop, "The Issue of Modernism in Colleges and Universities," *Christian Fundamentalist,* no. 3 (September 1927): 9.

13. Clara Winterton, "The Morals of the Movies," *Moody Bible Institute Monthly* 23 (May 1923): 422.

14. Talmage, "Are Theatres Improving?" *Christian Herald and Signs of Our Times* 7 (May 8, 1884): 292. See also "Current Events," *Christian Herald and Signs of Our Times* 4 (January 6, 1881): 8–9; "Mr. Moody on Church Fairs and Theatre-Going," *Christian Herald and Signs of Our Times* 4 (March 3, 1881): 141.

15. W. A. Betts, "Perils That Threaten the Future of the Home," *Western Recorder* 65, no. 13 (November 20, 1890) :2. See also "Popular Amusements," *Western Recorder* 47, no. 8 (October 28, 1880): 4; "A Divorced Wife Reclaimed from the Stage," *Western Recorder* 47, no. 35 (May 13, 1880): 6.

16. Josiah W. Leeds, "The Menace of the Theater," *Christian Cynosure* 23, no. 33 (April 30, 1891): 1.

17. T. L. Cuyler, "Should Christians Patronize the Theatre?" *Watchman* 77 (July 30, 1896): 10.

The fundamentalist attack on the theater changed little in the
early twentieth century. It was condemned for condoning "social vice,"
"laxity in the observance of the obligation of marriage relations," and
presenting material about sexuality and sexual behavior.[18] The sexual
behavior of women was the special focus of much of this fundamentalist
antitheater propaganda. J. B. Cranfill blamed "cultivated Christian
women" especially for patronizing "frivolous and ofttimes sinful indulgences" such as theater, dancing, cards, and gambling.[19] Another
author was "made uneasy" by the fact that women and women's concerns
had become a major topic for playwrights and novelists:

> When men begin to regard a woman as a curious and com-
> plex social enigma . . . , they cease to pay her the old-
> fashioned deference which we like to regard as her unques-
> tioned right. The less woman is considered as a "question"
> the surer she will be to fulfill her natural destiny.[20]

Followers were also told to avoid the "baneful effects of a debasing
literature" in novels and popular fiction.[21] The problem of contemporary
fiction and its immorality was usually couched in terms of a special
threat to women's virtue. Brookes attributed the increase in "infidel
women" to "novels, and a few magazine articles."[22] In another article
he likened contemporary women who read "unChristian" fiction to the
"silly women laden with sins, led away with divers lusts, never learning,
and never able to come to the knowledge of truth" of 2 Tim. 3:6-7.[23]
Talmage saw the devil and the "modern novel" as the orchestrators of
shameful "clandestine marriages" (elopements).[24]

18. "The Sanctity of Marriage," *Watchman-Examiner* 4 (March 9, 1916): 296. See
also "What an Expert Theater-Goer Says," *Moody Bible Institute Monthly* 26, no. 9 (May
1926): 413; "The Immoralities of the Theatre," *Our Hope* 15, no. 10 (April 1909):
709–10; "Is the Drama Morally Corrupt and Corrupting?" *King's Business* 8, no. 6
(June 1917) :485; "The Morality of the Theatre," *King's Business* 8, no. 4 (April 1917):
294–95; John Roach Straton, "Right Home Life," *King's Business* 12, no. 2 (February
1921): 116; "Demoralizing Effect of the Theatre," *King's Business* 8, no. 3 (March
1917): 195.
19. J. B. Cranfill, "Make Every Edge Cut," *Watchman-Examiner* 12 (October 16,
1924): 1342–43.
20. "A Woman's Career," *Western Recorder* 85, no. 14 (February 10, 1910): 10.
21. Betts, "Perils That Threaten the Future of the Home," *Western Recorder,* 2. See
also H. Gordon Ross, "Some Aspects of the Problem of Reading," *Record of Christian
Work* 45, no. 6 (June 1926): 399.
22. "Infidelity among Women," *Truth, or, Testimony for Christ* 12 (1885–1886): 385.
23. "Popular Books," *Truth, or, Testimony for Christ* 7 (1880–1881): 161–64.
24. Talmage, "Clandestine Marriage," *Christian Herald and Signs of Our Times* 9, no.
4 (January 28, 1886): 52.

Fundamentalists condemned the theater and late nineteenth-century literature because both media depicted and publicized changes in gender roles, domestic life, and the place of women that deeply threatened these conservative evangelicals. They confused the message with the messenger, and attacked the bearers of the ill tidings.

As dangerous as the live stage and the printed page seemed to conservative Protestants, the motion picture caused even more consternation. "Things are put on in moving picture shows that no one would have dared or dreamed of putting on the regular stage."[25] The movie industry developed rapidly during the same decades that spanned the revolution in social morality and customs. Weekly attendance at movies reached 100 to 115 million by 1930.[26] Movies were very popular among young women. Mary P. Ryan estimated that girls between the ages of eight and nineteen went to a movie nearly once a week during the 1920s. These movies often depicted near nudity and noncoital sexual activity. The film industry also made heroines of vamp figures like Theda Bara and Gloria Swanson.[27]

Because motion pictures reflected modern and controversial social behavior and attitudes, they were characterized by fundamentalists as one of the greatest dangers to public and private morality. "No pen can describe the harm which is being done and the evil seed which is sown into immature minds," concluded the author of a 1916 article in *Our Hope*.[28] One article attacked movies because theater owners did not go to church; actors were moral degenerates; "passion and thrills" dominated its advertising; producers were driven by the profit motive to produce trash rather than "wholesome" shows; and movie houses were open on Sundays.[29] Fundamentalists were particularly sensitive to "influences at work" for "the destruction of young girls." Movies,

25. "Demoralizing Effect of the Theatre," *King's Business*, 195. See also "Is the Drama Morally Corrupt and Corrupting?" *King's Business*, 485.

26. Nancy F. Cott, *The Grounding Modern Feminism* (New Haven: Yale Univ. Press, 1987), 147.

27. Mary P. Ryan, "The Projection of a New Womanhood: The Movie Moderns in the 1920s," in *Our American Sisters*, ed. Jean E. Friedman and William G. Shade (Lexington, Mass.: D. C. Heath and Company, 1982), 499–518. See also Lois W. Banner, *Women in Modern America: A Brief History* (New York: Harcourt Brace Jovanovich, 1974), 165.

28. "Moving Pictures," *Our Hope* 22, no. 12 (June 1916): 758. See also "The Morality of the Theatre," *King's Business*, 294–95; "Poisoned at the Source," *King's Business* 14, no. 1 (January 1923): 6–7; "Clean Up the Movies," *King's Business* 13, no. 10 (October 1922): 989–90.

29. L. Ray Miller, "May Christians Attend Picture Shows?" *Moody Bible Institute Monthly* 25, no. 7 (March 1925): 317–18.

with their "impure plots and familiarizing with sensual subjects," destroyed girls' "proper delicacy" and compounded the crisis of American
girls and their new "present-day freedom."[30]

Fundamentalist discourse against dancing carried even stronger
emphasis on female morality. Dancing, "with its increased modern
liberties of personal contact, breaks down personal barriers of safety."[31]
Dancing represented a "terrible peril to purity and to Christian character" because "it inflames passion. It kindles salacious thoughts."[32]
Virtually every fundamentalist critic of dancing cited the lewdness and
excessive sensuality of popular dances. These religious leaders threatened
hell and damnation:

> Worst of all, are those who instigate . . . these outrageous
> orgies. The moral leper and the libertine are well aware that
> the turkey trot and kindred dances constitute one of the
> surest means of accomplishing their vile purposes. The glare
> of hell already gleams in the serpent-eye of the devilish
> debauchee, as he watches the innocent victim that he hopes
> to lure to wreck and ruin.[33]

Because the antidance spokesmen emphasized the corruptive influence dancing had on women, the connection between dancing and
prostitution was made. The editor of the *Western Recorder* in 1919
cautioned that there were two well-worn paths: from dance hall to
drinking, and from dance hall to red-light district.[34] Dancing "was

30. "The Protection of Girlhood," *Herald and Presbyter* 92, no. 37 (September 14,
1921): 2. See also "Menace of the Movies," *King's Business* 7, no. 5 (1916): 389.
31. "The Protection of Girlhood," *Herald and Presbyter*, 2. See also Betts, "Perils
That Threaten the Future of the Home," *Western Recorder*, 2.
32. "Popular Amusements," *Western Recorder*, 4. See also J. T. Larsen, "What Is
Becoming of the Christian Home?" *King's Business* 19, no. 6 (June 1928): 346; A. C.
Dixon, "May I Dance?" *Western Recorder* 85, no. 39 (July 21, 1910): 1; "The Dancing
Church," *King's Business* 7, no. 12 (December 1921): 1186–87; "Question Drawer,"
Truth, or, Testimony for Christ 6 (1879–1880): 218; "Facts about Dancing," *Western
Recorder* 66, no. 36 (May 20, 1880): 1; Straton, "Right Home Life," *King's Business,*
116.
33. "The Dance of Death," *Western Recorder* 88, no. 35 (July 13, 1913): 8. See also
"Dangers of the Dance," *Christian Cynosure* 23, no. 20 (January 29, 1891): 10; W. J.
Puckett, "Dancing," *Western Recorder* 94, no. 42 (July 24, 1919): 2; Reuben A. Torrey,
"Practical and Perplexing Questions," *Institute Tie,* new series, 7, no. 12 (August 1907):
564; E. P. Marvin, "Why Not Dance?" *Christian Cynosure* 24, no. 3 (October 1, 1891):
10; "From the Dance Hall into Eternity," *Our Hope* 32, no. 3 (September 1925): 162–
63.
34. "Good, Better, Best!" *Western Recorder* 94, no. 25 (March 27, 1919): 8.

born in a brothel, and can never escape the odium of its origin."[35] Will women never learn, questioned an editor of the *King's Business:*

> that thousands upon thousands of girls that were once pure are now in houses of ill repute because they took their first steps in some select parlor dance? The modern dances . . . are designed to kindle the passions of young men.[36]

J. Frank Norris painted a garish picture of the fate of a girl who took her "first step on the dance floor" and "finds herself in the lustful embrace of a man that is no kin to her." She "abhors" the experience, but goes:

> on and on until she, at last can dance her way into hell. . . , and the wreck and ruin of a once fair and beautiful girl is cast out to be trodden under foot of men.[37]

Billy Sunday's language was just as extreme:

> And I say to you, young girl. . . . Don't go to that dance. Don't you know that it is the most damnable, low-down institution on the face of God's earth, that it causes more ruin than anything this side of hell? Don't you go with that young man; don't you go to that dance. I say, young girl, don't go to that dance; it has proven to be the moral grave-yard that has caused more ruination than anything that was ever spewed out of the mouth of hell.[38]

These religious writers and evangelists used the force of religious sanction to keep the younger generation out of new twentieth-century activities, especially movies and dancing. The social customs depicted in the movies and the new social setting created in the dance hall were both reflections of and contributing factors to the revolution in manners and morals. Although fundamentalists expressed some concern for the morals of young men, those who condemned these social innovations

35. "School Dancing," *Western Recorder* 94, no. 33 (May 22, 1919): 8.
36. "The Amusement Pestilence," *King's Business* 14, no. 3 (March 1923): 233.
37. J. Frank Norris, "From San Antonio Daily Light," *Searchlight* 6, no. 29 (May 30, 1924): 4. See also Norris, "J. Frank Norris Flays Deacons Who Dance," *Searchlight* 8, no. 10 (January 23, 1925): 3.
38. Sunday, quoted in Ellis, *"Billy" Sunday,* 223.

did so primarily on the basis of the supposed damage done to female virtue.[39]

"Vulgar Young Women"

One major theme in fundamentalist rhetoric during the first decades of the twentieth century was focused, however, entirely on the social behavior of women: immodest dress and "flapperism."[40] In the 1910s, fundamentalists published articles on the issue of "dress reform." In particular, fundamentalists disparaged "forms of indecency in dress" such as "the tight skirt."[41] In 1916, an editorial in *The Christian Workers Magazine* called attention to the rising rates of illegitimate births (to "the vice baby farm in Baltimore") and placed

> no small share of the responsibility on the way our young women have come to dress. If they insist on going to their shops and factories, and stores and offices arrayed in clothes short at both ends, and skimpy in the middle, they may expect to attract the unworthy attention of ungodly men and to inflame their passion to direful results.[42]

In 1919, a writer for the *Herald and Presbyter* linked "public morals" directly to "public dress" of women.[43]

39. Fundamentalists were not the only critics of the dance hall between 1900 and 1920. For example, Elisabeth Israels Perry documented the progressive dance-hall reform movement led by Belle Israels (Moskowitz) and her Committee on Amusements in New York City. These women advocated less suggestive dances and tried to make dance halls a safer place of recreation for young women. See "The Motherhood of the Commonwealth," *Belle Moskowitz: Feminine Politics and the Exercise of Power in the Age of Alfred E. Smith* (New York: Oxford Univ. Press, 1987), 41–57.

40. As early as 1892, Brookes published a warning of the relaxation of the "old fashioned rules and restraints which governed society." He pointed to young women as the prime culprits in this social decay. "Nowhere is this more conspicuous than among girls. . . . The young lady of today reads the newspapers, what books she chooses, and discusses with equal frankness the last scandal and the latest French mode; . . . she dances with partners who do not care to be introduced to her mother, and she leaves her chaperon, not to dance . . . but to retire to some leafy corner . . . where she can, to use the modern phrase, 'sit out' . . . . She spends her own money and dresses as she likes." Consequently, although most of the literature foretelling and bemoaning the decline of conventional morality among women comes from the 1910s and 1920s, it was not a totally new phenomenon. See "Signs of the Times," *Truth, or, Testimony for Christ* 18, no. 10 (October 1892): 649.

41. See "Dress Reform," *Western Recorder* 86, no. 31 (June 8, 1911): 8; "Washington Women," *Western Recorder* 88, no. 21 (March 27, 1913): 8.

42. "Lewd Dressing," *Christian Workers Magazine* 16 (February 1916): 430. See also Mrs. Henry W. Peabody, "The Enlarged Sphere of Woman's Work in Its Relation to the Church," *Record of Christian Work* 37, no. 9 (September 1918): 632–33.

43. B. E. P. Prugh, "Public Morals and Public Dress," *Herald and Presbyter* 90, no.

The biggest flurry of articles about women's dress came between 1920 and 1925. It was part of a larger assault on the flapper, the modern young woman who made headlines throughout the U.S. in the 1920s. The flapper was attacked for "immodest dress, improper dancing, frequenting immoral plays, and indulging in smoking, gambling, swearing, and joyriding."[44] An article in the *Searchlight* in 1922 made a "startling disclosure" that "the majority of girls who go wrong is far ahead of the number of boys."[45] The flapper was called "a coarse, daring, vulgar young woman of questionable morals. One who cared nothing about modesty, or propriety, or virtue, or righteousness, or God."[46] So strong was fundamentalists' distaste for and fear of the flapper and what she represented that the Moody Bible Institute ignored its differences with Roman Catholicism long enough to praise a Catholic bishop for his stand against the revolution in manners and morality represented by young women.[47]

Particularly offensive to the critics of the flapper was her attire. The new "immodesty" in women's dress was blamed for the deterioration of "the nice sense of modesty which is the greatest safeguard of feminine virtue," and for the "incitement and excitement" of men.[48] Margaret C. Worthington, writing for the *Moody Bible Institute Monthly,* compared current immodest women's apparel to "grave-clothes," garments worn by the dead in the tomb.[49] William Hiram Foulkes, in another Moody

34 (August 20, 1919): 10. This article contained a more sophisticated analysis of the subject of women's dress than did others. Prugh was aware that feminine fashion was "decreed largely by men designers and manufacturers," that high heels caused "permanent disfigurement of feminine feet and limbs," and that male designers dictated female fashion "for the purpose both of making a sensation and bleeding them [women] of their money."

44. "Is Respect for Women Waning?" *Watchman-Examiner* 9 (September 8, 1921): 1142. See also "Moral Clean-ups," *Record of Christian Work* 40, no. 6 (June 1921): 423; Don O. Shelton, "The Modern Drift; Shall We Not Face the Facts and Note the Fruitage of Christless Philosophies?" *King's Business* 8, no. 9 (September 1922): 912–13.

45. "Mothers, Take Warning!" *Searchlight* 4, no. 17 (March 10, 1922): 1.

46. A. R. Funderburk, "Serving the God of Fashion," *Moody Bible Institute Monthly* 25 (July 1925): 500. See also Norris, "Burdened for the Lost," *Fundamentalist* 10 (July 8, 1927): 4; "Editorial," *Bibliotheca Sacra* 86, no. 342 (April 1929): 133–34.

47. "The Roman Catholic Church and Dress Reform," *Christian Workers Magazine* 16 (August 1916): 912. See also " 'Cult of the Body'," *Moody Bible Institute Monthly* 26, no. 9 (May 1926): 412.

48. "The Protection of Girlhood," *Herald and Presbyter,* 2. See also "Feminine Pride," *Christian Workers Magazine* 20, no. 5 (January 1920): 361; "Man's Moral Machinery," *King's Business* 11, no. 12 (December 1920): 1143; Leora M. Blanchard, "Bathsheba— A Study of an Immodest Woman," *Moody Bible Institute Monthly* 21, no. 9 (May 1921): 396–97.

49. Worthington, "Are Grave-Clothes Becoming to Christian Women?" *Moody Bible Institute Monthly* 21 (October 1921): 617.

publication, told the story of two young soldiers at a street corner who were watching as two young women passed by. The women "were not modestly attired, and their demeanor was not chaste." One soldier then said to the other, "with a curl of his lip: 'And we went over to fight for that!' "[50] A 1923 editorial in the *Christian Cynosure* contained a list of current fads that were most offensive: "peek-a-boo waists," "short skirts," "rolled hose, sheer hose, or scrolled hose," and rouge and powder.[51]

The two major arguments against women's fashions of the 1920s were that such clothing destroyed women's natural modesty and that it corrupted the morality of men. The charge of immodesty was given moral weight by reference to 1 Tim. 2:9, in which women are told to "adorn themselves in modest apparel." Consequently, the fashions of the flapper are "in direct violation of the teaching of God's Word."[52] William Parker lamented in 1915 that

> We find less . . . of that modest, retiring spirit [in women] that suffers long and is kind. We miss that indescribable flush of the cheek, trembling of the lip, or drooping of the eyelids, the natural coquetry of the heart.[53]

A. R. Funderburk was certain that "the present style of dress" worn by young women "tends to destroy the sense of modesty that God has implanted in the heart of every pure woman." Without that sense of modesty, he feared, "she is left defenseless, and it is an easy matter for the Devil in the form of a human friend to rob her of a priceless jewel."[54] An editorial in *Bibliotheca Sacra* postulated that "decline in the modesty of women in conduct and apparel has ever marked the downfall of empires, Egypt, Rome, the French Monarchy, Russia, and the German Empire."[55]

The second major objection voiced against the fashion of the flapper was that such clothing styles and social behavior by women undermined the morality of men by arousing men's sexual appetites. The writers of fundamentalist popular literature repeatedly contended that "the

50. William Hiram Foulkes, "Consecration," *Record of Christian Work* 44, no. 10 (October 1925): 752.
51. "Decency in Dress," *Christian Cynosure* 61, no. 5 (September 1923): 139.
52. Funderburk, "Serving the God of Fashion," *Moody Bible Institute Monthly*, 499.
53. William Parker, "True Womanhood," *Christian Workers Magazine* 16 (November 1915): 185.
54. Funderburk, "Serving the God of Fashion," *Moody Bible Institute Monthly*, 500. See also "The Protection of Girlhood," *Herald and Presbyter*, 2.
55. "Editorial," *Bibliotheca Sacra* 86, no. 342 (April 1929): 135.

exposure of the female person" was "an incitement and excitement to those of the opposite sex."[56] The readers of *Our Hope* in 1921 were told that men talked about immodestly dressed women in a "shockingly lustful way," and that such dress "called out all the beastly" in men.[57] Another article contained the claim that these styles of dress "have an immoral effect upon men, arousing the passions of the lower nature and causing impure thoughts."[58] The same article contained within it a clear and precise description of the understanding of human sexuality on which the Victorian gender ideology was based:

> Every man has a quantity of dynamite . . . in him. It did not come to him by cultivation, and it will not leave him by combatting. The frequent explosion of that dynamite and its result is a tragic part of the world's history. . . . Many men are made to commit sin in their hearts by the unclothed bodies of women who may be professed Christians and ignorant of the evil they are doing in causing a brother to stumble and become weak.[59]

Because Victorian gender ideology set women up as the pure and chaste guardians of public morality,[60] the flagrant violation of established conventions and *mores* by the young women of the twentieth century threatened, in the minds of many, the very fabric of private life and public virtue.[61] The immodesty of the flapper placed male character and restraint in peril. Madison C. Peters, writing for the *Watchman-Examiner*, surmised that woman's task was to control base men and influence them toward the good. He concluded the article with the observation that the current generation of women were not performing that task.[62] George Wharton Pepper addressed the Northfield Young Women's Conference on the same theme in 1914. He told his audience that:

> the men in any community will be exactly what the women in that community expect them to be. . . . We are in your

56. "The Protection of Girlhood," *Herald and Presbyter,* 2.
57. "Indecent Dress and Lust," *Our Hope* 27, no. 10 (April 1921): 618.
58. Funderburk, "Serving the God of Fashion," *Moody Bible Institute Monthly,* 499.
59. Funderburk, "The Word of God on Women's Dress," *Moody Bible Institute Monthly* 22 (January 1922): 759.
60. See Sondra R. Herman, "Loving Courtship or the Marriage Market? The Ideal and Its Critics," in *Our American Sisters,* 33.
61. See Peter G. Filene, *Him/Her/Self: Sex Roles in Modern America,* 2d ed. (Baltimore: John Hopkins Univ. Press, 1986), 92–93, 129–30.
62. Madison C. Peters, "Woman's Influence," *Watchman-Examiner* 6 (January 24, 1918): 114.

hands . . . . If you want the men who come within the
sphere of your influence to be wholesome-minded and clean,
. . . you could accomplish the result single-handed.[63]

The next year the same conference was told that "men are a thousand
times more dependent upon you than you upon them. . . . You can
make young men just what you want them to be."[64] In 1918, Mrs.
Henry W. Peabody said at the Northfield General Conference for Christian Workers that "the boys are going to do what the girls want them
to do and women have got to keep the standards high."[65] In an article
entitled "Man's Moral Machinery," the *King's Business* ran a letter from
"a young college man" who described himself as mentally unclean
because "the women I know will not let me be clean." The "biggest
stumbling block is the manner in which our women folks clothe themselves":

> What is a fellow going to do? We don't go around looking
> for these things, but we cannot help seeing them. No matter
> how much one may respect a girl, it is an effort for him to
> keep his thoughts from straying when she exposes too much
> of her body. . . . Why should they go on dressing in a way
> to aggravate the sex tendency? The young man who is trying
> his utmost to keep himself clean for the sake of the woman
> he will marry . . . has trouble enough without his sisters
> throwing a monkey wrench into his moral machinery.[66]

J. Frank Norris sermonized in 1922 that the girl who insists on dancing's
"insidious lure wrecks the downfall of man. . . . Girls are good influence on man in so far as they stick to their duties of motherhood and
wifehood. Any influence that works counter to this is damaging."[67] In
another sermon, he compared America to Rome in decline, and blamed
the "little bobbed-haired, frizzle-headed, gum chewing, painted-
lipped, flapper-tailed girl."[68]

63. George Wharton Pepper, "A Fourth of July Address," *Record of Christian Work*
33, no. 9 (September 1914): 544.
    64. J. G. K. McClure, "Abraham and the Home," *Record of Christian Work* 34, no.
8 (August 1915): 488. See also Parker, "True Womanhood," *Christian Workers Magazine*,
184; "Lewd Dressing," *Christian Workers Magazine*, 430.
    65. Peabody, "The Enlarged Sphere," *Record of Christian Work*, 633. See also Prugh,
"Public Morals and Public Dress," *Herald and Presbyter*, 10.
    66. "Man's Moral Machinery," *King's Business*, 1143. See also Blanchard, "Bathsheba,"
Moody Bible Institute Monthly, 397.
    67. "J. Frank Norris Declares Dancing Cause of Sin," *Searchlight* 4, no. 3 (January
13, 1922): 6.
    68. Norris, "Concrete Sin and Concrete Remedy," *Searchlight* 6, no. 34 (July 6,
1923): 3. See also "Preservation of American Womanhood," *Moody Bible Institute Monthly*
31, no. 5 (January 1931): 253.

Fundamentalists also feared that the flapper destroyed distinctions between the genders. Funderburk noticed the relatively androgynous fashions of the flapper: her short hair, coarse language, and "men's clothes," and responded by articulating a key principle of the separate-spheres ideology:

> Purity and morality can never be maintained except there be a distinct line of demarcation between the sexes. There must be that which will differentiate a man from a woman at all times.[69]

Fear was expressed in this literature that women's moral standards would sink to the level of men's rather than draw men's standards upward:

> We have a double standard. . . . Will the men come up to the women, or will the women come down to the men? I have hoped and prayed that when that challenge came you women would stand fast. . . . There are altogether too many of your sex who are taking a flying leap and landing on a platform down below where not the best men are.[70]

Fundamentalists in the 1910s and 1920s were alarmed "that the conventions . . . practiced for the protection of womanhood" were losing their hold on the behavior of young women.[71]

"Marital Crimes"

Much of this conservative religious rhetoric consisted of denials of the appropriateness of the flapper's image or style. The flapper's persona consisted, in part, of what we now believe are superficial characteristics: smoking, strong language, clothing fads, and dancing. There were, however, much more significant changes occurring in women's (and men's) behavior during the early decades of the twentieth century—changes that were more than stylistic. Researchers were investigating human sexuality scientifically, and sex education became a topic for public lectures, school classrooms, and women's clubs and

69. Funderburk, "Serving the God of Fashion," *Moody Bible Institute Monthly,* 500.
70. Beaven, "The Building of an Efficient Christian Life," *Record of Christian Work* 43, no. 2 (February 1924): 119. See also Norris, "Concrete Sin and Concrete Remedy," *Searchlight,* 1; Margaret Slattery, "What the Modern Girl Thinks," *Watchman-Examiner* 11 (January 11, 1923): 50; "Marriage and Related Problems," *Record of Christian Work* 47, no. 4 (April 1928): 209–10.
71. Beaven, "The Challenges of a World in the Remaking of the Christian Womanhood of Today: Third Address," *Record of Christian Work* 41, no. 12 (December 1922): 894.

organizations. The use of birth control increased as the nineteenth century progressed (the middle class had an interest throughout the century in a low birthrate). Margaret Sanger's public movement for birth control legislative reform and the distribution of birth control information and devices brought that particular issue, as well as more amorphous concerns about human sexuality in general, to national attention in the 1920s. Abortion was also a topic of concern to many, especially since a relaxation of some conventions of propriety allowed more direct treatment of the subject by the public media.

Fundamentalists enthusiastically entered the fray on all fronts. They defended feminine purity and innocence against the assault of the sexologists and the sex educators. They championed the holy estate of motherhood against all who would control reproduction through any means other than abstinence.

Against "eugenics" (birth-control) lecturers, the editors of the *Western Recorder* alleged that the lectures "are too graphic about sex and reproduction," and that "these sexual seances are, more than any other cause, contributing to the destruction of the modesty of womanhood."[72] The same editors described a "sex hygiene" class in the schools as "a nauseating account of sinful indulgences" and "nothing less than a villainously vulgar performance." The editorial concluded that "unless a muzzle is placed on some of our effeminate and foolish men, and mannish and improper women, modesty will soon cease to command its accustomed premium."[73] The editors of *King's Business* in 1915 wrote that:

> One of the most dangerous tendencies of the present day is the emphasis put upon sex. We have numberless books on sex written and advertised. . . . We are attempting to have sexual hygiene taught in schools, and these questions are constantly referred to in sermons. The net result is a frightful epidemic of immorality and sex abnormality and morbidness.[74]

In 1929, an editorial in the *Christian Fundamentalist* decried research on human sexuality undertaken by university professors (a certain "sex

72. "Eugenics," *Western Recorder* 89, no. 8 (December 25, 1913): 8.
73. "Sex Hygiene," *Western Recorder* 88, no. 41 (August 14, 1913): 8.
74. "Undue Emphasis on Sex Problems the Devil's Snare," *King's Business* 6, no. 6 (June 1915): 466. See also "Instruction in Sex Hygiene," *Christian Workers Magazine* 16 (January 1916): 348.

questionnaire" distributed to students at Bucknell University, Carleton College, and the University of Montana):

> Any man who has ever seen one of these questionnaires felt his blood boil if he were the father of a daughter . . . who was subjected to such insulting questions by the modernistic half man, whose curiosity concerning the opposite sex had so far consumed him as to force from his pen a hundred insulting interrogations.[75]

The Victorian gender ideology included a specific set of assumptions regarding human sexuality: Women should be innocent of sexual knowledge and chaste, and sexual conduct should be dictated by tradition and religious sanction rather than by rational and scientific conclusions. The new approach to sex based on scientific research helped make women more aware of and comfortable with their own sexual natures. Consequently, it was unacceptable to defenders of traditional gender expectations.

New comfort and familiarity with sex both contributed to and was a result of changes in sexual behavior, especially among young women. A sexual revolution occurred after 1920 when more and more middle-class women engaged in premarital sex. Women, flappers in particular, received the blame for all these disruptions in sexual conventions and *mores*. The public image and sexual experience of the flapper were disconcerting to both men and women because the flapper proved to them that no one was left to enforce conventional sexual *mores*. Middle-class men could no longer turn the responsibility of controlling sexual desire over to their female peers.[76]

The public debate over birth control aroused many of the same fears. Birth control gave both men and women new freedom to explore sexuality apart from family and reproductive contexts. The *Western Recorder* contained one of the earliest references to birth control to appear after 1880. The author used only euphemisms: "Parisian licentiousness," and "marital crimes." Although it "is a delicate matter to allude to, . . . everyone knows that native American stock is rapidly diminishing," largely because many "think they 'cannot afford to have large families in these extravagant times!' "[77] After 1915, birth control and

75. "The Sex Questionnaire," *Christian Fundamentalist* 3, no. 5 (November 1929): 405.

76. Filene, *Him/Her/Self*, 84. See also William O'Neill, *Everyone Was Brave: The Rise and Fall of Feminism in America* (Chicago: Quadrangle Books, 1969), 298.

77. Cuyler, "Moral and Spiritual Dangers of Young Men," *Western Recorder* 63, no. 27 (February 28, 1889): 1.

abortion became more important themes in fundamentalist literature,
as they did in American society at large.[78]

Fundamentalists advanced two arguments against birth control.
The primary one labeled birth control a sin. An editorial in the *Christian
Workers Magazine* used scriptural precedent: "The subject of birth control
dates back to the time when God slew Onan for his detestable act." It
accused birth-control advocates of using "the mails, the press, the
platform and the clinics, as a means of teaching the poor the detestable
immoralities of the Godless rich."[79] Another writer used the scriptural
command "be fruitful and multiply" as grounds for the proper prohibition of birth control.[80] Another portrayed the sinful nature of birth
control as stemming from the selfishness of married couples.[81] The
editor of *Our Hope* understood birth control as just another "sign of the
times," times that were replete with sin and infidelity.[82] Another fundamentalist argued that birth control

> defies the Divine Legislator by completely and wantonly
> defeating His purpose in establishing and sanctifying mar-
> riage. There is no moral difference between denying birth
> to little ones and robbing them of existence after they are
> born. . . .[83]

78. There were many reasons why Americans rejected the use of artificial contraception. Some historians argued that late nineteenth-century women's rights activists
were opposed to it because it threatened the stability of marriages (women were
economically dependent on marriage in the nineteenth century) because conception
often "was a guarantee that men would marry" and stay married. Also, the idea of
voluntary motherhood threatened the cult of motherhood, from which many women
drew power and self-esteem. See Linda Gordon, *Woman's Body, Woman's Right: A Social
History of Birth Control in America* (New York: Penguin Books, 1977), 99–111; Sheila
M. Rothman, *Woman's Proper Place: A History of Changing Ideals and Practices, 1870 to
the Present* (New York: Basic Books, 1978), 82–83; Daniel Scott Smith, "Family
Limitation, Sexual Control, and Domestic Feminism in Victorian America," in *A
Heritage of Her Own: Toward a New Social History of American Women*, ed. Nancy F. Cott
and Elizabeth Pleck (New York: Simon & Schuster, 1979), 236; John D'Emilio and
Estelle Freedman, *Intimate Matters: A History of Sexuality in America* (New York: Harper
& Row, 1988), 64.
79. "Birth Control," *Christian Workers Magazine* 27, new series, no. 3 (November
1916): 175. See also Dudley Joseph Whitney, "The Moral Teaching of the Bible," *Bible
Champion* 35, no. 9 (September 1929): 486–87.
80. K. L. Brooks, "Comment from Many Sources," *King's Business* 10, no. 5 (May
1919): 443.
81. "Childless Marriages," *Christian Workers Magazine* 20, no. 5 (January 1920):
360.
82. "The Agitation for Birth-Control," *Our Hope* 31, no. 12 (June 1925): 746.
83. Thomas M. O'Leary, "Companionate Marriage," *Christian Fundamentalist* 3, no.
10 (April 1930): 628.

Billy Sunday called birth-control activists "the devil's mouthpiece."[84]

On the issue of birth control, as on divorce and dress reform, fundamentalists were in public agreement with Roman Catholicism. In 1929, John Roach Straton stood with William J. Duane, Catholic president of Fordham University, against "artificial interference with the sources of life."[85] Editors of the *Moody Bible Institute* in 1931 praised the papal encyclical condemning birth control.[86]

The second major argument fundamentalists lodged against artificial birth control was sociological. It was well known that the birth rate was declining more rapidly among "native" middle-class whites than among other segments of the population. Fundamentalists saw the destruction of the "race" and of American society in the decreasing birthrate of the white, "native" middle-class and in the higher birthrate of the foreign-born, black, and lower-class segments of the population:

> The voice of history warns us that God will not be mocked, and the nations that practice birth control soon disappear from the stage of life. . . . The birth control of the individual becomes the suicide of the race.[87]

Fundamentalists used both religious and sociological appeals to prevent women from using artificial birth control.

Abortion was not a major topic in popular fundamentalist literature from the period, although the "soaring incidence" of abortions between 1840 and 1888 were performed on married, middle- and upper-class white Protestant women.[88] What references exist acknowledged the use of abortion by American women and condemned that practice severely.[89] Abortion in these fundamentalist periodicals was almost

84. Sunday, quoted in William G. McLoughlin, *Billy Sunday Was His Real Name* (Chicago: Univ. of Chicago Press, 1955), 132.

85. C. Allyn Russell, *Voices of American Fundamentalism* (Philadelphia: Westminster Press, 1976), 62–64.

86. "Birth Control," *Moody Bible Institute Monthly* 31, no. 7 (March 1931): 336.

87. O'Leary, "Companionate Marriage," *Christian Fundamentalist,* 629. See also Norris, "The Woman Thou Gavest Me," *Fundamentalist of Texas* 7, no. 40 (August 16, 1929): 2; H. J. Ockenga, "The Ideal Home," *Christian Faith and Life* 37, no. 4 (April 1931): 96.

88. James C. Mohr, *Abortion in America: The Origins and Evolution of National Policy* (New York: Oxford Univ. Press, 1978), 183. See also D'Emilio and Freedman, *Intimate Matters,* 65.

89. Fundamentalists were not alone in their condemnation of abortion. In the 1860s and 1870s campaigns to outlaw abortion were led by physicians. See Rothman, *Woman's Proper Place,* 82–84; Carroll Smith-Rosenberg, *Disorderly Conduct: Visions of Gender in Victorian America* (New York: Alfred A. Knopf, 1985), 46; Gordon, *Woman's Body, Woman's Right,* 59–60.

always referred to as murder.[90] A relatively early statement was found in a 1913 editorial in the *Watchman-Examiner* in which abortion was called a "grave crime."[91] Billy Sunday's standard sermon to women contained statistics indicating that one-third of all pregnancies ended in abortions. As many of Sunday's addresses did, this sermon condemned wealthy women[92] who "spend their time touring in their automobiles and out at the golf links and drinking wine and playing cards and cruising in yachts with their miserable hands red with blood."[93]

Frank, in his history of early fundamentalism, also noted Sunday's diatribes against "society women" and interpreted such rhetoric and the exaltation of Christian manhood, which was also conspicuous in Sunday's revivals, as "a male uneasiness at a time when great social pressures were being marshalled to redefine woman's role as that of household consumer."[94] The emphasis on Christian manliness and character building, according to Frank, was posed by Sunday and others like him as a rival "morality" to emerging consumerism and advertising. This is a questionable interpretation for two reasons.

First, an important mark of "successful" middle-class masculinity during the period was a wife who was not employed outside the home—someone who spent income but did not earn it directly. It seems unlikely that middle-class men and Billy Sunday would launch an attack on the wife-at-home when she was the cornerstone of the separate-spheres ideology.

Second, Frank himself admitted that on the topic of consumerism Billy Sunday was deeply ambivalent; there is no wholesale rejection of those values. Sunday loved to be well-dressed and told his audiences so. He made no secret of his enthusiasm for the new automobiles rolling off the assembly lines.[95] Although there may have been some class variety and antagonism in his crowds, during his heyday campaigns in large cities Sunday was the toast of high society and depended on the wealthy, many of them men, for moral and financial support.[96]

90. See "A Timely Warning," *Western Recorder* 94, no. 40 (July 10, 1919): 8; B. F. McLendon, "Where Art Thou?" *Searchlight* 6, no. 18 (March 16, 1923): 1.
91. "Editorial Comments on Current Events," *Watchman-Examiner* 1, no. 7 (October 16, 1913): 201. See also "Infidelity among Women," *Truth, or, Testimony for Christ* (1885–1886), 388.
92. Class antagonism was evident in fundamentalist rhetoric, especially in attacks on middle- and upper-class women who could afford leisure activities, volunteer reform work, higher education, high fashion and abortions.
93. McLoughlin, *Billy Sunday Was His Real Name*, 132–33.
94. Frank, *Less than Conquerors*, 218.
95. Frank, *Less than Conquerors*, 219–20.
96. McLoughlin, *Billy Sunday Was His Real Name*, xxiv, 69.

Although it is likely that Sunday's attacks on women did indeed express "male uneasiness," the direct cause of the distress was not so much the new consumer economy *per se* as it was the rapid changes in women's roles and behaviors. And middle-class American men, their masculinity threatened on every front, used women—in this case wealthy women— as a scapegoat for the other social ills they perceived around them.

In conclusion, if any social phenomenon made fundamentalists aware of how far from the middle-class mainstream they had slipped it was the flapper of the late 1910s and 1920s. She was the daughter of the middle-class urban establishment, and she, not the fundamentalists, carried the day. Sheila Rothman reviewed 1920s marriage manuals and discovered that in these books the most significant theme for female identity within marriage, motherhood, had given way to the "modern" or "romantic" marriage that "the birth of a child might complicate." The same advice books counseled women to "enjoy at least some form of premarital sexual activity." "Indeed," concluded Rothman, "it is difficult to imagine a more shocking piece of advice to a generation trained to the precepts of virtuous womanhood."[97]

The flappers, too, with their "mannish bob, cigarette smoking, boyish figures," rejected gender distinction. Consequently, argued historian Smith-Rosenberg, "Not one shred of the Cult of True Womanhood remained to cloak their life in the symbols of respectability."[98] No wonder the defenders of Victorian gender roles and conventions were so dismayed by these young women.

The rise to power and popularity of fundamentalism coincided exactly with the emergence of the flapper. Threatened and shocked by the revolution in manners and morals after 1910, fundamentalists denounced it. They were preoccupied with the destruction of Victorian social conventions and *mores*. Rhetoric condemning new popular amusements, women's fashions and demeanor, and attitudes toward sexuality constituted a major part of fundamentalist popular literature after 1910. Many Americans shared the same concerns, and therein lay much of fundamentalism's appeal.

97. Rothman, *Woman's Proper Place,* 178. See also Filene, *Him/Her/Self,* 449.
98. Smith-Rosenberg, *Disorderly Conduct,* 177–78.

CHAPTER SIX

Fundamentalist Theology and Gender Roles

THE HISTORY OF THE FUN-
damentalist movement in late nineteenth- and early twentieth-century
America has generally been told from the perspective of issues pre-
eminent in the public theological debates between 1880 and 1930.
This set of essential theological issues most often included dispensational
premillennialism, biblical inerrancy, evolution, and modernism. Yet
accounts of fundamentalism that have concentrated on these or a range
of other issues associated with antimodernism have consistently ignored
the impact on theology of the disruptions in gender roles that occurred
during the period. Fundamentalists were profoundly affected by the
dismantling of the Victorian gender ideology. Acknowledgment of and
reaction to those strains on gender-role conventions were part and parcel
of fundamentalist theological formulations, whether ostensibly concerned with the end of time, the truth of the Bible, or the dangers of
evolutionary theory and modern theology.

Dispensational Premillennialism

For several important chroniclers of the fundamentalist movement,
dispensational premillennialism was a key element in identifying and
defining the movement. This apocalyptic schema divided history from
beginning to end into several distinct stages or dispensations. Rudnick's
definition of fundamentalist theology was "nineteenth-century Presbyterian or Baptist orthodoxy modified by the inclusion of dispensationalism, with special emphasis on premillennialism."[1] Hunter

1. Milton L. Rudnick, *Fundamentalism and the Missouri Synod: A Historical Study of*

concluded that "the movement derived its structure and direction principally from the premillennialists."[2] Marsden argued that "dispensationalism was . . . the most distinctive intellectual product of emerging fundamentalism."[3] And in fact, from 1880 to the end of the period, the vast majority of fundamentalist leaders were premillennialists.

Dispensational premillennialism stood out as a new and noteworthy development because mainstream nineteenth-century Protestant evangelicalism was postmillennialist; that is, most American Protestants believed that the era in which they lived was one of steady progress toward the Kingdom of God and the return of Christ. Premillennialists, on the other hand, believed that the millennium of peace and blessing would be established only after the second coming of Christ, and that the present age was one of corruption and apostasy, an era of violence and foreboding during which Christians were to wait, watch, and preach the gospel of repentance. Postmillennialists "viewed God's redemptive work as manifested in the spiritual and moral progress of American society."[4] Such was not true of the premillennialists. Sandeen concluded that

> in the face of American nationalism, [late nineteenth-century millenarians] . . . offered a sober and pessimistic view of the future of all human society, including the United States. . . . The mood of Protestant evangelicals changed in response to the tensions of industrialization and immigration from one of cocky optimism to chastened uncertainty."[5]

The premillennialists condemned the age and American society for its immorality and infidelity.[6]

Fundamentalist popular literature did, indeed, contain pessimistic assessments of American society. Throughout the period from 1880 to 1930, fundamentalists rejected the notion of moral and social progress

Their Interaction and Mutual Influence (St. Louis: Concordia Publishing House, 1966), 54.

2. James Davison Hunter, *American Evangelicalism: Conservative Religion and the Quandary of Modernity* (New Brunswick, N.J.: Rutgers Univ. Press, 1983), 30.

3. George M. Marsden, *Fundamentalism and American Culture: The Shaping of Twentieth Century Evangelicalism, 1870–1925* (New York: Oxford Univ. Press, 1980), 44.

4. Marsden, *Fundamentalism and American Culture*, 38.

5. Ernest R. Sandeen, *The Roots of Fundamentalism: British and American Millenarianism, 1800–1930* (Chicago: Univ. of Chicago Press, 1970), xvi.

6. See also Hunter, *American Evangelicalism*, 30; Willard B. Gatewood, *Controversy in the Twenties: Fundamentalism, Modernism, and Evolution* (Nashville: Vanderbilt Univ. Press, 1969), 11.

and contended instead that the country was slipping from its religious and ethical moorings. In 1880, an article in the *Watchman* carried one writer's observations that "the standard of Christian living is lower than it was thirty or forty years ago." The culprits cited were dancing, card-playing, and the theater.[7] The *Truth, or, Testimony for Christ,* edited by James L. Brookes, a leader of the premillennial Niagara conferences, ran articles throughout the last two decades of the nineteenth century that were very critical of the culture. Given all the murders, suicides, and divorces, Brookes marvelled that "there are 'multitudes of Christians, who, in the face of the most patent occurrences, and the most abundant testimonies of the Scriptures, persist in saying that there is progress in the right direction everywhere."[8] By 1892, Brookes had expanded his list of blatant immoralities to include drinking, political revolution, "the adulteries of rich society women," and homosexuality. "Truly," he concluded, "society is evoluting backwards."[9] The editors of *Our Hope,* a radical premillennialist journal, were also convinced "that the worst is yet to come," and they, too, could not understand

> how our post millennial friends, with their optimistic dreams can dream on and continue to speak of the glories of the present age, and the increasing righteousness of the age, when all about us goes the other way. . . .[10]

In 1917, the *King's Business* pronounced "our civilization a dead failure."[11]

Fundamentalists believed that the cause of social decay was a breakdown in faith and morals. An article published in the *Bible Champion* in 1914 noted that "never before, perhaps since civilization began, has there been less regard for the outward symbols of religion and government."[12] Ten years later, J. Frank Norris contended that the "breakdown of civilization, of home life . . . is because we have left

7. Mallah, "Lowering the Standard," *Watchman* n.v. (January 8, 1880): 2.
8. "What Awaits the World," *Truth, or, Testimony for Christ* 11 (1884–1885): 294.
9. "Civilization and Crime," *Truth, or, Testimony for Christ* 18 (1892): 363–64. See also George A. Lofton, "General Corruption," *Western Recorder* 63, no. 27 (February 28, 1889): 1.
10. "Increase of Iniquities and Corruption," *Our Hope* 26, no. 7 (January 1910): 444. See also *Our Hope* 30, no. 6 (December 1923): 362–65.
11. "Our Civilization a Dead Failure," *King's Business* 8, no. 5 (May 1917): 390. See also William Bell Riley, "Is Society Rotting?" *Christian Fundamentalist* 1, no. 9 (March 1928): 6–7.
12. "Authority Declines," *Bible Champion* 17, no. 4 (April 1914): 173.

off the worship of the living God."[13] The connection between conservative evangelical religion and the maintenance of Victorian morality was made frequently and consistently in this literature. In 1911, a writer for the *Herald and Presbyter* put the matter succinctly:

> Religion and morality go hand in hand. . . . Men will not long continue to live well and purely if they are destitute of religious principles and motives. . . . He who breaks down the sanctions of holy religion is helping inaugurate an era of immorality.[14]

Two years later, the journal reiterated its position.[15] In 1917, the *Bible Champion* carried an article by fundamentalist John A. Grose in which he remarked that "the analogy between faith and morals is close and real."[16] There seems no doubt that the characterization of premillennial fundamentalism as pessimistic is accurate. The source of their alarm was, in general, an impression that civilization, religion, and morality were in serious and unprecedented decline.

Historians of premillennialism have tried to understand just which late nineteenth-century social phenomena were the most frightening to these conservative Protestants. What aspects of their culture led them to conclude that society was rotting and that the end was near? Evidence from popular premillennial literature indicates that disruptions in middle-class gender roles and ideology constituted a primary source of social pessimism and discomfort. Inherent in the fundamentalist attack on the current state of religion was an attack on the current state of morality. In these materials, "morality" is often just a code word for conventional gender behavior, and "immorality" a code word for sexual and gender impropriety. Hence, in fundamentalists' theological discourse on morality, such gender issues as marriage and divorce, women in public life, women's fashion, and birth control were the major concerns, and defense of the Victorian gender ideology a primary social and religious goal.

Premillennialist theorizing about the end times contained illuminating claims. Two leading premillennialist journals, Brookes's *Truth, or, Testimony for Christ* and Gaebelein's *Our Hope,* declared that

13. J. Frank Norris, "Shouldst Thou Help the Ungodly?" *Fundamentalist* 10, no. 33 (June 12, 1927): 2.
14. "Irreligion and Crime," *Herald and Presbyter* 82, no. 34 (August 23, 1911): 3.
15. See "Religion and Morality," *Herald and Presbyter* 84, no. 37 (September 10, 1913): 2.
16. John A. Grose, "Christ or the Higher Critic?" *Bible Champion* 23, no. 3–4 (March–April 1917): 127.

the new boldness and infidelity evident among women was a clear sign of the "end times." *Our Hope* took occasion on publication of the *Woman's Bible* to condemn that feminist book and the New Woman it represented:

> If this is the way in which the wives and mothers of this land are being trained to look at and speak of God's Word, how long it will be before we are ready for the utter collapse and corruption of organized society? . . . If woman saps the foundation of the family, how can society and the state continue to stand? The pillar of the church is the headship of Christ. The pillar of the family is the headship of the man. Truly perilous times are upon us. Let us watch and be sober.[17]

Although the publishing of the *Woman's Bible* may have prompted a particular set of editorials, the grave concern about the emerging New Woman and her apparent lack of concern for convention, religious as well as social, is apparent in much of the end-times discourse. In the mid-1880s, the *Truth, or, Testimony for Christ* printed an article entitled "Infidelity among Women." The author attacked women who were educated and kept up with current intellectual debates:

> They [women] understand from the books and book notices they read, that "people of culchah" have outgrown faith in the Bible, and they are determined to keep up with the times, particularly when they find that they can live without prayer, without watchfulness over their conduct, without the necessity of listening to dull and orthodox sermons, without a thought of eternity.

The author warned that "the rapid increase of such women" was a sign that the last perilous days were approaching.[18] Two years later, the journal published another article entitled "Infidelity among Women." There, too, "literary female infidels" were condemned as signs of the end times. The future looked even more ominous than the present: "God pity the church and the country, when such women have the training of the next generation!"[19]

17. "A Striking Sign of the Times: A Chapter from the Woman's Bible," *Our Hope* 2, no. 2 (August 1896): 33–34.
18. "Infidelity among Women," *Truth, or, Testimony for Christ* 12 (1885–1886): 385–86.
19. "Infidelity among Women," *Truth, or, Testimony for Christ* 25 (1888–1889): 246.

Late nineteenth-century premillennialists believed that women in leadership roles within the church were another ominous sign of the tribulation to come:

> But the prominence of women in a sphere inconsistent with nature and with the meekness and quietness, which are the ornament of a Christian woman (I Pet. iii:4), is one of the signs of the times.

As further evidence of the danger of women's religious leadership, the author noted that in "all the wicked and pernicious movements such as Spiritualism, Christian Science and Theosophy, women are in authority."[20] Similar disapproval was expressed in an article entitled "The New Woman." The author, expecting "to find women preachers among the Unitarians and Universalists, for they care nothing for the Bible," was "disgusted" to find them in the Salvation Army and among the Cumberland Presbyterians and Methodists. "Oh well," the writer concluded, "it will only hasten the appearing of the antichrist. . . . As it was with the first woman, so shall it be with the woman at the close of the age, listening to the tempter."[21] There is ample evidence from two leading premillennialist journals in the 1880s and 1890s that the New Woman, both within the church and without, was a cause of no little disturbance. Her education, free-thinking, and prominence within the religious realm were considered evidence of social decay and the approaching apocalypse.

The New Woman caused apocalyptic alarm and theological consternation for another reason, too. Although the author of an article entitled "Signs of the Times," published in the *Truth, or, Testimony for Christ* in 1892, spoke of riots, violence, and crime as signs of the end times, most space was given to a discussion of the social behavior of the New Woman: the "easy-going manner in which women of the highest rank and culture have allowed the old-fashioned rules and restraints which governed society to be relaxed."[22] Specifically, premillennialists contended that there was "an appalling increase of drunkenness among women,"[23] that too many marriages ended in divorce,

20. "1 Corinthians xiv:34," *Our Hope* 14, no. 12 (June 1908): 770.
21. "The New Woman," *Truth, or, Testimony for Christ* 22, no. 7 (July 1896): 369–70.
22. "Signs of the Times," *Truth, or, Testimony for Christ* 18 (1892): 679.
23. "Infidelity among Women," (1885–1886): 387.

that too few women were choosing to have children,[24] and that "immodest fashions" for women were "outward evidence of the hidden lasciviousness and corruption" of "the days of Lot."[25]

The premillennialists in the fundamentalist movement (and most of the fundamentalists were premillennialists[26]) in the early twentieth century continued to find in changing gender roles and the revolution in women's manners and morals foundations for their fears and predictions of the pending doom. In a defense of the ideology of female subordination printed in a Moody publication in 1915, William Parker argued that when woman "assumes the prerogative of power which belongs to man and seeks to dominate the world in all of its activities, as she is doing today, she then possesses the spirit of the beast."[27] In 1923, J. Frank Norris surmised that "never before in the history of the world were certain classes of women becoming so bold and so defiant and so abandoned." "How long," he asked, "can the angel of time withhold his trumpet?"[28]

Like their nineteenth-century counterparts, twentieth-century premillennialists pointed to specific social phenomena as proof of their claims that civilization was in a state of decay and that the era was drawing to a close. These social phenomena were often identified as disruptions in Victorian domestic patterns. An article in the *Western Recorder* in 1917 declared that "the surest sign of the deterioration of our civilization may be seen in the disintegration of the American home."[29] Free-love, companionate marriage, and divorce were "links in one chain," "another sign . . . that the end of the age is upon us and that the predicted lawlessness is fast approaching."[30] The editors of *Our Hope* gave birth control special attention in 1925. The article concluded that "surely the whole scheme is another sign of the times."[31] Changing marriage patterns and customs were key ingredients of the

24. Jesse Hill, "A Plea for the Family," *Bibliotheca Sacra* 62 (1905): 628–29.
25. "Immodest Fashions and Luxuries," *Our Hope* 16, no. 4 (October 1909): 249–50.
26. Gatewood, *Controversy in the Twenties*, 11.
27. William Parker, "True Womanhood," *Christian Workers Magazine* 16 (November 1915): 185.
28. Norris, "The Last Days," *Searchlight* 6, no. 16 (March 2, 1923): 3.
29. "The Decadence of the Home," *Western Recorder* 92, no. 32 (May 17, 1917): 8.
30. "The Abolishment of Marriage and the Home Demanded," *Our Hope* 32, no. 2 (August 1925): 105. See also Norris, "The Messenger and His Message, or The Book of Malachi," *Searchlight* 5, no. 35 (July 14, 1922): 1; Clarence H. Benson, "Our Monthly Potpourri: Wake Up, America!" *Moody Bible Institute Monthly* 32, no. 11 (July 1932): 540.
31. "The Agitation for Birth Control," *Our Hope* 31, no. 21 (June 1925): 745–50.

pessimism of the premillennialist message throughout the early decades of the 1900s.

Premillennialists also attacked "the emancipation of woman" as a "bad sign" that we are "living in the last days, the perilous times."[32] Suffrage was singled out. In these last days women

> will be tempted to take part in this or that social reform, to give their sex the ballot and place them on political equality with men, for their own protection, and to reform society.[33]

Such "silly women" who participated in the "Suffragist movement" were the " 'silly women' of the last days. Confusion worse confounded, moral corruption of the most awful nature, will surely come if woman leaves her sphere."[34] Another article called the movement for women's suffrage "another sinister movement which will hasten the final conditions of the last days."[35] A. C. Dorris claimed that "woman in politics is not an advance . . . , but a return toward . . . savagery."[36]

Although historians traditionally have given little attention to the premillennialist and fundamentalist reaction to disruptions in gender roles and identity from 1880 to 1930, there is strong evidence that such social and cultural dynamics contributed significantly to the deep pessimism that has been associated repeatedly with this religious movement. Yet there was a telling inconsistency in their pessimism. In popular fundamentalist literature, theological orthodoxy—salvation itself—was inexorably connected to the morality and social conventions of the Victorian middle-class. Premillennialists were not pessimistic about the possibilities for salvation inherent in a return to the nostalgic home and family of their yesteryear. Often represented by historians as being other-worldly and uninterested in social policy and institutions,[37] the premillennialists within the fundamentalist movement were neither. Their rhetoric depicted the divinized "Christian" home—the white, middle-class, evangelical, nuclear family, in which husband works and wife remains at home subject to the husband's authority—as the one social institution capable of saving both individuals and the

32. "The Christian Home," *Our Hope* 30, no. 4 (October 1923): 202.

33. "Bible Notes," *Record of Christian Work* 26, no. 6 (June 1907): 559.

34. "Foolish Women," *Our Hope* 29, no. 8 (February 1913): 462–63.

35. "Current Events and Signs of the Times in Light of the Word of God," *Our Hope* 28, no. 11 (May 1912): 717–18.

36. A. C. Dorris, "Woman Suffrage," *Western Recorder*, 86, no. 27 (May 11, 1911): 3.

37. See Marsden, *Fundamentalism and American Culture*, 66–67.

nation from sin and decline. A major part of their agenda—to salvage the gender ideology and conventions of midcentury, thereby defending exclusive male access to the public realm, supporting male domination within the home, and reclaiming the church for men—was radically political and deeply concerned about the maintenance of social institutions.

As the middle-class ideology of separate spheres gave way, religious people responded in religious language to their sense of unease and uncertainty.[38] One such response was interest in the various premillennialist theories that gained new prominence and a wide audience after 1880. Not only did such theories give a religious explanation of the chaos and turmoil so many Americans experienced so close to home, and in the marriage bed itself,[39] but premillennialist organizations and rhetoric supported the crumbling gender order with religious and moral sanctions and attempted to halt its corruption for decades after 1880.

Biblical Inerrancy

No other theological position has been so closely associated with the fundamentalist movement as biblical inerrancy, the claim, against

38. Both Sandeen and Marsden have made reference to certain inconsistencies among premillennialists that would lend further credence to the nontheological foundations of premillennial dispensationalism. Marsden commented how "anomalous" it was "that the premillennial leaders should fall all over themselves in their enthusiasm to enlist Bryan, [a postmillennialist], as leader of their organizations." *Fundamentalism and American Culture,* 208.

A more important inconsistency observed by Marsden is that despite the perceived "hopeless corruption of the world," premillennialists registered "no demand to abandon most of the standards of the respectable American middle-class way of life. It was to these standards, in f act, that people were to be converted." *Fundamentalism and American Culture,* 38.

Sandeen observed the basic incompatibility between the total rejection of American culture advocated by many premillennialists and the activist political agenda of Bryan's antievolution campaign, which was testimony to "American faith that legislative action can bring into being pure morals." Sandeen, *The Roots of Fundamentalism,* 267.

39. G. J. Barker-Benfield argued that nineteenth-century men interpreted changes in sex roles as "tantamount to social anarchy." Although he did not use nineteenth-century premillennialists as a case in point, I think it is a very important one. See Baker-Benfield, *The Horrors of the Half-Known Life: Male Attitudes toward Women and Sexuality in Nineteenth-Century America* (New York: Harper & Row, 1976), xiii.

Douglas W. Frank, on the other hand, missed in the opposite direction. His chapter devoted to premillennialism poignantly portrayed their fear of losing control in a society when so much was in flux and out of their control. He doesn't take the radical changes in gender relations and conventions into account, and hence his analysis is incomplete. Men were literally losing control of women. See Frank, *Less than Conquerors: How Evangelicals Entered the Twentieth Century* (Grand Rapids, Mich.: Wm. B. Eerdmans, 1986), 30–59.

the new "higher criticism," that the Bible was historically accurate and
inspired by God in its every word. This issue has been a major inter-
pretive principle for most of the historians of conservative evangelical
Protestantism between 1880 and 1930. According to Marsden, the
"infallible authority of Scripture" was

> the central feature of the evangelicalism that has survived
> through fundamentalism and into the twentieth century; it
> is a crucial factor in defining its current distinctiveness and
> certainly has something to do with its success.[40]

Virtually every other historian agreed. The traditional interpretation
of fundamentalism is that it was an organized and often militant movement to protect the Bible from any that might question its historical
accuracy and moral integrity—"higher criticism, evolution, Bolshevism, modernism, public education, or any other."[41]

As one would expect, there was a great deal of discussion in
fundamentalist popular literature about the proper role and interpretation of the Bible. Yet it is readily apparent that the Bible was not
defended, revered, or exegeted simply for its own sake nor for the sake
of abstract theological disputations. The Bible was of such concern to
these conservative evangelical Protestants because they saw in it the
basis for a set of eternal and unchanging social norms, most of which
set boundaries on private, gender-related behaviors and attitudes. An
inerrant Bible was the major weapon fielded in the fundamentalist
battle for the conventions of the Victorian separate-spheres ideology.
A significant amount of the inerrancy rhetoric used in the fundamentalist argument was designed to promote and defend this social agenda.

Fundamentalists gave the Bible unique status because they believed it was the only source of eternal divine law. G. Campbell Morgan
contrasted the *New York Times* to the Bible: "The Times is a mirror in
which we see daily change, the Bible is a mirror in which we see things

40. Marsden, "From Fundamentalism to Evangelicalism," in *The Evangelicals: What
They Believe, Who They Are, Where They Are Changing*, rev. ed., ed. David R. Wells
and John Woodbridge (Grand Rapids, Mich.: Baker Book House, 1977), 156–57.
    41. Timothy P. Weber, "The Two-Edged Sword: The Fundamentalist Use of the
Bible," in *The Bible in America*, ed. Nathan O. Hatch and Mark A. Noll (Oxford Univ.
Press, 1982), 102. See also Louis Gasper, *The Fundamentalist Movement, 1930–1965*
(Grand Rapids, Mich.: Baker Book House, 1981), v-vi, 13; Rudnick, *Fundamentalism
and the Missouri Synod*, ix–x; Grant Wacker, *Augustus H. Strong and the Dilemma of
Historical Consciousness* (Macon, Ga.: Mercer Univ. Press, 1985), 17–18, 111; Ferenc
Morton Szasz, *The Divided Mind of Protestant America* (University, Ala.: Univ. of Alabama
Press, 1982), 1; Gatewood, *Controversy in the Twenties*, 12.

that never change—the practices of Time contrasted with the principles of Eternity."[42] Readers of the *Herald and Presbyter* in 1920 were reminded that the Ten Commandments "have never been repealed. . . . We are, everyone of us, whether converted or not, absolutely under the Moral Law, as found in the Ten Commandments."[43] In 1925, the organization known as the Christian Fundamentalists introduced itself in an article in the *Bible Champion.* Its doctrinal statement consisted of nine points of faith. The first was:

> We believe in the Scriptures of the Old and New Testaments as verbally inspired of God and inerrant in the original writings, and that they are of supreme and final authority in faith and life.[44]

Fundamentalists believed that the Bible was the source of knowledge about the divine will and purpose. Such knowledge had primarily moral implications:

> Christian Morality has adopted as its standard the Person of Jesus Christ. We have the record of Christ's . . . teaching in the . . . Scriptures. This standard is not variable. It is fixed and final. . . . Morality . . . is not the unstable and uncertain thing that many people today declare it to be. In the main, the practices which have been socially adopted in Christian communities have reference to the requirements of the Gospel of Christ.[45]

The divine origin and verbal accuracy of the Bible were important to these conservative religious leaders because it was upon scriptural authority that the fundamentalists defended their standards of morality—the social conventions of the late-Victorian middle-class to which they belonged.

The destruction of biblical faith and authority through higher critical methods would have two perilous and direct results, according

42. G. Campbell Morgan, "The Bible and National Life," *King's Business* 2, no. 2 (February 1911): 30.
43. "Changeless Laws of God," *Herald and Presbyter* 91, no. 21 (May 26, 1920): 3.
44. "The Christian Fundamentalists," *Bible Champion* 31, no. 1 (January 1925): 45. See also Mrs. Henry W. Peabody, "The Bible and Women," *Record of Christian Work* 45, no. 3 (March 1926): 154; Arthur T. Pierson, "God's Word to Woman," *Northfield Echoes* 3, no. 3 (1896): 253; D. S. K., "An Important Survey," *Bible Champion* 35, no. 1 (January 1927): 10; "The Bible and Public Safety," *Herald and Presbyter* 92, no. 44 (November 2, 1921): 3; Riley, "Is Society Rotting?" *Christian Fundamentalist*, 10–11.
45. "The New Morality," *Bible Champion* 35, no. 12 (December 1929): 622. See also "Have Times Changed?" *Record of Christian Work* 41, no. 1 (January 1922): 21.

to fundamentalist argument. First, a fall away from faith in and obedience to the Bible would lead to the corruption of individual character and virtue. This was a primary theme in early twentieth-century issues of the *Bible Student and Teacher*. In 1904, E. Fitch Burr warned that "the Higher Criticism" has "in practice conducted [*sic*] to the abandonment of the most fundamental Christian doctrines," and that "if universally accepted" will "leave all men to believe and do according to their liking."[46] In the same year, Francis L. Patton spoke of the relationship between biblical inerrancy and individual virtue:

> The essence of Christianity is that these [biblical] judgments of value . . . are anchored in judgments of fact; *it is the fact that gives them value.* . . . [Without the Bible] your Christianity drops down into moral philosophy. And your morality goes to pieces, except as morality is an instinct, except as virtue happens to be an appetite.[47]

Another writer for the magazine theorized that "ethics that do not rest upon religion are unable to check immorality and sin," and that once the "supernatural sanctions" of "immorality and future judgment, which are found in the Bible only" are weakened, "there is no adequate deterrent from wrong-doing."[48] In 1909, an author for the magazine told his readers that higher criticism has "destroyed moral authority," that "it kills the soul," and "destroys the conscience."[49]

The same concern for individual character and virtue was expressed rather frequently in the *Bible Champion* during the 1910s. An article published in 1913 concluded that

> in the same proportion that men and women have been influenced by these assaults [of higher criticism against the Bible], or ignore the precepts and rules and laws of the Bible, personal morals and piety have declined and vice and irreligion have correspondingly increased.[50]

46. E. Fitch Burr, "To Christian Laymen: Concerning the Higher Criticism," *Bible Student and Teacher* 1, new series, no. 3 (March 1904): 118.

47. Francis L. Patton, "The Present Assault of the Bible: The Issue between Supernaturalism and Atheism," *Bible Student and Teacher*, new series, no. 5 (May 1904): 271.

48. J. B. Remsnyder, "Christianity Placed on Trial," *Bible Student and Teacher* 1, new series, no. 5 (May 1904): 284. See also Albert H. Plumb, "Practical Consequences of the Attack on the Bible: What I Have Seen of the Results," *Bible Student and Teacher* 1, new series, no. 7 (July 1904): 387–95.

49. J. J. Summerbell, "Destructive Criticism Suicidal—Why?" *Bible Student and Teacher* 10, no. 6 (June 1909): 401.

50. "Back to the Old Faith and the Old Book," *Bible Champion* 16, no. 2 (September 1913): 71–72.

Another in the same issue conjectured that "when a boy's faith in the Biblical narratives totters his faith in morality will totter also."[51] A botanical analogy made the same point in 1915: "ethics is a feeble plant. . . . Ethics must draw constant life from religion. . . . Ethics without religion is like fruit without a tree."[52] So impressed with the efficacy of biblical faith, fundamentalists called the Bible the "best crime-deterrent."[53]

In a period of rapid social change, conservative evangelical Protestants used the rhetoric of biblical inerrancy to lend the authority of divine sanction to social convention. They attacked higher criticism of the Bible as "one of the most immoral forces in the world to-day."[54] Absolute belief in and obedience to biblical codes, as interpreted by the fundamentalists, was the only source of individual morality and virtue. Within this system the authority of the Bible was not given practical value apart from its role in undergirding individual piety and the corresponding obedience to certain social conventions and codes of conduct.

The second major theme in the inerrancy rhetoric was that an infallible Bible was the only true source of stability for the larger community—church, nation, and civilization itself. In 1906, A. C. Dixon attributed "a disintegration and a degeneration of public morality" in "some New England communities" to the religion and ethics of "New England Liberalism" because it "attempted to transfer the seat of authority from the will of God as revealed in the Bible to each one's inner consciousness."[55] In 1913, Dixon reasoned that "if the Bible is lost, so is the Sabbath, the home, the church, and finally the nation."[56] An editor of the *Bible Champion* declared that the "Bible is the bulwark of civilization, and if this bulwark is overthrown our civilization must go with it."[57] W. Leon Tucker, a writer for Norris's *Searchlight,* declared that the Bible and the men who believe in its "authenticity" were "the greatest conservers of Government, or civil order and law authority,"

51. L. T. T., "Perils of Non-Belief," *Bible Champion* 16, no. 2 (September 1913): 89.
52. "Ethics and Religion," *Bible Champion* 19, no. 1 (January 1915): 29–30.
53. "The Malicious Menace of Atheism," *Bible Champion* 34, no. 7 (July 1928): 357.
54. "Moral Decline," *Our Hope* 10, no. 5 (November 1913): 273. See also "Christianity and Civilization," *Herald and Presbyter* 85, no. 23 (June 10, 1914): 3–4.
55. A. C. Dixon, "The Fruits of Liberalism in New England," *Bible Student and Teacher* 4, no. 3 (March 1906): 216.
56. Dixon, "The Bible and the Origin of Life," *Western Recorder* 88, no. 39 (July 31, 1913): 1.
57. "Current Comment," *Bible Champion* 19, no. 1 (January 1915): 29.

and that "the Bible is the sheet anchor of liberty."[58] The same appeal
to the national welfare was made in the *Herald and Presbyter:*

> Our nation can exist only as its people have the proper
> character, and this character can be attained and maintained
> only as the people are acquainted with the truths and teach-
> ings of the Bible. From the Bible come the only sufficient
> teachings as to God and truth and justice and law and
> obedience and order and human welfare.[59]

Already by 1913, fundamentalists blamed the "disregard, dis-
belief, and denial of the Holy Scriptures as the Word of God" for
changes in gender-related *mores*—"the gross sins of private life, the
appalling corruption in public life, the indecency and licentiousness of
popular amusements, the profanation of the Sabbath, the indifference
and contempt of the majority for religion."[60] By 1920, fundamentalists
blamed higher criticism of the Bible for the revolution in manners and
morals. Much of this material consisted of commentary on changes in
the attitudes and behavior of women. Fundamentalists heralded faith
in the infallibility of the Bible as the only cure. Norris preached that
the flapper—"the little bobbed-haired, frizzle-headed, gum chewing,
painted-lipped, flapper-tailed girl"—was a product of a moral breakdown: "There was a time . . . that people believed the Bible was the
Word of God. . . . What do you find now? . . . You find the Bible
torn to shreds."[61] In 1929, John Roach Straton yearned for a return to
"the old-fashioned home, where children were taught to obey their
parents; where there was a family altar; and where the members of the
home found their chief satisfaction within the home." He attributed
the decay of society to a shortage of "men who believed the Bible" and
women

58. W. Leon Tucker, "Unmakable, Unbreakable, and Unshakable Book," *Searchlight*
2, no. 20 (April 4, 1924): 2.

59. "The Bible and Public Safety," *Herald and Presbyter*, 3. See also Philip Mauro,
" 'We Want a Bible!': H. G. Wells, in 'The Salvaging of Civilization,' Recognizes the
Great Need of These Times," *Moody Bible Institute Monthly* 21, no. 11 (July 1921):
472–73.

60. "Appeal to the Christian Ministry and Laity," *Bible Champion* 16, no. 1 (August
1913): 31. This is an extract from an appeal to ministers and lay people to join the
Bible League of North America and to subscribe to its journal, the *Bible Champion*.
See also " 'The Bible Champion' Dons Armor to Gird against Skeptics," *Bible Champion*
17, no. 4 (April 1914): 168–69.

61. Norris, "Concrete Sin and Concrete Remedy," *Searchlight* 6, no. 34 (July 6,
1923): 1. See also "Have Times Changed?" *Record of Christian Work* 41, no. 1 (January
1922): 21.

who did not wear their complexions in the bureau drawer; who were not past-masters in bridge-whist, nor finished artists in the foxtrot, . . . women who would not brook familiarities from men; who found their homes more attractive than the playhouses; who knew more about their Bible than about Ibsen; who did not qualify for high society by a record in the divorce courts; . . . who would rather own a baby than a pug dog.[62]

Every ill suffered by the middle-class Victorian family at the turn of the century was attributed to a departure from absolute faith in the truth and accuracy of the Bible. Norris blamed it for the decrease in birthrates and a "revolt against motherhood" on the part of American women.[63] The rapid increase in the divorce rate was explained as a logical result of the "revolt" against Paul's teachings in the Bible.[64] The cure for divorce, said an article in the *Western Recorder*, "is the restoration of the Bible to its proper place. . . . Let the husband and wife realize their God-appointed sphere and duties."[65] The "new morality" was decried in the *Bible Champion* in 1929 because it "totally repudiates the Bible as a guide to life" and because within it "the marriage bond is very loosely held or not regarded at all in many instances."[66] An anonymous author in the *Bible Champion* in 1927 accused "the wave of anti-Scripture" of destroying "the sanctity of the home" and the institution of marriage.[67] An editorial in the *Western Recorder* cited the replacing of the Bible with sociology as a source of knowledge about the family as one of the main dangers to the family. "Back to the Bible," it concluded, "means back to the home and the God-ordained family."[68] The appeal to scripture constituted an appeal to the fundamentalists' interpretation of scripture, in this case to supposedly scriptural foundations of the conventional gender roles and

62. Straton, "A Plea for the Old Fashion," *Watchman-Examiner* 7 (May 29, 1919): 864.
63. Norris, "Concrete Sin and Concrete Remedy," *Searchlight,* 1.
64. See H. W. Tilden, "Paul's Idea of Woman and of Marriage," *Western Recorder* 69, no. 31 (June 13, 1895): 1.
65. "Divorce," *Western Recorder* 86, no. 52 (November 2, 1911): 8.
66. A. Z. C., "The New Morality," *Bible Champion* 35, no. 12 (December 1929): 623. See also Norris, "Home Foundation of All Things, Says Rev. J. Frank Norris," *Searchlight* 2, no. 25 (April 22, 1920): 2; Cassius Wakefield, "Value of Biblical Supernatural," *Call to the Colors* 1, no. 12 (April 1926): 188–90.
67. D. S. K., "An Important Survey," *Bible Champion* 35, no. 1 (January 1927): 9–11.
68. "The Family," *Western Recorder* 86, no. 15 (February 16, 1911): 8. See also Richard W. Lewis, "A Family Forum," *Moody Bible Institute Monthly* 31, no. 9 (May 1931): 447.

social codes of the Victorian Protestant middle class. As A. C. Dixon put it, "this Bible has decided what home means, what motherhood means, what wife-hood means."[69]

The new openness about sexuality, particularly female sexuality, evident after 1910 fueled a fundamentalist outcry against "sex hygiene" classes and other public discussions of sexual behavior, venereal disease, and reproductive anatomy. The only "anti-toxin" recommended for the "plague of sexology" was religion, and "the book which society needs to study is not so much physiology, as the Bible."[70] One Bible champion told of his avoidance of sexual impurity:

> . . . into his youthful hands there had come no books on the sex problem; that he had never been privileged in his youth to visit a museum of anatomy, but that the Bible had been read through and through in his home in family worship; that he had been introduced to the problems of sex life by its sacred literature; that he had learned of God's ideal for the fellowship of men and women in domestic life.[71]

Fundamentalists looked to the Bible for answers and armor against the frightening social disruptions of the period. They needed an infallible Bible because their defense of Victorian social and sexual conventions depended heavily on the authority of divine revelation—in this case, divine revelation of social relations and morality. The controversy over the Bible was more than an intellectual or theological debate. It was related to a larger and, to the general American public, more personal and concrete disruption in gender roles and identity.[72] Americans after

69. Dixon, "Sermon," *Western Recorder* 92, no. 20 (February 22, 1917): 6–7.
70. "Sex Hygiene," *Herald and Presbyter* 83, no. 29 (July 17, 1912): n.p.
71. Robert McWatty Russell, "Christian Education: Its Relation to Modern World Life," *Christian Workers Magazine* 20, no. 3 (November 1919): 182.
72. Other historians have expressed some skepticism about the purely theological nature of the inerrancy debate. Lefferts A. Loetscher was troubled by the timing of the controversy—at least a decade after the 1880s when the first articles about the new criticism were published in the *Presbyterian Review*. He concluded that such a lag "is indication that the onset of this kind of theological warfare was motivated by something other or at least more than the theological issues themselves." Loetscher, *The Broadening Church* (Philadelphia: Univ. of Pennsylvania Press, 1954), 35.
Virginia Lieson Brereton discovered a great deal of inconsistency in fundamentalists' interpretation of biblical texts. She concluded that the doctrine of inerrancy "served more as a protective barrier between the faithful and the 'apostate' than as a true predictor of how fundamentalists would interpret scripture. As long as they were combatting the higher critics and their attitudes, fundamentalists could easily unite around the standard of inerrancy. However, their response on anything but a symbolic

1880 began to feel "cut loose from this sure anchor"—the Bible and all the self-understandings and social conventions that Bible-based Protestant evangelicalism represented. "As a consequence," wrote an editor for the *Bible Student and Teacher*, "a great mass of thoughtless people—and of thoughtful people too—have had their faith in the claims of the Bible weakened or destroyed, and are aimlessly asking what they are to believe and whom they are to believe."[73]

Evolution

In the 1920s, fundamentalists chose evolutionary theory as one of their major battlegrounds, and historians interpreted fundamentalism since 1920 as essentially opposed to evolutionary theory. Szasz listed evolution among the three major issues facing American churches during the period.[74] Marsden observed that the "most evident" component of fundamentalists' alarm during the 1920s was their struggle against evolutionism.[75] Gatewood characterized the evolution controversy as the climax of "the martial quality of their combat," their use of military language and biblical symbols calculated to "conjure up the image of . . . epic struggle between rival contenders for the faith."[76] James R. Moore's study of post-Darwinian controversies assumed that there was something normative, or at least especially revealing, about the Fundamentalist-Modernist dispute over evolutionary theory because it marked an important final collision between modernity and older "beliefs about certainty and fixity."[77]

---

level hardly constituted a united front." Virginia Lieson Brereton, "Protestant Fundamentalist Bible Schools, 1882–1940" (Ph.D. diss., Columbia Univ., 1984), 70–71.

An example of the inconsistency with which fundamentalists employed the inerrancy argument—and the consistency with which they affirmed standard Victorian gender roles and morality—is obvious in the following attack on Mormonism. "The Mormons are great literalists. They believe in the literal interpretation of the Bible. Hence when they read how Abraham had more wives than one; that he was the friend of God; that he at last is to sit down in the Kingdom, that seems to be good evidence that they should follow suit and do likewise. They take little account of the progress of the human race and of knowledge. Their ideal is to return to past conceptions rather than to go forward to a higher type of life." William E. La Rue, "The Menace of Mormonism," *Watchman-Examiner* 9, no. 2 (January 13, 1921): 46.

73. "Noted Editorial and Critical: Cutting Loose from Authority," *Bible Student and Teacher* 6, no. 6 (June 1907): 409.

74. Szasz, *The Divided Mind of American Protestantism*, 1.

75. Marsden, *Fundamentalism and American Culture*, 141.

76. Gatewood, *Controversy in the Twenties*, 6.

77. James R. Moore, *The Post-Darwinian Controversies: A Study of the Protestant Struggle to Come to Terms with Darwin in Great Britain and America, 1870–1900* (New York: Cambridge Univ. Press, 1979), 14–15.

Fundamentalists did not, however, attack evolutionary theory so much for its own sake as for the threat it posed to social conventions and *mores*. Fundamentalists approached evolution in the same way they did higher criticism of the Bible. They postulated a direct and necessary link between faith (their brand of conservative Protestant evangelicalism) and morals, and then proceeded to demonstrate that evolutionary theory destroyed both. Dixon, for example, argued that evolutionary theory had its roots in "paganism" (Greek philosophy) and was, therefore, antithetic to Christianity.[78] A constant theme of J. Frank Norris's during the 1920s was that evolutionary theory destroyed faith. "Evolution," he declared, "has our schools by the throat . . . destroying the faith of our young people in the faith of our Fathers."[79]

For fundamentalists, Christian faith was impossible without a corresponding affirmation of the inerrant truth of the Bible. Because evolutionary theory posited a "nonbiblical" understanding of the origin of life, particulary human life, the fundamentalists could and did use their entire arsenal of biblical inerrancy rhetoric against it. And like their inerrancy rhetoric, the attack on evolution functioned to reinforce conventional Victorian gender ideology and roles. In an antievolution speech before the Texas legislature in 1923, Norris rejected evolutionary theory because it denied the Genesis account of creation, which "is the foundation upon which everything rests." He reiterated his position: "The primary danger of evolution is that it will destroy faith in the Bible."[80] From Norris's perspective, anarchy was to government what evolution was to religion; "they are Siamese twins."[81] It was telling that Norris concluded his antievolution address to his state legislature with conventional home-protection language, arguing that the defense of the Christian home was the primary objective of antievolution legislation: "The home is God's first institution. . . . Let us do all we can to protect that institution, pass . . . laws to protect it and let none invade its sacred precincts."[82] For Norris, the issues of evolution and the Christian home were inseparable.

78. Dixon, "Evangelism Old and New II," *Watchman* 86, no. 6 (February 11, 1904): 10–11.

79. Norris, *Searchlight* 6, no. 14 (February 16, 1923): 4.

80. Norris, "Address on Evolution before Texas Legislature," *Searchlight* 6, no. 15 (February 23, 1923): 3.

81. Norris, "The Reign of Law vs. the Reign of Anarchy," *Baptist Fundamentalist* 10, no. 40 (August 12, 1927): 4.

82. Norris, "Address on Evolution before Texas Legislature," *Searchlight,* 3. See also Norris, "The Reign of Law vs. the Reign of Anarchy," *Baptist Fundamentalist,* 4.

The second major contention of antievolution fundamentalists was that evolutionary theory destroyed morality because it reduced human beings to the status of animals or machines, thereby destroying their responsibility as moral agents.[83] In 1913, a writer for the *Western Recorder* alerted his readers to the true character of evolutionary theory: Evolution said there was no such thing as free will and, hence, "there is no such thing as moral responsibility."[84] Similarly, the *Watchman* concluded that evolutionists "have contended that man is no more accountable for his nature, his acts and his products than an animal or a tree."[85] The first of a list of destructive principles promulgated by modernist "jazz theologians," according to *Herald and Presbyter* writer John C. King, was that humankind was "just an improved beast."[86] Norris complained that within evolutionary theory "man is reduced to a mere machine. There is no longer any personal accountability of the soul to its God."[87] Because evolutionary theory, according to fundamentalists, portrayed human nature as bestial and arbitrary, it destroyed the basis on which moral responsibility and action rested.

Just what kinds of evolution-induced immorality concerned fundamentalists most? Their antievolutionary strategy had practical as well as theoretical ramifications because they often directly linked evolutionary theory to the decline of conventional gender indoctrination and behavior. Norris was very graphic: "It [evolution] breeds free-loveism. The apes . . . have never had a marriage license. . . . They change mates frequently."[88] Evolution, he preached, leads to "liberalism of the Sabbath, liberalism of the law, liberalism on love, liberalism on divorce, liberalism on morals, liberalism on doctrine."[89] Within these discussions of morality, consistent reference is made particularly to the moral conditions of girls and women—to the revolution in manners and morals

83. See Gatewood, *Controversy in the Twenties*, 22–23.

84. "The Causes of Social Degeneration," *Western Recorder* 88, no. 10 (January 9, 1913): 2.

85. "The Causes of Social Degeneration," *Watchman* 94 (August 29, 1912): 7.

86. John C. King, "Jazz Theology," *Herald and Presbyter* 93, no. 27 (July 5, 1922): 6.

87. Norris, "Address on Evolution before Texas Legislature," *Searchlight*, 3. See also S. M. Ellis, "Secularized Public Schools—The Nation's Menace," *King's Business* 15, no. 10 (October 1924): 622–24; I. W. Canfield, "The 'New System of Morals'!" *Western Recorder* 52, no. 14 (December 3, 1885): 1; "Prof. Dana on Evolution," *Western Recorder* 46, no. 18 (January 15, 1880): 4; "The Vile Corruption of the Young," *Our Hope* 34, no. 8 (February 1928): 467.

88. Norris, "Another Example," *Searchlight* 6, no. 22 (April 13, 1923): 6.

89. Norris, "The First and Second Creations," *Searchlight* 5, no. 48 (October 13, 1922): 2.

of the 1910s and 1920s. Norris's list included divorce, crimes committed by women, and girls who were drinking and smoking.[90] In a
well-publicized and well-attended debate on evolution, John Roach
Straton began his speech this way:

> The wave of animalism which is sweeping over the world
> today, and the degradation of the modern dance, the sen-
> sualism of the modern theater, the glorification of the flesh
> in modern styles, the sex suggestion of modern literature,
> the substitution of dogs for babies, the appalling divorce
> evil, have all come about because of this degrading philos-
> ophy of animalism which evolution is spreading over the
> earth.[91]

Straton was a gifted rhetorician. One must assume that the changing
mores of the 1920s were both a primary concern and his most effective
and popular case against evolution because he began his part of the
debate with such an appeal.

Straton was not the only fundamentalist to use such an appeal.
Evolution was the most "fundamental cause" of "social degeneracy"
because, in an article published in the *Western Recorder,* evolution was
associated with unconventional behavior on the part of women. It was
linked with the writings of Henrik Ibsen and "other unmoral and
immoral plays and novels of the day" that contain the message that
"loving wives and mothers [should] forsake the home and children in
order to 'live their life' as vanity and selfishness ordain."[92] "Materialistic
education," warned a writer for the *Watchman-Examiner* in 1921, has
been the cause of a "moral letdown in the habits of women," including
immodest dress, improper dancing, frequenting immoral plays, and
indulging in smoking, gambling, swearing, and joy-riding."[93] The
same fear was mirrored in a 1928 issue of the *Bible Champion.* It predicted
that because of evolution "we are at the present time on the verge of
a moral breakdown among women."[94]

Two conclusions can be drawn about the close rhetorical link
between antievolutionism and women's manners and morality. First,

90. Norris, "Address on Evolution before Texas Legislature," *Searchlight,* 3.
91. Straton, "Straton Wins Evolution Debate: 3000 Cheer and Laugh," *Searchlight*
7, no. 12 (February 8, 1924): 4.
92. "The Causes of Social Degeneration," *Western Recorder,* 2.
93. "Is Respect for Women Waning?" *Watchman-Examiner* 9 (September 8, 1921):
1142.
94. W. G. Bennett, "Evolution versus Civilization," *King's Business* 34, no. 9 (September 1928): 489.

evolution was not bothersome to fundamentalists simply as a set of scientific, philosophical, or theological principles. They repeatedly and explicitly pointed to a concrete source of their disagreement with and fear of evolutionary theory: the effect they believed the theory had on morality and social conventions regarding family life and gender roles. Second, the widespread appeal of the antievolutionary movement[95] rested, to a significant degree, on its defense of Victorian gender roles and domestic conventions because gender issues were such a central part of popular antievolution rhetoric. Americans may not have been able or inclined to follow the convoluted intellectual debates over Darwinian theory, but they were aware of the shifts and disruptions occurring in their domestic lives and in their own understanding of who they were as men and as women and what they were to do.[96]

Modernism

Marsden defined fundamentalism as "originally a broad coalition of anti-modernists," composed of elements of revivalism, Keswick holiness, dispensationalism, and Princeton orthodoxy that "were united

95. Robert E. Wenger noted that several contemporary observers emphasized the popularity of antievolutionism in the 1920s. One writer for *The Nation* in 1923 concluded that such feelings were "the normal American condition"; another that "ninety percent of the population was fundamentalist on the evolution issue, either actively or by its silence." *The Nation* 116 (June 6, 1923): 645; and Miriam Allen DeFord, "The War against Evolution," *The Nation* 120 (May 20, 1925): 565. Both were quoted in Wenger, "Social Thought in American Fundamentalism," (Ph.D. diss., Univ. of Nebraska, 1973), 56.

Marsden, too, concluded that antievolution was the issue that really brought the general public into the fundamentalist camp. "Both the premillennial movement and denominational fundamentalism had been confined mostly to the Northern states, but antievolution swept throught the South and found new constituencies in rural areas everywhere. Many people with little or no interest in fundamentalism's doctrinal concerns were drawn into the campaign to keep Darwinism out of America's churches." He attributed the "meteoric rise" of the antievolution issue to prominence to the "World War I notion of saving civilization from German theology and its superman philosophy." Yet, Marsden already admitted that many followers had little or no interest in matters of doctrine. Hence, I think the disruptions in gender roles provide a better explanation. See *Fundamentalism and American Culture,* 170.

96. Gatewood recognized the symbolic nature of the evolution controversy. "Since such fundamentalist crusaders as Martin made virtually no distinction between organic evolution, Darwinism, and evolutionary philosophy, they found little difficulty in linking evolution with atheism, secularistic trends, 'godless education,' sexual immorality, disintegration of the family, German militarism, and Communism. In their vocabulary, evolution became a catchall, scare word meaning modern evils in general." *Controversy in the Twenties,* 20.

in their common resolve to concede nothing to the inroads of modernism."[97] So central have theological issues been to the interpretation of the fundamentalist movement that the emergence of fundamentalism during our period was most often referred to in histories of American religion as the "fundamentalist-modernist controversy."[98]

Yet, as Sandeen has convincingly argued, the fundamentalist party did not defend Christian tradition against innovation, despite their claims to be the only true defenders of orthodoxy.

> Both dispensationalism and the Princeton Theology were marked by doctrinal innovations and emphases which must not be confused with apostolic belief, Reformation theology, or nineteenth-century evangelicalism. . . . The assumption that only the modernists reconstructed their theological position during the intellectual crisis of the late nineteenth century cannot be maintained.[99]

Both sides of the controversy were innovators. One cannot take fundamentalist claims to theological orthodoxy at face value.

Another important interpreter of fundamentalism, Marsden, attributed the hardening of fundamentalism into theological and political reaction—the "great reversal" of the 1920s—to theological debates. Marsden claimed that because the rise of the Social Gospel and the fundamentalist's great reversal occurred simultaneously in the late 1910s and 1920s, the new militant defensiveness on the fundamentalist side must be a reaction to the liberal theology preached by Social Gospel advocates.[100] This explanation of the great reversal is doubtful. First, there is little indication that more technical theological disputes between the two parties could account for the remarkable popularity of fundamentalism across such a broad spectrum of the American population in the early twentieth century. Janet Forsythe Fishburn's investigation of the Social Gospel movement indicated, on the other hand, that at the level of regular church membership, Social Gospel Chris-

97. Marsden, *Reforming Fundamentalism: Fuller Seminary and the New Evangelicalism* (Grand Rapids, Mich.: Wm. B. Eerdmans, 1987), 10, 32.

98. The term *modernism,* when referring only to liberal or modern theology, was used infrequently in these materials. Generally the term functioned as a label for a wide range of phenomena such as higher criticism, evolution, and Bolshevism. Consequently, there is less fundamentalist discussion of liberal or modern theology than one might expect.

99. Sandeen, "Toward a Historical Interpretation of the Origins of Fundamentalism," *Church History* 36 (1967): 83.

100. Marsden, *Fundamentalism and American Culture,* 90–92.

tianity differed little from "the practice and methods of the conservative evangelical tradition." "In practice," she argued, like the conservative evangelicals "the salvation of the social order depended [for the Social Gospelers] on the influence of individual Christians as the primary mode of evangelism."[101] The Social Gospel as such simply did not have the same impact on the public as did fundamentalism, nor the same impact on ordinary church people as it did on fundamentalist scholars and church professionals, and there is little mention of the Social Gospel by name in the popular fundamentalist press.

Second, Fishburn also cited evidence that the Social Gospel movement, like fundamentalism, was in its own way a reaction to changes in gender roles and ideology prompted by the social turmoil of the last decades of the nineteenth century. She observed the emphasis on moral heroism and Christian manhood, and the staunch defense of the middle-class "Christian" family by the Social Gospel leaders, and concluded that the Social Gospel was to a considerable extent a reaction, particularly for the men, to gender disruptions and insecurities.[102] Although a detailed analysis of the Social Gospel movement is beyond the scope of this study, it is interesting to hypothesize that this "liberal" movement could be understood not so much as a primary enemy against which the fundamentalists marshalled themselves but rather as a related, parallel but not identical, response by church people to the same late nineteenth-century gender crisis compounded by the revolution in manners and morals of the 1910s and 1920s.

So, while the fundamentalists presented themselves as the preservers of the true Protestant heritage—the fundamentals of the faith—the popular literature on the fundamentalists' side indicates that the debate was not particularly theological, especially as the conservative case was presented to the general membership of the churches. The rhetoric used by the fundamentalists in their attacks on modern or liberal theology expressed the same deep uneasiness with new currents in gender roles and social codes as did their language in the evolution and inerrancy debates. It was not so much traditional theology they were defending as it was traditional gender ideology.

As early as 1886, the link between modernism and immorality was established by a writer for the journal *Bibliotheca Sacra*. In an article critical of the "new theology," John F. Todd discerned that

101. Janet Forsythe Fishburn, *The Fatherhood of God and the Victorian Family*, (Philadelphia: Fortress Press, 1981): 166.
102. Fishburn, *The Fatherhood of God and the Victorian Family*, 95–96, 102–27, 156–66.

the inevitable tendency of these doctrines is to lessen men's
sense of accountability, and to encourage them in sin and
impenitence. . . . The very foundations of society are
threatened by men in multitudes who have cast off all faith
in God, all fear of judgment to come, all sense of moral
obligation. [103]

By 1920, fundamentalists spoke often of modernism and the deterioration of morality. Some estimated that "modernism has done more
to bring about the present moral degeneracy than all other influences
brought together." [104] "Bad practice," another warned, "has its roots in
bad philosophy, and the social disorders and mischief that abound will
never be corrected until the false philosophy which breeds them is
exposed." [105] The Bible Crusaders blamed liberal theology for World
War I and a grave "moral breakdown," the result of which "the nation
is inundated by a great tidal wave of crime, embracing law violations
of all kinds. Sabbath desecration, an alarming increase in divorces, and
a tremendous drop in moral standards." [106] Modern or liberal theology
was also associated with higher criticism of the Bible and was accused
of destroying morality because it destroyed faith in the Bible. [107]

Fundamentalists leveled these charges against modernism with
concrete breaches of conventional morality in mind. They did not ask
their readers and listeners to engage in abstract philosophical or theological speculation. Rather, a direct connection was established between modern theology and the deterioration of home life and
conventional marriage:

Today some of the blessed sacred meanings of [love and
home] . . . are being tainted and spoiled. Those among us
today who would take away Christ's distinctly supernatural

103. John E. Todd, "New Theology," *Bibliotheca Sacra* 43 (1886): 355. See also
Clarence Bouma, "The Educational Challenge to Fundamental Christianity," *Christian
Fundamentalist* 2, no. 5 (November 1928): 23; "The New Morality," *Bible Champion*,
623; "Dickey Burton's Divorce," *Christian Fundamentalist* 5, no. 4 (October 1931):
126.
104. A. Z. Conrad, "Fatal Errors of Modernism, " *Herald and Presbyter* 93, no. 28
(July 12, 1922): 7.
105. John McDowell, "Christ and National Unrest," *Record of Christian Work* 41,
no. 1 (January 1922): 29.
106. "The Bible Crusader's Challenge," *Christian Fundamentals in School and Church*
8, no. 2 (April–June 1926): 54.
107. See N. S. McPherson, "Why I Am a Fundamentalist," *Moody Bible Institute
Monthly* 31, no. 5 (January 1931): 254; "The Crime Wave," *Call to the Colors* 1, no.
7 (November 1925): 116.

meaning may well stop and weigh the influence of merely cultural religion as seen in this most sensitive thermometer.[108]

One fundamentalist leader reduced the decline of Christendom into heathenism to the fact that "family life is increasingly desecrated."[109] Still another blamed the "revolt of youth" which occurred in the 1910s and 1920s on modernists.[110] The "crimes" for which modernism or liberal theology was blamed were not felonious or violent; the "crimes" mentioned were almost always deviations from conventional Victorian domestic patterns and sexual *mores*. Like higher criticism of the Bible and evolutionary theory, modernist theology was scapegoated by fundamentalist leaders and their followers who were afraid and angered by social disruptions, chief among them vast changes in cultural gender ideology and in the actual behavior of men and women around them. By locating an enemy, a source of the evil, perhaps they thought themselves closer to annihilating it.

Seen in the context of gender-role disruptions, fundamentalist theology can be understood more fully. Like all theological formulations, fundamentalist doctrine was profoundly influenced by its social environment. Conservative evangelical Protestant theology reflected real concern and alienation caused by the rapid and unprecedented changes in American society. Disruptions in gender ideology and roles were only part of the social turmoil, yet they affected people in profoundly intense and personal ways. Religious language has often been used to express that which is profoundly intense and personal. It has often been used, as well, to reinforce social structures, hierarchies, and conventions. Fundamentalist theology must be interpreted as the complex phenomenon that it was.

108. S. D. Gordon, "Quiet Talks on the Simple Essentials: Six Woman Words," *Watchman-Examiner* 11 (October 10, 1923): 1330. See also Norris, "The Breakdown of Modern Education," *Searchlight* 2, no. 4 (December 7, 1923): 1; Dixon, "Why I Am an Evangelical Christian and Not a Modernist," *Searchlight* 6, no. 39 (August 10, 1923): 2; Riley, "Is Society Rotting?" *Christian Fundamentalist*, 8–9.

109. "Christendom under the spell of rationalism (or modernism) is becoming more and more akin to the heathen world. The difference between an educated 'heathen' and an educated 'Christian' is being reduced. Family life is increasingly desecrated." "Dr. Reuben Saillens on Modernism," *Christian Fundamentalist* 2, no. 1 (July 1928): 19.

110. "The Revolt of Youth," *Call to the Colors* 2, no. 8 (November 1926): 109. See also "The Vile Corruption of the Young," *Our Hope*, 466–67.

CHAPTER SEVEN

Religion and the Gender Agenda

I DO NOT WANT TO LEAVE this analysis of the rhetoric about gender used by the fundamentalists and their turn-of-the-century predecessors without looking closely at one historian's interpretation of some of the same phenomena. Douglas W. Frank's study, *Less than Conquerors: How Evangelicals Entered the Twentieth Century,* is a sensitive account of the rise of fundamentalism among white North American Protestants. In his discussion of the Keswick movement, Frank took seriously the psychological and emotional impact of corporate industrialization, urbanization, immigration, and other social disruptions as well as the ways in which people meet emotional needs and handle psychological stress by thinking in religious categories and participating in religious communities and causes. The same assumptions ground my own analysis of fundamentalism, so I find much of Frank's work congenial.

What makes Frank's conclusions especially interesting is that they are some ways consistent with mine and yet devoid of attention to the dynamics of gender and the impact they had on late nineteenth-century life in the United States. For example, he wrote accurately of middle-class male life without seeming to know that men's lives differed in significant ways from women's lives. Hence, his description is rendered in artificially gender-neutral terms:

> The middle-class *person* was one—most often male during this time—who saw the opportunities and took them for himself: he grasped his own individual capacities as his only

true endowment and resolved to use that endowment to
enter on a life-time of continual self-expansion, self-
expression, and self-enrichment. To accomplish those ends,
the middle-class *person* had to become a calculating, willful,
and often ruthless individual. . . . He functioned with a
certain abandon, competing shamelessly against his rivals,
undermining any opposition to his self-serving innovations. . . . Bereft of the inherited standards of status or
worth that predominated in a simpler age, the middle-class
person was caught up in a mad race for self-esteem and self-
glory based on his mastery and development of unique
personal characteristics [emphasis mine].[1]

This is a deft description not of the life of the middle-class *person,* but
of the life of the middle-class man, for women were not bereft of their
traditional sources of self-identity and worth (mothering and housekeeping), nor were women encouraged to be competitive, self-expan-
sive, ruthless, or willful. The culturally dominant separate-spheres
ideology dictated just the opposite. Only men cultivated the identity
of the business warrior and the professional elite in order to shore up
their failing sense of gender identity and self-esteem. Keeping women
out of the male sphere was part and parcel of the larger strategy initiated
by middle-class men. Therefore, while Frank perceived accurately that
the middle class was stressed and uncertain because "competitive failure
. . . could easily be construed as personal inferiority," he did not take
it a step further: men, not women, were at risk in business and political
competition. Further, failure in competition with other men was one
thing—disappointing but still manly—but failure to compete suc-
cessfully against the women who were hired into clerical and other
business and industrial positions, or who entered higher education and
the professions, meant for men a loss of clear gender identity itself.
The breakdown of the separate spheres during the period was an in-
tensely unsettling experience, especially so for men, and one overlooked
by Frank. In the end, even Frank's historical interpretation remains a
part of the dominant historiographical tradition in that it ignores
dynamics of gender. It assumes that male selfhood and culture are
universal and normative and that human ideas and behavior are somehow
free of gender packaging.

Frank expanded the discussion of the Keswick movement in a very
helpful way, however, by perceiving in Keswick's emphasis on "the

1. Douglas W. Frank, *Less than Conquerors: How Evangelicals Entered the Twentieth
Century* (Grand Rapids, Mich.: Wm. B. Eerdmans, 1986), 128–29.

victorious life" a response to and defense against a growing sense of failure. Evangelicals—the white, Protestant, "native" middle class— experienced a defeat, "a kind of nest-shaking," because, according to Frank, "they identified themselves with a God who was letting Catholics and Jews take over their political institutions."[2] Although both evangelical men and women must have felt a deep sense of unease over their loss of this kind of cultural and political hegemony, imagine how that sense of defeat was compounded for men who were, at the same time, losing *gender* hegemony—losing their sphere of business, politics and the professions to women. No wonder, among all the holiness groups of the nineteenth century, the one most dominated by middle-class men, the Keswick movement, became militantly fundamentalist in the twentieth century.[3] No wonder, as Frank documented, the rhetoric of the Keswick movement was so full of allusions to failure and defeat.[4]

Had Frank and historians before him considered gender itself— the sets of symbols and taboos that constitute a culture's gender ideology, and the social behaviors and roles determined by culture—he might have discovered a source both of widespread alarm and anger, and of internal unity and motivation, that could account for fundamentalism's wide and popular appeal. Every American of the late-Victorian era faced rapid and unprecedented changes in gender ideology and roles. Every American, rich or poor, postmillennialist or premillennialist, educated or uneducated, in cities or on farms, from the North or from the South, lived at a time when it no longer was clear just what it meant to be male or female.[5] This uncertainty rocked the most basic aspects of human life and experience—self-understanding and esteem, sexual attitudes and behaviors, power and intimacy between mates, and bonds between parent and child.

Religion has always been one of the ways in which humans have understood sexuality and controlled sexual behavior. Fundamentalism

2. Frank, *Less than Conquerors,* 138.

3. George M. Marsden noted how Keswick was a middle-class version of "separatist Holiness groups and Pentecostalism," which, unlike Keswick, appealed to the "socially and economically disinherited." He also observed that, unlike holiness movements of midcentury, Keswick was distinctively "male-dominated and masculinity was equated with power and action." *Fundamentalism and American Culture: The Shaping of Twentieth-Century Evangelicalism, 1870–1925* (New York: Oxford Univ. Press, 1980), 96, 80.

4. See Frank, *Less than Conquerors,* 141–43.

5. An assumption here is that nonwhite Americans were affected by the shifts in traditional gender roles brought about by industrialization and urbanization. A study of gender roles within nonwhite subcultures in this country and of fundamentalism that emerged within nonwhite churches is, however, beyond the scope of this study.

as a religious system functioned in popular American culture to support the gender roles and ideology of the Victorian era well into post-Victorian times. The prevalence of Victorian gender ideology in fundamentalist discourse was consistent through 1930. The fundamentalists used religious appeals and sanctions to reinforce the sexual and social conventions of the separate spheres and to attack woman's movement outside her sphere into paid employment, social reform, electoral politics, and higher education.

One of the most prominent symbols in fundamentalist rhetoric was the divinized home. In their popular discourse, fundamentalists replaced the church with the Victorian home as the primary religious institution. Language investing the home with sacred meaning and qualities reinforced both the location of religion and morality within the home and the election of woman as religious agent and moral guardian. Fundamentalists used divinized-home rhetoric to weight their arguments against divorce and other threats to conventional Victorian marriage and family life. Also, by emphasizing the holiness of the home and domestic duties over the church and ministerial duties, fundamentalists encouraged even the most religious and reform-minded women to choose marriage and motherhood over church ministry and social mission.

Fundamentalist ministers were especially eager to reduce the influence of women in the church because it had, over the course of the nineteenth century, become a feminized institution. Churchmen had a very difficult time achieving a sense of manhood within such a professional *ethos.* Consequently, fundamentalist clergymen attempted to reclaim American Protestantism for men and masculinity. They fought feminized religion by trying to limit women's access to positions of church leadership and by engaging in aggressive and militant polemic. Christianity and church ministry were recast as truly masculine pursuits; the ideal Christian as a warrior.

The most rigid and belligerent phase of fundamentalism coincided with the revolution in manners and morals from 1910 to 1930. Fundamentalists' alarm increased dramatically, and they issued shrill denunciations of new amusements for young people such as the theater, popular fiction, movies, and dance halls. Fundamentalists expressed intense dismay at changes occurring in the sexual behavior and social manners of young women. Middle-class women after 1910 more frequently engaged in premarital sex, used artificial birth control, and underwent abortions. The flapper of the 1920s was an affront to the Victorian ideal of virtuous womanhood. Fundamentalists saw in her a sure indication of personal and social corruption.

Fundamentalists responded to late- and post-Victorian developments in gender roles and ideology by reasserting the ideology of female subordination and separate gender-related spheres that gained cultural dominance before the Civil War. This social agenda was reflected even in the central theological tenets of fundamentalism. The New Woman of the 1880s and 1890s contributed significantly to dispensationalists' distaste for their times and pessimism about their future. Virtually any behavior that departed from Victorian sexual norms and domestic conventions was decried as a sign of the end times. Although pessimistic about changes in gender ideology and roles, premillennialists were optimistic about the power of salvation inherent in the separate-spheres ideology and middle-class Victorian family conventions of their recent past.

Fundamentalists based most of their attacks on gender-related social change on the premise of divine law revealed in an infallible Bible. Conversely, the rhetoric of biblical inerrancy derived its vitality and salience from the way it functioned to reinforce the fundamentalists' popular social agenda. Similarly, fundamentalist refutation of evolutionary theory and modernist theology reflected the same complexity. Fundamentalists identified Christian faith and morality with Victorian gender ideology and domestic conventions. They represented evolution and modernism as destroyers of faith and morality. Consequently, the practical outcome of their theological and moral discourse about evolution and modernism was a religiously sanctioned defense of a particular set of social hierarchies, norms, and values.

The maintenance of Victorian gender ideology and roles was a political agenda with far-reaching consequences for the distribution of wealth, electoral politics, social policy, the labor movement, health care delivery, public education, and economic growth. Yet George M. Marsden and others have concluded that, with few exceptions, fundamentalism "does not appear to have been identified with any political stand." He surmised that fundamentalists advocated only "personal ethics."[6] Such a conclusion was possible only because he did not consider

6. Marsden, *Fundamentalism and American Culture*, 208. Hardesty interpreted fundamentalism in the same way. "A large segment of the church became fundamentalist, more concerned with theological, intellectual questions than with ethical, social issues; more concerned with preserving the faith than Christianizing society." Nancy A. Hardesty, *Women Called to Witness: Evangelical Feminism in the 19th Century* (Nashville: Abingdon Press, 1984), 157. Robert E. Wenger, too, characterized fundamentalists as "preachers who saw their primary duty as one of converting individuals to Christ, rather than revising the social structure." "Social Thought in American Fundamentalism" (Ph.D. diss., Univ. of Nebraska, 1973), 216.

the powerful and systematic political nature of fundamentalism's gender agenda. To the extent that fundamentalism can be identified by and with a staunchly conservative defense of the ideology of female subordination and the separate spheres of activity, it was thoroughly political.

Fundamentalism was not, of course, the only movement in America intent on preserving the subordination of women and the Victorian separate spheres. Although a broader analysis of American culture from 1880 to 1930 is beyond the scope of this study, some examples are both illuminating and tantalizing. One dedicated defender of Victorian gender ideology during the period was the medical profession. In many respects, physicians replaced ministers as the real holy men, the priests of industrial and technological society as it stabilized in the nineteenth century.

> The medical system is not just a service industry. It is a powerful instrument of social control, replacing organized religion as a prime source of sexist ideology and an enforcer of sex roles.[7]

Historians have documented how medical doctors sanctioned and preserved domesticity with their medical theories and advice.[8] The medical profession after the turn of the century began adopting standards of professional qualification that moved against "irregular" medical practitioners (many of them women, especially the midwives), and medical schools began to limit or to deny completely women's access to medical training.[9]

There was also a backlash against women in higher education and teaching. A full-scale campaign was waged during the period to counter

7. Barbara Ehrenreich and Deidre English, *Complaints and Disorders: The Sexual Politics of Sickness* (Old Westbury, N.Y.: The Feminist Press, 1973), 83. See also James Reed, *From Private Vice to Public Virtue: The Birth Control Movement in American Society since 1830* (New York: Basic Books, 1978), 40ff; Linda Gordon, *Woman's Body, Woman's Right: A Social History of Birth Control in America* (New York: Penguin Books, 1977), 170–71; John D'Emilio and Estelle Freedman, *Intimate Matters: A History of Sexuality in America* (New York: Harper & Row, 1986), 67, 146–48.

8. See Carroll Smith-Rosenberg, "Puberty to Menopause: The Cycle of Femininity in Nineteenth-Century America," in *Clio's Consciousness Raised*, ed. Mary S. Hartman and Lois Banner (New York: Harper & Row, 1974), 23–37. Smith-Rosenberg, *Disorderly Conduct: Visions of Gender in Victorian America* (New York: Alfred A. Knopf, 1985), 11; William Leach, *True Love and Perfect Union: The Feminist Reform of Sex and Society* (New York: Basic Books, 1980), 350.

9. Catherine Clinton, *The Other Civil War: American Women in the Nineteenth Century* (New York: Hill & Wang, 1984), 145.

the feminization of education by reducing the number of women school-teachers.[10] Schools forced women into "home economics" tracks, and many married women lost their teaching positions.[11]

There was a secular glorification of the home, too. In the 1920s the home was glamorized with new "time-saving" household appliances and theories of childrearing.[12]

Fundamentalist ministers were not the only men who tried to reassert traditional notions of masculinity during this time of cultural and social stress. For example, Ernest Hemingway's exaggerated masculine demeanor and the style and content of his literature were a stark contrast to the sentimental stories and novels of the nineteenth century, many of which were written by and for women.[13] Also, in the 1920s, men re-created exclusively male worlds and male competition. The post-World War I decade was the great age of spectator sports.

> Most men needed . . . a hero with whom to identify in order to clarify (or at least fabricate) their own identity. Not having found him on the battlefield, they looked to the gridiron and the [baseball] diamond.[14]

In the academy, programs encouraging competitive male athletics sprang up all over the country during the period, providing "warrior" activities for even refined, educated men.[15] And between 1918 and 1930 the number of male "service clubs" quintupled, recreating a place from which women were banned.[16]

Within American Protestantism, fundamentalists were not alone in their attempt to reclaim the church for men. Methods and rhetoric varied, but Social Gospel theologians and ministers supported the separate-spheres ideology, too. Like the fundamentalists, these "liberal" churchmen spoke of the home as the most sacred and important social

10. Clinton, *The Other Civil War,* 127.
11. See Leach, *True Love and Perfect Union,* 349; D'Emilio and Freedman, *Intimate Matters,* 146, 190; Clinton, *The Other Civil War,* 127.
12. See Lois Banner, *Women in Modern America: A Brief History* (New York: Harcourt Brace Jovanovich, 1974), 142–44; W. Elliot Brownlee and Mary M. Brownlee, *Women in the American Economy: A Documentary History, 1675–1929* (New Haven: Yale Univ. Press, 1976), 38.
13. See Diane Johnson, "Mama and Papa," *New York Times Book Review* (July 19, 1987): 3.
14. Peter G. Filene, *Him/Her/Self: Sex Roles in Modern America,* 2d ed. (Baltimore: Johns Hopkins Univ. Press, 1986), 138–39.
15. Peter N. Stearns, *Be a Man! Males in Modern Society* (New York: Holmes and Meier Publishing, 1979), 102–3.
16. Stearns, *Be a Man!* 142.

institution and recommended that women remain within its confines. Unlike fundamentalists, who tried to remasculinize the church with aggressive language and militant posturing, Social Gospelers countered the feminization of religion by reasserting the church's role in the public, political world of men. The Social Gospel theologians wanted the church and its male ministers active again "at the very center of society," and they wanted women at home. Liberal ministers asserted their masculinity by claiming their proper place in the exclusively male world of urban politics, social reform, and public service.[17]

Fundamentalism was not the only conservative reaction to changes in gender ideology and roles, but it was an unusually popular one. Fundamentalists defended the "old fashioned" ways with the symbols of evangelical Protestantism, and they used evangelicalism's most successful campaign tactic, the revival. To the revival they added a host of popular magazines and newsletters; hundreds of conferences, summer camps, and retreats; radio shows and networks; and finally television campaigns and stations. Conservative Protestant evangelicalism, with a world-view, a vocabulary, and a variety of effective institutional and communal options widely understood and affirmed by Americans up and down the social scale, was one of the most accessible protest movements for that sizable chunk of the population that identified itself in some way with Protestantism.

When Marsden wrote about the re-emergence of fundamentalism as a major social and political force in the 1970s and 1980s, he made comparisons between current fundamentalism and the first wave of fundamentalism at the turn of the century. "Many themes and causes were the same," he concluded. "The renewal of a 'Christian America' was a frequent refrain. The call for return to evangelical-Victorian *mores* and economic orthodoxy was also heard." But several of the themes in the fundamentalism of the 1970s and 1980s struck Marsden's ear as new: "the Christian school movement"; "the fundamentalist opposition to the women's movement and abortion"; and "the breakup of the family [interpreted as] an important new symbol of the demise of the Christian heritage." He also believed that the fundamentalist-Roman Catholic alliance on gender issues was a recent arrangement.[18] Frank, too, in making the same comparison gave the contemporary "Religious

17. Janet Forsythe Fishburn, *The Fatherhood of God and the Victorian Family* (Philadelphia: Fortress Press, 1981), 28–33, 122–24, 161–65. See also Colleen McDannell, *The Christian Home in Victorian America, 1840–1900* (Bloomington, Ind.: Indiana Univ. Press, 1986), 100–1, 116.

18. Marsden, *Fundamentalism and American Culture*, 228.

Right" credit for adding the gender concerns of homosexuality and the Equal Rights Amendment to the platform inherited from their first-wave forebears.[19] Yet this analysis of the popular literature of fundamentalism between 1880 and 1930 has revealed that opposition to feminism and abortion, and the interpretation of the breakup of the family as a threat to Christian society are not creations of the Christian Right of the 1970s and 1980s. Nor is the willingness to side with Roman Catholics an innovation. These matters, and many others relating to gender identity and roles, are part of a large and constitutive legacy inherited from turn-of-the- century conservative Protestant evangelicalism and the first wave of fundamentalism. Regarding matters of gender, perhaps especially so, late twentieth-century evangelicalism is truly the heir of its own past.

19. Frank, *Less than Conquerors*, 274–76.

APPENDIX

Primary Sources
1880–1900

1. *Bibliotheca Sacra* was edited until 1921 by George F. Wright of Oberlin College, who was described by Marsden as "a product of the old intellectually sophisticated New England Calvinism. . . . Under Wright's editorship, *Bibliotheca Sacra* stood with the emerging fundamentalist movement." Upon Wright's death in 1921, the journal moved to "the new dispensationalist seminary in Dallas. There it remained as an at least symbolic link between militant fundamentalism and the former days of the scholarly New England battles for the faith."[1] This periodical is among the most scholarly of any included in this study.

2. *Christian Cynosure* was the official publication of the National Christian Association, headed by Jonathan Blanchard until 1892 and his son Charles after that. Jonathan Blanchard became president of the Illinois Institute in Wheaton in 1860, and founded the National Christian Association in 1868, the primary purpose of which was to speak out against Masons and other secret societies. The elder Blanchard was drawn to Moody revivalism in the 1870s and 1880s, and he attended Northfield conferences thereafter. Charles Blanchard assumed the presidency of Wheaton College and of the association in 1892 and became a leader in the emerging fundamentalist movement. He preached often at Moody Church, and by 1919 he was a founding member of the World's Christian Fundamentalist Association. He died in 1925.

3. *Christian Herald and Signs of Our Times* was a very popular premillennialist journal edited until the early 1920s by T. DeWitt Talmage out of the Brooklyn Tabernacle. Charles M. Sheldon then took over the editorial reins. Its circulation in 1890 was 30,000, with contributions from key premillennialist leaders as A. J. Gordon and

---

1. George M. Marsden, *Fundamentalism and American Culture: The Shaping of Twentieth-Century Evangelicalism, 1870–1925* (New York: Oxford Univ. Press, 1980), 123.

A. T. Pierson. The period of its largest growth was from 1890 to 1910. Marsden concluded that by 1910, when its circulation had gone up to about 250,000, much of the narrower premillennialist teachings were dropped, and that the journal became "distinctly progressive in politics. It endorsed labor unions, worked for legislation concerning women's and children's labor, advocated better treatment of immigrants and blacks, and waged an unceasing campaign for world peace."[2]

4. *Northfield Echoes* was published by the Moody Bible Institute from 1894 to 1900. It contains articles of general interest to evangelicals as well as the text of addresses delivered at various conferences held at Northfield every summer. Historians such as Carroll E. Harrington[3] and Marsden understand Moody and his colleagues as the first generation of fundamentalists whose evangelical revivalism was a fertile seedbed for later fundamentalism.

5. *Record of Christian Work* is another Moody publication, which ran from 1887 to 1933. It was intended for a general evangelical audience.

6. *Truth, or, Testimony for Christ* was edited by James H. Brookes, the chief organizer of Niagara prophetic conferences. Cole reported that "no Christian leaders were better known in the late seventies and eighties than J. H. Brookes and A. J. Gordon."[4] This journal was published from 1874 to 1897; when Brookes died, it was merged with *Watchword* to become *Watchword and Truth*.

7. *Watchman-Examiner* was a popular journal that came out of Boston's Tremont Temple, the "largest Church in New England of any denomination" in 1924.[5] J. C. Massee, a very important leader of the conservative faction within the Northern Baptist Convention, was minister there during the 1920s. Curtis Lee Laws became editor-in-chief in 1913 when the *Watchman* was merged with the *Examiner.* He coined the term *fundamentalist,*[6] and he saw that the journal continued to be a mouthpiece for the fundamentalists within Baptist circles, although Laws was a moderate who preferred to remain within the Convention rather than leave it.[7]

2. Marsden, *Fundamentalism and American Culture,* 85.

3. See Carroll E. Harrington, "The Fundamentalist Movement in America, 1870–1921" (Ph.D. diss., Univ. of California, Berkeley, 1959).

4. Steward G. Cole, *The History of Fundamentalism* (New York: R. R. Smith, 1931), 45.

5. Arthur Leonard Wadsworth, "Dr. J. C. Massee and the Tremont Temple Church," *Watchman-Examiner* 12 (December 11, 1924): 1605–6.

6. George Marsden found the reference in "Convention Side Lights," *Watchman-Examiner* 8 (July 1, 1920): 834.

7. "Our Kind of Fundamentalism," *Watchman-Examiner* 19, no. 4 (January 22, 1931): 103.

8. *Western Recorder* was a Southern Baptist journal edited after 1910 by one of the most influential Southern Baptist fundamentalists, John W. Porter, in Louisville, Kentucky. Porter, in 1924, became the first president of the Anti-Evolution League of America.[8] Along with T. T. Martin, Porter represented Southern Baptists on the roster of the Baptist Bible Union at its first annual meeting in 1924.

1900–1930

9. *Billy Sunday's sermons* represent religious rhetoric that was very popular and had an immense circulation. Most of his standard sermons were published in pamphlet form or were carried in the newspapers of the cities in which he held campaigns. Most of the sermons surveyed were from the 1916 campaign in Trenton, New Jersey.

10. *American Fundamentalist* was edited by John Roach Straton, called the "fundamentalist pope" by Gatewood,[9] and the "most important fundamentalist clergyman of his generation" by Russell.[10] Straton was an aggressive premillennialist[11] who in 1918 became minister of Calvary Baptist Church in New York City, a national center of fundamentalist organizing and activity. Public debates between him and Unitarian Charles Francis Potter in New York in 1924 made him a well-known and widely read religious leader.[12] In the mid-1920s he was an officer of the Bible Crusaders of America, which fought to keep evolution out of public schools by passing state legislation. He was one of the leaders of the Baptist Bible Union and "commanded the reactionary churches of the eastern metropolitan area through the channel of the Baptist Fundamentalist League of Greater New York and Vicinity."[13] Marsden claimed that Sinclair Lewis's character, Elmer Gantry, was in part modeled after Straton.[14] Only two issues of this journal were published before it was absorbed by another magazine.

11. *Bible Student and Teacher* was published by the American Bible League, a conservative and primarily Presbyterian body, from 1911 to 1913. The journal's intended audience was ministers, so it is more

8. See Cole, *The History of Fundamentalism*, 261.
9. William B. Gatewood, *Controversy in the Twenties: Fundamentalism, Modernism, and Evolution* (Nashville: Vanderbilt Univ. Press, 1969), 130.
10. C. Allyn Russell, *Voices of American Fundamentalism* (Philadelphia: Westminster Press, 1976), 85.
11. Marsden, *Fundamentalism and American Culture*, 162.
12. See Cole, *The History of Fundamentalism*, 244; and Marsden, *Fundamentalism and American Culture*, 176.
13. Cole, *The History of Fundamentalism*, 284.
14. Marsden, *Fundamentalism and American Culture*, 188.

technical than most others. When the League passed into the hands of new leadership in 1913 it changed its name to the Bible League of North America and that of its magazine to the *Bible Champion,* which was continuously published until 1930. In 1914, it counted 2,500 subscribers.[15]

12. *Call to the Colors* was published by the Methodist League for Faith and Life and edited by Harold Paul Sloan, a major spokesman for fundamentalism within the Northern Methodist Church. It was issued for one year, 1925 to 1926.

13. *Christian Fundamentalist* was the official publication of the World's Christian Fundamentalist Association, the principal organization of the premillennialist wing of the fundamentalist movement.[16] William Bell Riley of Minneapolis, Minnesota, was its editor-in-chief, and "the activating force" within the association.[17] Riley also founded the Anti-Evolution League in 1923, which became the Anti-Evolution League of America when leadership changed hands from Riley to J. W. Porter and T. T. Martin.

14. *Christian Fundamentals in School and Church* was also edited by William Bell Riley. It was published from 1918 to 1927.

15. *Christian Workers Magazine* is another Moody publication, published for ten years from 1910 to 1920.

16. *Herald and Presbyter* was a Presbyterian weekly that staunchly defended the "orthodox" position during the controversies.[18] It ran from 1869 to 1925, when it merged with the *Philadelphia Presbyterian.*

17. *Institute Tie* described itself as "A monthly devoted to the interests of Moody Bible Institute, Its Students, Supporters and Friends," and is the closest thing to an alumni/ae magazine I surveyed. James M. Gray was editor-in-chief. It was published from 1901 to 1910.

18. *King's Business* was the official publication of the Bible Institute of Los Angeles (BIOLA), the school funded by the same Stewart family that financed the publication of *The Fundamentals.* Southern California was the home of an especially strong conservative element, and BIOLA was its center. Reuben A. Torrey, a revivalist and one of Moody's successors, was its dean from 1912 to 1924. Torrey was himself one of three editors of *The Fundamentals.* Marsden judged the *King's Business*

---

15. *Bible Student and Teacher* 17, no. 6 (June 1914): 272.
16. Marsden, *Fundamentalism and American Culture,* 152.
17. Norman F. Furniss, *The Fundamentalist Controversy 1918–1931* (New Haven: Yale Univ. Press, 1954), 49.
18. Furniss, *The Fundamentalist Controversy,* 129.

the "leading premillennial journal" during the 1910s, and in 1922 J. Frank Norris's newsletter reported a circulation for the journal of 40,000.[19] Marsden used it a great deal in his own analysis of fundamentalism.[20]

19. *Moody Bible Institute Monthly* was published from 1920 to 1938 for a general evangelical audience. Brereton estimated that in the late 1920s it had between 20,000 and 30,000 subscribers.[21]

20. *Our Hope* was one of the most extreme premillennialist periodicals published. It was edited by Arno C. Gaebelein. Its primary focus was on the status and movement of the Jews, because some premillennialists, Gaebelein a leader among them, looked for the return of the Jews to Palestine as a sign of the second coming of Christ.

21. *Searchlight* was the weekly publication of J. Frank Norris's large Southern Baptist church in Fort Worth, Texas. This church in the 1920s boasted the largest Sunday school in the world, with attendance well over 5,000 each week by 1928.[22] The newsletter enjoyed wide circulation. In 1923, its own estimate was 55,000.[23] Russell estimated 80,000 and called it "the most widely circulated religious journal in the South." Norris also held hundreds of revivals around the country, and at his peak, broadcast weekly over twenty-seven radio stations.[24] Publication of the newsletter began in 1917. In 1927 the title was changed to *The Fundamentalist,* later to the *Baptist Fundamentalist,* and the *Baptist Fundamentalist of Texas.*

19. *Searchlight* 5, no. 50 (October 27, 1922): 4.
20. Marsden, *Fundamentalism and American Culture,* 144.
21. Virginia Lieson Brereton, "Protestant Fundamentalist Bible Schools, 1882–1940" (Ph.D. diss., Columbia Univ., 1981), 241.
22. Russell, *Voices of American Fundamentalism,* 31.
23. *Searchlight* 6, no. 22 (April 13, 1923): 6.
24. Russell, *Voices of American Fundamentalism,* 24, 29.

INDEX

161